BRIMSTONE CORNER

BRIMSTONE CORNER

CORNER

Park Street Church
BOSTON

By H. CROSBY ENGLIZIAN

Foreword by HAROLD JOHN OCKENGA

MOODY PRESS

CHICAGO

To my wife, Eleanor,
with love and admiration

BRIMSTONE CORNER, by H. Crosby Englizian
Copyright © 1968 by The Moody Bible Institute of Chicago

Library of Congress Catalog Card Number 68-18882

Manufactured in the United States of America

Contents

39174

PHOTO SECTION FOLLOWS PAGE 80

Foreword

CHURCHES, like nations, are judged in time rather than at a great future judgment day. Nations have their formative period, their birth, their growth, their flowering, their fructification, their decay and their oblivion. Many nations have moved in and off the scene of human history. So it is with churches.

In Revelation 2 and 3, we have letters from the resurrected Christ to seven churches which existed in Asia Minor at the time of John the beloved's ministry. Undoubtedly each of those existent churches at that time had need for the encouragement, instruction and admonition of the letter addressed to it. One interpretation of Revelation would make each of these churches represent a period in church history. Although these periods are hard to define, this very well may be the case. However, it is patent that all seven types of churches exist simultaneously in the world at this time and the warnings are given to the churches lest they be judged and their candlestick, or witness, be taken away. Historically, this has happened in Asia Minor, in North Africa, and in other parts of the earth. Churches are judged in time.

This leads me to say that Jesus' promises apply to churches as well as to individuals. When He said, "Seek ye first the kingdom of God and his righteousness, and all these things shall be added unto you," He was giving a promise which can be claimed by individual congregations. The added things about which Jesus was speaking were raiment, shelter, food and all that satisfies material needs. Is there a program of the kingdom which is such that if we follow it as churches we will be assured of God's blessing upon

7

us? I think that program has been given to the churches by the resurrected Christ between the time of His resurrection and the time of His ascension. There He reiterated most often the Great Commission in its various forms. This commission emphasized world missions, first; evangelism, second; teaching, third; humanitarian action, fourth; and it rested worship and fellowship upon the following of this program. Park Street Church has taken this seriously and for more than a quarter of a century has applied it effectively to this program.

Missions make the church. This is literally true with Park Street Church. It is not the architecture of the church which makes it famous, although the building is a landmark in Boston, is visited by tens of thousands of sightseers on the Freedom Trail, and was said by Henry James to be the most impressive mass of brick and mortar in America. It is not because of the many historical events which have occurred in connection with the church, such as the storing of powder in its crypt for the War of 1812, the orations of William Lloyd Garrison against slavery in 1829, the first singing of "America" in its sanctuary on July 4, 1831, the famous oration of Charles Sumner on the war system of the nations in 1849, or the founding of many national societies which makes Park Street Church famous. It is not the series of revivals that have occurred, beginning in 1823 and continuing to 1964, under men like Charles G. Finney, Dwight L. Moody, William Sunday, J. Wilbur Chapman, Billy Graham and others which makes our church known. It is not our orthodox commitment which stemmed the tide of Unitarianism and gave rebirth to Trinitarianism in New England which makes us famous. Park Street Church is most known because of its missionary program and interest which began in 1819 with the formation of the Sandwich Islands Church in the church vestry, and it continues to the present time when ninety-two missionaries are supported in forty-eight countries of the world by this congregation. The story of this work is well told by Dr. Englizian.

The second emphasis in the church program is evangelism. From the beginning, daily prayer meetings and concerts of prayer have been held at Park Street Church for evangelistic emphasis and for revival. Time after time such revivals have broken out, the greatest of which, no doubt, was in the days of the Mid-Century Campaign under Billy Graham which began in Park Street Church and extended into sixteen cities of New England where the largest auditoriums were insufficient to contain the crowds of people and where over ten thousand people made profession of faith in Jesus Christ.

The third point in that program is that of teaching. Ours has been a teaching ministry in which we have expounded the Scripture, proclaimed the doctrines, described the biographies of biblical characters and inculcated biblical principles in all who came. This has been done by public preaching, by the Sunday school movement which is one of the earliest in America, by the Boston Bible School and by radio and television.

Humanitarian activity has been diverse. The Boston chapter of the NAACP was founded in Park Street Church, as was the Animal Rescue League; the abolition movement had its beginnings at Park Street Church with William Lloyd Garrison, and the church's congregation yearly engages in a fasting program to save money to give to relieve hunger in various parts of the world. The witness of the church has constantly been connected with humanitarian activity.

The framework of this program is made up of the large assemblies that worship the Lord on Sunday mornings and evenings. The morning services crowd the auditorium and send an overflow into a closed-circuit television room. The evening attendance has sustained a large congregation in the midst of the many competitive interests and the declining attendance in evening services in other churches. The fellowship of the congregation in this program is such that loyalty is maintained regardless of the area to which our people move around the Boston area. At one time we had 144 towns represented in our membership. This increases or decreases according to the moving of the people but they remain loyal to the church.

Due to the hundreds of requests which I have had from people concerning our program, I have had it in mind to write the history of Park Street Church, especially the modern missionary story, but demands of maintaining the program have prevented my research and writing. I am extremely happy that Dr. Crosby

Englizian has undertaken this task and has done it so acceptably and accurately. I trust that the history of Park Street Church will be a source of blessing and inspiration to many other churches, but especially to those in the core of the city.

HAROLD JOHN OCKENGA

Preface

The public presentation of the history of Park Street Church has been long overdue. Although today in America there exists a large number of historic churches, each having provided its own peculiar strand to the overall fabric of the nation, Park Street's contributions since the first decade of the nineteenth century are so significant that its achievements and the honor of its clerical and lay leadership demand the telling.

Over the past 159 years, thousands have reflected upon the glory of this institution and have given expression to its Christian mission in Boston and beyond. These expressions have come from nonmembers and non-Christians as well as from its own fellowship, at times as an encomium or a pecuniary gift, and at other times in the form of civic approbation, or even a gubernatorial proclamation. They suggest the many-sided historic importance of this citadel of orthodoxy.

The American novelist Henry James observed that the edifice of Park Street Church is "the most interesting mass of brick and mortar . . . in America."[1] Others also, not of the congregation, but with the same sense of appreciation for its colonial architectural beauty, once subscribed the sum of $10,000 during a low period in the church's life to preserve the famous landmark and save it from proposed dismantling.

Its unique and unparalleled location on its original site in downtown Boston, flanked on the south by the Boston Common and on the north by the Granary Burial Ground, has captured the

[1]Henry James, *The American Scene* (New York: Harper & Bros., 1907), p. 231.

11

eye of architects, historians, artists and thousands of tourists who come to the Hub City annually to visit its historic attractions. National magazines have featured the church in pictures and in text. Park Street Church, however, is more than a famous meeting-house with a magnificent spire. The early decades of the nineteenth century saw the rise and growth of numerous societies within the prevailing orthodox framework: The American Board of Commissioners for Foreign Missions, Andover Theological Seminary, The Foreign Missionary Society of Boston, The American Education Society, The Park Street Singing Society (a forerunner of the Handel and Haydn Society), The Prison Discipline Society, The American Peace Society, The American Temperance Society, and The City Missionary Society. Park Street Church became indissolubly associated with these organizations. Its pastors and lay leaders provided invaluable services in various official and unofficial capacities. Whenever the cause of Christ required laborers and support, whether in the missionary enterprise, evangelism, Christian education, benevolences, or in founding local churches—in its own community, on the expanding Western frontier, or on some distant shore—Park Street Church showed itself ready to serve.

Prominent nineteenth century movements of a moral or religious nature with which the church has been identified include the revival of Trinitarianism in the second decade, the development of church music, the antislavery agitation, and the introduction of Sabbath schools.

In the present day its vision and service, its readiness to face challenge, continues apace. Evangelist Billy Graham commented during his 1964 visit to Boston that of all the churches he knew, Park Street Church was the finest in membership, spiritual life, dedication and service.

Since this work was prepared originally as a doctoral dissertation for Dallas Theological Seminary, Dallas, Texas, the author wishes to extend his thanks to its faculty for permission to publish this history in slightly altered form, and for including in its curriculum, doctoral studies in American Christianity, which, among schools of its type, are practically nonexistent. A debt of gratitude is due also to Dr. George W. Dollar, chairman of the Department of Historical Theology, for inciting interest in this general area of scholarship.

Dr. Harold John Ockenga, minister of Park Street Church, and his staff have been most gracious in permitting free access to the church's archives and in providing necessary tools for research.

The fine facilities of the Congregational Library, Boston, Massachusetts, were wholeheartedly made available by its librarian and her assistants.

Sincere thanks is expressed also to the following institutions: Boston Public Library, New England Historic and Genealogical Society, Massachusetts Historical Society, Boston Athenaeum, Massachusetts State Library, Harvard Divinity School Library, Andover-Newton Theological Seminary Library, and the library facilities of Harvard University; also Yale University Library and the Beinecke Rare Book and Manuscript Library, New Haven, Connecticut; the New York Public Library and the New York Historical Society in New York City; and in Worcester, Massachusetts, the American Antiquarian Society and the Worcester City Library. For permission to use "A Legend of Brimstone Corner," a note of thanks is due to Mark Howe, Cambridge, Massachusetts.

The author presents this historical record in a spirit of admiration and respect for those who perhaps knew Park Street Church best—its historians—after being nurtured on the manuscript evidence of a great past.

A Legend of Brimstone Corner

The Devil and a Gale of Wind
    Danced hand in hand up Winter Street.
The Devil like his demons grinned
    To have for comrade so complete
A rascal and a mischief-maker
Who'd drag an oath from any Quaker.

The Wind made sport of hats and hair
    That ladies deemed their ornament;
With skirts that frolicked everywhere
    Away their prim decorum went;
And worthy citizens lamented
The public spectacles presented.

The Devil beamed with horrid joy,
    Till to the Common's rim they came,
Then chuckled, "Wait you here, my boy,
    For duties now my presence claim
In yonder church on Brimstone Corner
Where Pleasure's dead and lacks a mourner;

"But play about till I come back."
    With that he vanished through the doors,
And since that day the almanac
    Has marked the years by tens and scores,
Yet never from those sacred portals
Returns the Enemy of Mortals.

And that is why the faithful Gale
    Round Park Street Corner still must blow,
Waiting for him with horns and tail—
    At least some people tell me so—
None of your famous antiquarians,
But just some wicked Unitarians.

                M. A. DeWolfe Howe

Introduction

The first generation of Massachusetts Bay Puritans felt that God led them to build in eastern Massachusetts a civil-ecclesiastical order strong enough to withstand every antichristian (anti-Puritan) force. Although they built well, they utilized materials that eventually weakened and destroyed the edifice. Signs of such debility became increasingly evident in succeeding generations. The Half-Way Covenant of 1662 and the grievous lamentations of the Boston Synod of 1680 revealed the colony's distressing state of religion and the clergy's mounting concern.

This spiritually arid condition persisted until the 1740's when revival and salvation took place throughout New England under the preaching of George Whitefield, Gilbert Tennent and others. This Great Awakening, while producing much good fruit, laid bare a New England fact of life which previously had been of little concern to the clergy: the rising preponderance of opinions, among notable ministers, injurious to the accepted Calvinistic faith. In Boston the most notable of these clergymen were Jonathan Mayhew of the West Church, and Charles Chauncy, minister at the First Church under whose aegis the gathering forces of anti-Calvinism began their preliminary assault. Their distaste for the revival's excessive emotionalism was but the opening shot in the theological debates that followed in succeeding decades.

This theological fissure in the Calvinistic-structured New England Congregationalism remained unrepaired—a gaping and unsightly breach—as the colonists turned first to politics and to armed conflict, and then to constitution-making and the federalist system. The aftermath of the war for independence compounded the problems facing the remaining orthodox ministers of coastal Massachusetts. In addition to the unabated doctrinal schism, a period of spiritual declension set in to dry up the strains of piety in the pew and to bank the fires of Puritan preaching in the pulpit.

This declension was reflected in the neglect and abuse of catechetical instruction, a growing contempt for confessional statements, and the limp set of ministerial qualifications for ordination, wherein the candidate's personal accomplishments, rather than his doctrinal beliefs, carried more weight with the ordaining council. "Indeed, to question whether or not a candidate held to the orthodox understanding of the Scriptures was tantamount to an invitation to ridicule and contempt."[1] The prevailing view on creeds and confessions, as reported in *The Panoplist*, was that these symbols were but "useless inventions," "sources of debate and contention," "inconsistent with the natural liberty of mankind," "arbitrary impositions," and "engines of spiritual tyranny."

By 1800, in the wake of recent libertarian movements throughout the colonies, both political and religious, the once-rigid polity and practice of Boston's Congregational churches had been relaxed. The aristocratic features of seventeenth century Puritanism had been displaced by a more democratic and more truly Congregational system. The laity were discovering a new and larger role in church life. Furthermore, the economic, social and intellectual aspects of civic and community life began to occupy more importance in the ever broadening cultural pattern. Boston's horizons seemed unlimited; her citizens stood ready to confront the challenges of the time and make their town a place of unparalleled power and affluence, a mercantile and maritime center second to none.

To those few evangelicals who clung to their biblical faith, however, the times looked dark and bleak. Deacon Nathaniel Willis of Park Street Church, and editor of the *Boston Recorder*, deplored the deep spiritual declension which characterized the city's Congregational churches. The piety, fidelity and spirituality of the members flickered like a dying lamp. The Christianity of the day retained in its external forms and aspects much that was venerable and conservative, but its life and power were gone; its

[1]"Survey of Churches," *The Panoplist*, October, 1806, p. 210.

real throbbing, earnest soul was stifled and palsied. The pulpit was not without strength and cogency; the decencies, charities and virtues of a high-toned morality were still being heard, but seldom echoed the thunders of a violated law or the melting accents of Calvary.

What caused this apostasy and general religious decline? These were contributory factors: (1) Popular reaction against the rigidity of the early Puritan church-state combine: the New England Way of John Cotton and John Winthrop proved unpalatable to their grandchildren's generation. (2) The excesses associated with the Great Awakening: the high level of enthusiasm, the overly censorious spirit of the evangelists, plus the radical rantings of men such as Rev. James Davenport of Long Island combined to arouse the ire of friend and foe alike. To the staid and starched clergyman of New England, who valued decorum as much as doctrine, the many incidents of emotionalism and parish encroachment by itinerant preachers seemed well beyond the legitimate bounds of sober religion. (3) Preoccupation with political and military problems: from 1754-63, during the French and Indian Wars, the colonists were called upon for heavy supplies of men and materiel in order to end the threat of French imperial power from the North and West. In the years following 1775, the Revolutionary War was fought and won, constitutional conventions were convened, and political party alignments adjusted to the new national government. (4) Religious liberalism, an expression of the European Enlightenment: humanistic, philosophical and scientific concepts from England, plus rationalistic thought from France, combined with other nonchristian importations to vie for the minds of young intellectuals, including some of Boston's ministerial elite, early in the nineteenth century.

Rev. Silas Aiken, Park Street's fifth pastor, recalled how infidel philosophy like an unclean spirit had gathered its disciples to the battle and in their endeavors to destroy the credit of God's revelation no weapon of ribald jest or blasphemy had been left unemployed. Reason was exalted above revelation. Orthodox doctrines were claimed to be antiquated notions, while philanthropy was substituted for regeneration. (5) The Bible Commonwealth: although the grievances of individual citizens throughout the seventeenth and eighteenth centuries were necessary to the final overthrow of the church-state system in Massachusetts, and although the Great Awakening, through its individualization of personal religious experience aided in this overthrow, there remained, nevertheless, in the offices of civil leadership churchmen, who, as officials representative of all the people, liberal and orthodox, were obliged to bear an image suitable to all. (6) Pulpit exchanges: the time-honored ministerial practice of exchanging pulpits turned many from orthodoxy to Unitarianism. At first the evangelical clergy did not denounce or discontinue fellowship with those who tended toward another gospel, though they disliked their theological peculiarities (which were supposedly to be confined to the study). For half a century these unorthodox, compromising views were heard in orthodox pulpits, though it was understood that no minister would expound doctrine unacceptable to a given congregation. This gave the impression that the liberal was essentially no different than his orthodox counterpart, and that his views, though not entirely correct, were not deeply erroneous. Since it was possible that a minister's sermon might be heard in liberal surroundings as well as among the orthodox, the clergy fell into the habit of giving offense to none. It was almost impossible for a staunch evangelical to refrain from participation in these exchanges without violating some rule of social courtesy or appearing overly exclusive.

Thus, the leaven spread throughout the whole lump. Though there had been no direct avowal of any dereliction of evangelical principles—except perhaps on the part of a single church—probably not more than one or two Boston pulpits taught the primitive orthodoxy of New England. No decree of banishment had been formally and openly issued against this system of doctrine; and many maintained that it was the system still in vogue, except perhaps being a little pruned of some of its more offensive forms of phraseology. But actually, it had been silently, and by almost common consent, driven into exile; at length it was as much as a man's reputation was worth to appear openly as its advocate.[2]

With the arrival of the nineteenth century the various theologi-

[2]William B. Sprague, *Memoir of The Rev. Edward D. Griffin, D. D.* (New York: Taylor & Dodd, 1839), p. 101.

cal views in the Boston Association of Congregational Ministers made cooperation increasingly unlikely. Ecclesiastical business relative to ministerial exchanges, councils and ordination proceedings was carried on in a spirit which made harmony difficult.

Admittedly, New England had never before been at a lower religious point than in the earliest years of the nineteenth century.

1. The Faithful Remnant

The flame of Christian orthodoxy was sputtering in the churches of Boston Proper in the year 1803. The churches numbered sixteen: nine Congregational, three Episcopal, two Baptist, one Methodist and one Quaker. But certain persons within three of these sixteen churches—Old South Congregational Church, and the First and Second Baptist churches—refused to permit this small fire of orthodoxy to be extinguished. These faithful Christians, each acting independently of the other, became instrumental in beginning three important religious movements: a Congregational women's prayer circle, the Baptist revival of 1803-4, and the Religious Improvement Society.

In describing the religious state of Boston's Congregational churches, Deacon Nathaniel Willis made known the dire need for an association of praying women. He emphasized that there were no weekly lectures; conference meetings; foreign missions; education, tract or Bible societies; Sabbath schools; monthly concerts; or religious newspapers. Though the form of public worship was maintained, the church appeared to be swallowed up in the world. He recalled that a number of pious "Mothers of Israel" had met for several years to plead the cause of evangelical religion, to mourn over Zion's desolations, and to ask God for an old-time revival. According to Rev. Benjamin Blydenburg Wisner, these prayer warriors were largely from Old South Church, some of them having been converted during the Great Awakening. Although everything evangelical and vital in doctrine and practice was withering and dying, there remained this "one hope."

Boston's first revival in the nineteenth century, and the most

21

significant one after the days of George Whitefield, occurred in 1803 within the congregations of the First and Second Baptist churches. The revival's power and results were not due to an evangelist imported for the occasion, but to the quiet movement of the Spirit of God accompanying the preaching of the Baptist pastors Samuel Stillman and Thomas Baldwin. The meetings at the First Baptist Church attracted many hundreds of spiritually concerned persons. Numerous conversions and baptisms were recorded. Crowds consistently filled the auditorium with winter storms not preventing large numbers from filling every pew and sometimes the aisles. This greatly needed revival continued for two years. One hundred and thirty-five persons were baptized into the membership of the First Baptist Church, and an even larger number was added to its sister congregation.

The revival's ramifications are greatly enlarged by considering the impact of the services upon the Congregationalists who regularly attended. They were devout people who had been praying earnestly. Dr. Joseph Eckley, minister at Old South, who had been having trouble maintaining the faith in his church as well as in his own heart, attended the meetings and was personally strengthened. Undoubtedly Pastors Stillman and Baldwin were influential in encouraging Dr. Eckley in orthodox ways. Their encouragement paved the way for a renewed emphasis on the doctrine of grace at Old South, where an evangelical associate pastor was called, and Eckley led an important band of men who through their organization bridged the years between 1804 and 1809, the year Park Street Church was founded. A key role in evangelical religion was played by the Baptists of Boston at this time of crisis. The importance of this spiritual effusion was noted by Dr. Nathan E. Wood, a Baptist minister, who said the Baptists, under God, were the means of preserving orthodox Congregationalism in Boston, for Old South Church, when spiritually quickened, settled into the old faith and became the "mother" of new Congregational churches.

However, the years of diligent and persevering prayer by the city's devout women also was a key factor and of equal value to the revival.

In the wake of revival fervor, Dr. Eckley sought to enlist the

Old South Church in the movement by proposing that a public lecture be held during the winter of 1803-4. The church members voted to accept the proposal; but due to strong opposition from the society,[1] that is, the pewholders, the plan did not materialize. But the society's action proved to be momentous, for it caused eight members to form the Religious Improvement Society on March 13, 1804. This society was organized in the home of Deacon Josiah Bumstead. Others taking part were: Ebenezer Waters, Jeremiah Bumstead, Jr., John E. Tyler, Josiah Vinton, Joseph W. Jenkins, Henry Homes and Elisha Hunt. In time, others joined these men to play a major role in the founding of Park Street Church.

Tyler, Jenkins and Jeremiah Bumstead, Jr., were appointed as a committee to make the society's rules. Dr. Eckley was asked to preside at the meetings and to preach, pray or converse on religious topics of value. Dr. Eckley gladly accepted the invitation, and a Tuesday evening lecture series was begun. In addition, the men met regularly for prayer and business. The semicentennial booklet of Park Street Church tells of the level of spiritual freedom which characterized their devotional activities:

> Such, however, was the lack of courage and confidence with private Christians of the time, and such the meager growth of Christian graces and accomplishments, that for several weeks no member of this little association could lead the devotions of his brethren in audible prayer in their meetings.

This low state of spiritual vitality was not surprising, considering the religious temper of the times. That Dr. Eckley himself was somewhat unsure of his doctrinal position undoubtedly contributed to the shaky and tenuous beginnings. Apart from internal problems tending to hinder spiritual movement in the early months of the society's existence, outside opposition began to heap ridicule and scorn. This negative reaction was a disheartening influence upon these well-meaning men.

Not long after the society had been established, tentative plans

[1]Note the distinction between the church (regenerate membership) and the society (pewholders: regenerate and unregenerate persons), as individual and separate entities within the congregation.

for a new meetinghouse were formulated and presented to the Old South Church for approval. But the church rejected the idea as harmful competition. Although the society continued to encounter reproaches and the fiercest opposition, its meetings were well attended and proved to be a blessing from the beginning.

Therefore, in spite of inner weaknesses and doubt, and in the face of hostile acts, the prayer meetings and lectures continued for six years until February 27, 1809, when Park Street Church was founded. The decision to build the church came from these prayer meetings. When first attempts to form a church were thwarted, the society continued planning. Their intercession resulted in a second attempt which, because of their improved faith and brightened vision, proved highly successful.

2. Beginnings on a Grand Scale

Increase Mather is credited with saying that if there are defections from orthodox doctrine then churches will be gathered out of churches; that is, doctrinal schism within local churches will lead to the formation of new churches. In the first decade of the nineteenth century this "recuperative process" began, interestingly enough, in the Mayflower Church. On October 1, 1801, a number of the more orthodox members of the First Church of Plymouth, Massachusetts, seceded to form the Third Congregational Church; on May 12, 1802, they called as their first pastor, Rev. Adoniram Judson, father of the famous missionary to Burma. Six years later and forty miles farther up the coast in the town of Boston a similar event, but on a larger scale, was about to occur.

Dr. Henry Kollock, minister of the Independent Presbyterian Church, Savannah, Georgia, spent occasional summer vacations in the cooler climate of the Northern states. In the summer of 1808 he was visiting and preaching throughout New England. His sermons among the Baptists of Boston were well received and attracted many from other churches who were hungry for the old-time religion, including the members of the Religious Improvement Society. Speaking with irresistible energy and conviction, his sermons attracted crowds who confessed the power of the truth he preached.

The men of the Religious Improvement Society had not heard such soul-stirring preaching for years. A delegation was sent to Dr. Kollock to invite him to become their leader. To their delight, he tentatively accepted the call and indicated that he would be pleased to move to Boston. He made two conditions before his final acceptance: A church must be gathered, and a meeting-house erected.

During the following early autumn ten persons met at the Beacon Hill house of William Thurston to discuss how to meet Dr. Kollock's conditions. A committee was chosen to sound out interest in the projects and to ascertain how much money would be subscribed. It was reported soon afterward that there appeared to be sufficient interest in the new meetinghouse to raise approximately $40,000, which was the amount required to proceed with the plans. Each potential contributor was told that the new church would have the exclusive power of choosing its pastor and making its own decisions. The founders of Park Street Church were determined to safeguard their institution against those elements which had either robbed or marred the biblical witness of Boston's Congregational churches. They built into the warp and woof of the church's fabric a higher style of orthodoxy than prevailed at that time in the other churches.

Knowing the unique image which the proposed church would bear before her sister congregations, seventy-three persons signed the subscription papers of November and December, 1808. The first subscription of November 28 listed twenty-three persons pledging $16,700. Within three weeks, subscribers had risen to seventy-one and the total pledge to $33,400. Since this amount was still below the necessary minimum, nine men, eight of whom had already promised to contribute generously, made special subscriptions totaling $8,300. This extra sacrificial effort made a grand total of $41,700. (Benajah Brigham, who did the masonry work on the edifice, later contributed $1,000 on January 13, 1810.) The historic preamble to the subscription paper declared in part:

> We the Subscribers impressed with the importance and benefit which the erecting a new Meeting House in Boston, and collecting therein a new Congregational Church on Evangelical principles, would be to the cause of Religion, and the welfare of the souls of many who are deprived of the privilege of attending public worship by want of Pews, do hereby associate together for the sole purpose of procuring a Lot of Land in Boston, and erecting a Meeting House thereon for the public worship of God, trusting that in this great

undertaking the blessing of the Head of the Church will be afforded to us.

And we do hereby severally promise to pay the sums set against our names respectively to such person or persons as shall by said Church when gathered be appointed to purchase the Land and superintend the erecting of said House, in the proportion of Ten percent of the sums subscribed, every month, commencing on the 10th of December, 1808, provided however, before any payment be made, the sum of Forty Thousand Dollars shall be subscribed for the sole purpose afforesaid [sic], and in order that no misconception may arise as to the principles on which said Church shall be established or to the object to be obtained by the erecting said House, it is hereby expressly agreed that said Church shall adopt as articles of faith that system of Religion which is Evangelical and those doctrines which in a proper sense are stiled [sic] the doctrines of grace.[1]

On Monday evening, February 16, 1809, ten subscribers met at the house of William Thurston to discuss the formation of a new church and ecclesiastical society based on evangelical principles. At this initial meeting moderated by Elisha Ticknor, a committee of five men was chosen to draw up articles of faith and a covenant, secure land and obtain plans for building a meetinghouse. This committee included Elisha Ticknor, William Thurston, John Tyler, Josiah Bumstead and Joseph Jenkins.

Two weeks later the subscribers gathered at the Henry Homes residence to continue organizational plans. Present by request were Rev. Jedidiah Morse of the Charlestown church and Rev. John Codman, minister of the Second Congregational Church, Dorchester. Dr. Morse served as moderator, and Thurston as clerk. Three key motions were passed: (1) to meet for the formal and official organization of the new church at the Thurston mansion on February 27, 1809, at 3 P.M.; (2) to plan the organizational service; (3) to invite the following five churches to assist in the formation of the church: Old South Church, Federal Street Church, and the churches at Charlestown, Cambridge and Dorchester.

With the exception of William Ellery Channing of the Federal

[1]Subscriptions to New Church Lot, December 5, 1808, Park Street Church.

Street Church, each invited minister was of the orthodox faith and
in sympathy with the strong confessional symbols which were to
be incorporated into the church's founding documents. The invitation to the Federal Street Church may have stemmed from the
fact that Channing had received his early religious education in
the Newport, Rhode Island, church of which Dr. Samuel Hopkins
was the strongly orthodox pastor.

During the evening of February 23, 1809, an adjourned meeting of the previous Monday was held at the house of Joseph Jenkins. The committee chosen to prepare articles of faith and a
church covenant presented their report which was unanimously
accepted. A committee of Bingham, Tyler and Thurston was
authorized to send letters to the five churches requesting them to
form an ecclesiastical council and to aid in founding the church.

At an Old South Church meeting on February 26 the invitation
was presented to the congregation for discussion. It was rejected
by a negative vote, accompanied by an amendment extending
Christian felicitations. The Federal Street Church also declined
to participate.

On February 27, 1809, at 3 P.M. the Park Street Church was
organized at the Bowdoin Street mansion of William Thurston,
which was one of the more prominent dwellings in Boston, due
not only to its lofty site but also to its stately elegance. It was
built by Thurston in 1804 on the highest point of Beacon Hill on a
lot adjoining the famous Revolutionary War Memorial Monument.

Author William W. Wheildon wrote of this residence:

> Not a few of the older inhabitants who were living at the
> commencement of the present century, remember well the
> lofty mansion house of William Thurston, Esq., as it pre-
> sented itself to the sight of all in the days of its magnificence,
> from its towering eminence just east of the monument; and
> many will never forget the same building shorn of its pristine
> glory, standing upon the high precipice formed by the re-
> moval of the greater part of the soil of the same hill, over-
> topping the chimnies of the neighboring houses.[2]

Dr. Andrew L. Stone, sixth pastor of Park Street Church, re-

[2]William W. Wheildon, *Sentry, or Beacon Hill* (Concord, Mass.: by the
author, 1877), p. 102.

called nostalgically that the house had long since disappeared, even its site having been scattered to the winds.. Within those walls, the resourcefulness and unswerving vision of a handful of men and women, united in their love for Christ, established a religious society that was to become the citadel of evangelical orthodoxy in New England.

With Dr. Abiel Holmes of the Cambridge Church as moderator and Rev. John Codman as scribe, proceedings began. Letters of dismission and recommendation were placed before the six-man ecclesiastical council: Dr. Holmes, Deacon John Walton, Dr. Morse, Deacon James Frothingham, Rev. John Codman and Dr. James Baker. Those unable to obtain official letters of dismission because of the opposition of their churches presented membership certificates instead. The founding exercises were opened with a prayer by Dr. Morse, followed by a Scripture reading of Acts 4 and the singing of a hymn. A talk was given by the Charlestown minister, who used a text from Psalm 118:25, which forms part of the Hallel sung at the triumphal entry of Christ into Jerusalem: "Save now, I beseech thee, O LORD: O LORD, I beseech thee, send now prosperity."

Afterward, the moderator reminded the group why the council had been convened, calling upon the proposed members to approve the Articles of Faith and the Church Covenant adopted on February 23. The members signed the document after hearing it read by the scribe. Then the moderator declared them to be a duly gathered church consonant with the ecclesiastical platform of Congregational churches. Following prayer, the fellowship of the churches was offered by John Codman.

The church having been formed with twenty-one persons, five additional persons were admitted upon their profession. The meeting was then dismissed, and the ecclesiastical council dissolved. Charter members of Park Street Church and their former religious affiliations were:

By Letter

William Thurston	Old South Church
Elizabeth Thurston	Old South Church
John Eugene Tyler	Old South Church
Hannah B. Tyler	Old South Church

Josiah Bumstead	Old South Church
Mary Greenough Bumstead	Old South Church
Caleb Bingham	Dresden
Hannah Bingham	Second Church
William Ladd	Brattle Street Church
Mary Ladd	Brattle Street Church
Daniel Baxter	Quincy
Sarah Baxter	Quincy
Joseph W. Jenkins	First Church
Abigail Jenkins	First Church
Andrew Colhoun	West Church
Martha Colhoun	West Church
John Holbrook	Weymouth
Hannah Haskins	New South Church
Elizabeth Haskins	Brattle Street Church
Fanny Haskins	Brattle Street Church
Mary Turner	Federal Street Church

By Profession

Henry Homes
Aaron Hardy
Ebenezer Parker
Asa Ward
George Homer

The last five persons listed made a profession of religion for the first time.

That same evening the fourteen male members held their first business meeting in the Thurston home. Officers elected were: Caleb Bingham, moderator; William Thurston, clerk; Elisha Ticknor, subscription treasurer.[3] Two key committees were also chosen: the Building and Lot Committee, and the Committee of Correspondence, which was instructed to give Dr. Kollock a unanimous call to the pulpit of Park Street Church, and to correspond with Dr. Edward Dorr Griffin of the First Presbyterian Church, Newark, New Jersey, requesting him to assist Dr. Kollock.

By the middle of March, 1809, the Building and Lot Committee had found a site for their meetinghouse at the corner of Centry (Park) and Common (Tremont) streets. On March 21 the male

[3]Ticknor served as subscription treasurer for one year without becoming a member and withdrew when Dr. Kollock declined to come. He was succeeded by Ebenezer Parker, February 27, 1810.

members voted to purchase this land from its owner, Hepzibah Clarke Swan, for $20,000, provided a mutually agreeable contract could be arranged. Their certainty that they would acquire the property is reflected in a March 14 vote to give the name, Park Street Church, to the new religious society.

The sale was consummated on April 13, 1809, between Caleb Bingham, bookseller; Andrew Colhoun, merchant; William Thurston; the sons-in-law of Mrs. Swan; John T. Sargent, merchant; John C. Howard, physician; and William Sullivan. The dimensions of the lot are given in the title deed:

> We do hereby acknowledge, do hereby give, grant, sell and convey unto the said Bingham, Colhoun, and Thurston, their heirs and assigns forever, in joint-tenancy, a certain tract or parcel of land, situated in Boston aforesaid, and bounded as follows: Viz: On Common Street, the length of the Granary, about eighty feet; then turning on a street formerly called Centry Street, and now called Park Place, there measuring one hundred and eighteen feet; then running from said Centry Street on land of Arnold Welles, to the burying ground, there measuring about eighty feet; then by the burying ground as the line runs down to the corner where the Granary meets the same burying ground, and to Common Street; with all the privileges thereto belonging, being the same premises conveyed to us by Hepzibah C. Swan.[4]

Thus, as "trustees" of Park Street Church, Bingham, Colhoun and Thurston received the title in their own names.

The next day, April 14, these three men entered into a second contract with the Swan family, delivering three promissory notes totaling $16,000 in exchange for a loan to be repaid at a rate of $5,333.33 per year at 6 percent interest. The remaining $4,000 of the purchase money had been borrowed earlier from the Boston Female Asylum. Howard, Sargent and Sullivan agreed not to require payment of the principal until 1813, when it was hoped the church would be on a more substantial financial footing.

In the March 21 business meeting the subscription treasurer, Elisha Ticknor, had been authorized to begin making his collections on March 25 on a monthly basis at the rate of 10 percent of

[4]Registry of Deeds, Suffolk County, Boston, Massachusetts, Libro 228, Folio 181.

the pledged amount. As each subscriber contributed his monthly assessment of 10 percent, the treasurer gave this receipt:

Boston_____ 180____.

Received of _____ $_____ being ten percent, and _____ instalment of his subscription, of the 5th of December last, for buying a lot of land, and erecting a meetinghouse thereon, etc.

Treasurer of the Subscribers and
/s/ Elisha Ticknor   appointed by the New Church,
                            organized 27th February, 1809.

The choice of the lot was excellent in that it placed the edifice in the very heart of the peninsula, on a main thoroughfare, with the beauty of the Common before it. On the north was a cemetery, with its "constant monitors of the short duration of earthly life, and the surety of an eternal departure from the endearments of this world."

Before building their meetinghouse, the twenty-six charter members met regularly for Sabbath worship in the Thurston house. Meanwhile, they looked for a larger hall. An offer by the Charlestown church was refused on grounds of inconvenience.

To assure Dr. Kollock's arrival in Boston, the church edifice needed to be constructed immediately, so the members gave this top priority. During negotiations with the Swan family, preliminary plans had already been made. Master craftsmen were engaged to erect the imposing structure: Peter Banner, an Englishman then residing in Boston, was hired as the architect and carpenter; Benajah Brigham was employed as chief mason, and Solomon Willard, as wood-carver and designer. The two-story brick building called for a steeple with bell. Surmounting the belfry was to be a delicate spire designed after a Christopher Wren creation in London.

Banner, who has been described as "an ingenious architect," and who built the new parsonages for Old South Church the same year, signed a contract with Park Street Church on March 10, 1809. The contract with Brigham was made at approximately the same time. The Park Street founders planned to erect a meetinghouse that would tower over all others, both in height and in architectural beauty. Had more money been available, the building would have been even larger. They later admitted their grandiose plan was dictated, in part, by pride: "But our *Great Leader* who went before us in the pillar of cloud by day, and the pillar of fire by night, did not suffer us to go farther on this *Worldly* policy and *Idolatry*."[5]

About mid-April, 1809, the construction work began with the dismantling of the old granary building which had occupied the site since 1728. In an April 12 meeting the proprietors requested of the town, liberty "to advance one angle of the porch into Common Street." The reply was that no portion of the building was to project into the street, and that "not more than three steps would be allowed to come beyond the Line."[6] However, the workmen proceeded with their original plan. The cornerstone was laid May 1, 1809, at the southeast corner of the foundation with ceremonies led by Dr. Morse and Dr. Holmes. On the stone was placed a plate, prepared by the two men, bearing this engraved inscription:

Jesus Christ, the chief corner-stone, in whom all the building fitly framed together groweth unto an holy temple in the Lord. This church formed February 27, and this foundation laid May 1, 1809.

When the city's board of selectmen heard of the church's intention to build over the sidewalk, they decided to look at the construction and forbid the sidewalk encroachments. At this point the church encountered difficulties with the board and particularly with its chairman, Charles Bulfinch. An anonymous letter from "A. B." to the famous architect, though undated, was probably written on May 4, 1809:

DEAR SIR,

Permit a friend to suggest to you not to make *more noise than is* REALLY EXPEDIENT, about the new church now building at the Granary. The stranger, who now addresses you, heard a Jacobin of some influence say he thought with the Republican party, and some hundred of Federalists, they could put you out. Indeed, a number of Federalists have already engaged to this effect; and as you will probably have

[5]Park Street Church, Proceedings of Business Meetings, 1834-54, p. 169.
[6]*A Volume of Records Relating to The Early History of Boston, with Selectmen's Minutes, 1799-1810* (Boston: Municipal Printing Office, 1904), XXXIII, 403.

the whole of two hundred pew owners against you, with all
their friends, 'tis not improbable. And perhaps there is two
or three hundreds building, where the trespass will be equally
great—all of which, should a Town Meeting be called, will
probably be against you.[7]

To this letter, which was made public, Bulfinch appended this
explanation:

That the public may be enabled to understand the above,
which was delivered this morning, as directed, it is necessary
to state, that a number of gentlemen, having purchased the
late Granary land for a new Meeting House, prepared their
plan on so extensive a scale, as to propose to project one angle
of the tower *six feet eight inches* into the street. A Committee
of the Selectmen had a conference with a Committee of the
Proprietors, and informed them, it was the unanimous opinion of the Board, that the building should not advance over
the line of so-frequented and important a street, and the steps
not more than three feet beyond the line. Notwithstanding
this, on Wednesday morning last, the workmen proceeded to
lay their foundation in a direction to advance at one end
three feet into the street, with the corner of the tower and
its ornaments. They were cautioned not to proceed; but
continuing their work, under the sanction of the Proprietors,
they were ordered to desist by the whole number of Selectmen present on the spot in the afternoon; and were informed
that anything placed beyond the line, would be forcibly removed.

These transactions have occasioned the above extraordinary letter. Without charging any of the Proprietors with the
folly of this production, I take this only method in my power
to inform the author and all concerned that a disinterested
regard for public ornament and convenience compels me to
resist such encroachments, which are daily becoming more
common; and as I have never courted a party, to be *put into
office*, I shall never crouch to anyone, political or religious,
from an apprehension of being "put out."

I am authorized to say the above are the unanimous sentiments of the Board of Selectmen.[8]

[7]Undated letter of A. B. to Charles Bulfinch, with explanation by Charles
Bulfinch, May 5, 1809, Massachusetts Historical Society.
[8]*Ibid.*

Evidently the proprietors had to meet the building code demands, for there is no further record of the dispute's continuation.

The building's exterior has been described as follows:

> The treatment of the front with high, simple central-entrance motive and the two curved vestibules with a slim colonnade, is unusually fresh, original, beautiful; the whole forms a pleasant foil to the arched windows and severe forms of the church proper.[9]

Descriptions of the interior are scant. The auditorium was quite commodious and very plain. In addition to the pews, other furniture included a communion table, mahogany baptismal stand, and two cast-iron stoves resting on stone hearths. The pulpit and platform were high above the pews, with curved stairways on either side of the pulpit. A gallery was on three sides. Beneath the sanctuary floor was an unfinished cellar. Above the main entrance hallway was a small finished room, the only one in the entire structure.

By the end of the year, the meetinghouse had been completed; however, "to pay for those proud steps we had taken," the church had to borrow an additional $30,000. After the church was opened, not all the pews could be sold; so pew taxes were not sufficient to meet current expenses. Mrs. Swan's interest money—approximately $960 annually—was covered by Henry Homes ($400), Josiah Bumstead ($300) and Andrew Colhoun ($260). Several other families helped meet due bills and pay off contracts. During the spring of 1810 the treasurer was authorized to borrow additional funds "to defray the present demands due on account of building Park Street Church." One year later the Ways and Means Committee was able to raise $26,500 in a new subscription on the condition that an equal sum be reserved in unsold pews for repayment. This sort of unparalleled liberality by men who had already given large sums resulted in Dr. Griffin's acceptance of May 1, 1811. Joseph W. Jenkins, a charter member, observed that the church had placed too much dependence on the elegance of the meetinghouse, its central and suitable location, the attrac-

[9]Talbot F. Hamlin, "Peter Banner," *Dictionary of American Biography*, ed. Allen Johnson (New York: Charles Scribner's Sons, 1927), I, 581.

tiveness of the choir—known as the best in New England—and
above all, the talents of their minister.

In the meantime, during the autumn and winter months of 1809,
a number of important church meetings were convened in which
several key votes were made. On October 19 it was voted to
make all the male members of Park Street Church trustees of
the land and meetinghouse in perpetuity; November 13 was set
apart as a day for prayer and fasting to seek divine guidance in
the choice of a pastor, the "sisters of the church" having been
invited to be present; on December 8, John E. Tyler and Josiah
Bumstead were chosen the first deacons. Caleb Bingham was
elected treasurer, and a standing committee composed of William Thurston and Ebenezer Parker was chosen to assist the
deacons. A third member, Aaron Hardy, was added to this committee on December 13. The date for the sale of the church pews
at public auction was set for the Monday after the meetinghouse
dedication. The first sexton, W. S. Claflin, was hired as of January 1, 1810, at an annual salary of $100.

During the initial subscriptions of November and December,
1808, the subscribers were clearly informed of the prohibitions
against all nonmembers: (1) the church alone was to enjoy the
exclusive power of choosing its ministers and opening the meetinghouse, (2) the deeds to the land and the house were to be
given into the hands of the male members.

At the advice of his legal colleagues, Thurston persuaded the
church to establish their property title so as to prevent any
possible loss of title in later years. To avoid uncertainties of the
law and to guarantee the perpetuity of their doctrines, the founders adopted a trust deed. With this they intended to make sure
that successive male members of the church would always have
the right of electing the minister, without respect to the pew-
holding society. The society would have no right in such an
election. This was on every pew deed, so that the purchaser signed
the contract with its full knowledge.

The two key paragraphs in the trust deed concern the selection
of ministers and the sale of pews:

> Said house and land at all times hereafter to be used, occu-
> pied and enjoyed as and for a Meeting House or place or

house for the public Protestant worship and service of God
by the Church aforesaid and such Society or congregation
as shall approve of the pastor or minister of the Gospel who
from time to time shall be elected by the male members of
said Church and shall suffer and permit such Protestant
pastor or minister of the Gospel as the male members of said
Church shall from time to time elect and engage and no
other to preach and perform religious exercises and services
therein, and shall and will suffer and permit the Deacons or
a committee of the Church aforesaid to sell, demise, and dispose or covenant and agree for the having, holding and en-
joying of the pews or seats in said Meeting House to such
persons, upon such tenure, terms and conditions and for such
prices and considerations as the male members of said Church
by a major vote thereof shall agree on or prescribe.[10]

Following the precedent established by Park Street Church, a
number of churches, Baptist and Congregational, adopted the
trust idea; however, it was not until after Lyman Beecher's Hanover Street Church had incorporated the scheme into its founding documents that the Unitarians began to protest the practice.
By 1830 orthodox Congregationalism had made significant progress on the comeback trail. Several new churches were functioning, revival fires were burning brightly, and many nonorthodox
people were visiting these churches. The Unitarian ministers,
unhappy with this revitalization of orthodoxy, built themselves a
straw man out of the trust scheme and in 1828 proceeded to cut
it to bits. The trust deed was called a tool for the "degradation
of the human mind," and as "moral and religious slavery."[11] An
anonymous author revealed the Unitarian mind:

The trust deed is the extraordinary attempt to bind to all
future generations . . . and to effect by forms of law what
*the inventors feel conscious they could not produce by
eloquence or the force of truth. . . . Certain persons, assured
that divine truths cannot possibly be better understood in
future ages, than they now are by themselves, or than they
were two hundred years ago by the Westminster Assembly*

[10]Registry of Deeds, Suffolk County, Boston, Massachusetts, Libro 237,
Folio 74.
[11]*Review of a Pamphlet on The Trust Deed of The Hanover Church* (Boston: T. R. Marvin, 1828), p. 6.

in England, have purchased land, and built churches, and granted pews, *on condition of perpetual servitude and submission.*[12]

The 1820 Dedham decision, which identified the church with the property, underlines the farsighted action of Park Street Church whose influence, in this regard, spread into the New England countryside. Even after the church was incorporated in 1835, thereby transferring certain responsibilities to the new Park Street Congregational Society, the sole right to choose the minister remained with the church body.

The cares and burdens surrounding these earliest labors were not easy to bear. Sympathizers were few, and detractors many. Others, if not altogether hostile, were indifferent and apathetic. Some, as Elisha Ticknor, who had been willing to support the work at first, turned away in the face of grinding discouragements, as when Dr. Kollock finally chose to remain in the South. Bumstead recorded some of the odds:

> When the Church began to build, many were looking upon us, as those Adversaries did on the feeble Jews, when they commenced their Temple, and saying it must soon fail, and there was a strong expectation of such an event, for we were indeed *very feeble,* and to all human appearance, both *in* and *out* of the Church, that we must be destroyed. The Church was *far* from being united, contention often arose in our little circle, and *pride,* that great adversary, was evidently in our midst.

A more encouraging experience faced the members on January 10, 1810, as they gathered in the crowded sanctuary of their new meetinghouse for its dedication. Dr. Edward Dorr Griffin, Bartlett Professor of Pulpit Eloquence at Andover Theological Seminary, was the principal speaker. His text was: "But will God in very deed dwell with men on the earth? Behold, heaven and the heaven of heavens cannot contain thee; how much less this house which I have built!" (II Chron. 6:18).

He posed three questions: (1) Does the omnipresent God dwell in any one place? (2) Will God dwell with men on the

[12]*Review of a Pamphlet on The Trust Deed of The Hanover Church* (Boston: T. R. Marvin, 1828), p. 6.

earth? (3) Can it be presumed that He will dwell in this house
which we have built? Responding affirmatively to each question,
Dr. Griffin proceeded to speak more particularly of Park Street
Church and the motivation behind its founding:

> This pulpit was not erected to hurl anathemas against men
> who to their own master must stand or fall. . . . The business
> to be transacted here lies not between us and our brethren of
> different names or opinions, but between God and our own
> souls.

> .   .   .   .

> This house, though not raised for controversial discussions,
> has been built by those who esteem it far from indifferent
> what doctrine a man believes; and who doubt that his reli-
> gion will take its shape from the articles of his faith.[13]

Expecting hostile criticism from the Boston clergy, he said:

> Those, therefore, who *stand in the ways, and ask for the
> good old paths, and walk therein,* will say, *Peace be to this
> house:* those only who have abandoned the religion of their
> fathers, will regard it with a cold or jealous eye.
> It is proper for me further to state, that if our earnest de-
> sires are accomplished, we shall see, in this house, the power
> and glory of the Lord, as our blessed ancestors beheld Him in
> the sanctuary. It shall not be concealed, it shall never call
> forth a blush, that this edifice was reared with many prayers
> and hopes that it might prove subservient to revivals of reli-
> gion. . . . Why should that be denounced as enthusiasm, in
> our days, which, in the days of the apostles, was the power of
> God? . . . I hope in God that this house will never be pro-
> faned by indecorous levity, nor stand for a handful of easy
> men to amuse themselves in for an hour, one half of the day;
> but that it will be crouded [*sic*] . . . with people who are
> conscious that they have souls, and must give account to
> God.[14]

Approaching the end of his discourse, Dr. Griffin offered these
words of dedication:

[13]Edward Dorr Griffin, *A Sermon Preached January 10, 1810, at The Dedication of The Church in Park Street, Boston* (Boston: Lincoln & Edmands,
n. d.), pp. 19-20.
[14]*Ibid.*, pp. 27-28.

We religiously devote this edifice to the Father, infinite
and self-existent; to the Son, the brightness of His Father's
glory; to the Holy Ghost, almighty and eternal. To the
honour and service of the ever blessed Trinity we solemnly
dedicate these walls, these arches, these columns, this pulpit,
that towering spire, and all that contains, with all that is
contained within these sacred limits. For the preaching of
the word, for the publick service of prayer and praise, for
the administration of the sacraments of the new testament,
and for the residence of the eternal God, we consecrate the
house. . . . And now, what wait we for? *Arise, O Lord, into
thy rest, thou and the ark of thy strength!* Behold Him here!
His glory fills the house! Bow yourselves before a present
God![15]

Looking forward into the future and beyond, into eternity, he
concluded:

Should this church stand a century and a half, and its seats
be generally filled, how many thousands will hear the gospel
within these walls! Millions of times will all those thousands
look back from eternity to this house, with inconceivable
pleasure or pain. By all those thousands, the effect of its
erection and dedication will be felt, millions of ages after
this world is no more. . . . The time will come when not a
tongue in the universe will make these measures the subject
of a jest.

.   .   .   .

And when the dust of this crumbled edifice shall be scattered upon the winds of heaven;—when the stones of the last
earthly sanctuary shall tremble in the convulsions of expiring
nature;—when the agonies of disappointment and despair
shall seize on those who reproached your religion; then, in
the full assembly of your fathers, and with all the triumphs
of victory, you shall ride the clouds with your victorious
Prince.[16]

The sermon was generally well received. Within a few hours
a thousand copies were ordered from the printer. However, the
liberal *Monthly Anthology*, commenting on the points of doctrine,

[15]*Ibid.*, p. 29.
[16]*Ibid.*, pp. 31-33.

viewed them as "technical babble" and "a frail and crumbling fabric."

Dr. Griffin remarked:

> The *Monthly Anthology* opened its mouth as wide as a shark's and devoured it at once. They have proved that the style is horrid, that the doctrines are worse, and that I have made at least four or five persons in the Trinity.[17]

Although it was an important day for the interests of orthodoxy, it was nevertheless an occasion unusually delicate and hazardous, for the church was looked upon by its enemies as a Gargantuan evil whose presence would serve only to bind helpless men and women. Dr. Griffin's task was extremely difficult, for he had to slacken the bands of prejudice encircling the undertaking, and at the same time expostulate on the disparities between orthodox and liberal religion.

As the men and women of Park Street Church returned to their houses that historic day, the ringing, pungent words of the minister accompanied them, and, though their enemies would continue to cast epithets, their hearts were lifted by such expressions of commendation as this: "That so small a number of men should complete so spacious and beautiful an edifice in the course of eight months is a wonder which has no parallel in the history of American churches."[18]

[17]Parsons Cooke, *Recollections of Rev. E. D. Griffin* (Boston: Massachusetts Sabbath School Society, 1855), p. 23.
[18]Griffin, *op. cit.,* p. 31.

3. Efforts to Obtain a Shepherd

In addition to the numerous details and difficulties normally attached to a venture of this magnitude, the new church was to experience repeated disappointments in obtaining its first minister. From the laying of the cornerstone in May, 1809, to the resolution of the problem in May, 1811, a series of calls were made to prominent men from New England to Gergia, but none accepted. Some were given repeated calls, but in every case the result was negative. Without Dr. Griffin's watchcare during this interim, the accelerated flounderings of the young church may have caused its eventual death. His leadership enabled the congregation to hold together; his guidance in the selection of ministerial candidates proved invaluable; and his eloquent preaching attracted hundreds to the Sabbath services, where many purchased pews—a most important factor for the financial health of the church.

From the earliest years of the Massachusetts Bay Colony, the Congregational clergy had received their monetary support through a general tax upon citizens. During the eighteenth century stiff and increasing opposition arose against this unjust law, especially from the Baptists. In 1754 the Massachusetts legislature passed a law whereby all religious societies could assess pew owners on the basis of a proper evaluation.

The Monday following the meetinghouse dedication was designated as the sale day, but it was postponed a week. The exact number of pews in the original seating plan is not known; however, the pew plan of 1838, made upon the completion of major alterations that year, shows approximately one hundred eighty-four pews. Dr. Griffin's correspondence reveals that nearly a hundred pews were sold or rented.

A financial statement of April 24, 1810, shows eighty-three pews unsold on the lower floor at an appraised value of $29,000, and a number of gallery pews yet unsold at a value of $6,000. Probably most of the gallery pews were unsold during the entire ministry of Dr. Griffin. Prices for pews on the main floor ranged from $100 to $460; those in the balcony, $100 to $300. In addition to the initial sale price, the pew proprietor was assessed a quarterly tax based upon the worth of his pew. These tax rates varied in the succeeding years depending upon the society's financial condition. During the Civil War years a $430 pew was taxed at a quarterly rate of $7.53, a $300 pew at $5.25.

The pews were offered for sale at public auction on January 22, 1810, under the gavel of Thomas Jones. The conditions of sale were 20 percent down and the residue payable with interest in three installments over the succeeding nine months. The purchaser received a pew deed upon his completed payment. This title deed was to be maintained under strict conditions governing regular payments of taxes. Failure to abide by the obligations resulted in loss or forfeiture of the pew. Those who had loaned money to the new church were permitted to receive pews in partial payment of their loans.

It was reported in a church business meeting of February 6, 1811, that on the basis of the pews already sold or rented, tax income totaled $1,800. The rental of a portion of the cellar underneath the sanctuary produced an additional $150 annually. It was hoped that with an increasing sale and rental of pews these sums would be sufficient to cover operating expenses and salaries. Several decades passed, however, before the church was free from debt and the burden of insufficient funds. Dr. Griffin was unsuccessful in his attempt to sell enough pews to establish a sound fiscal structure, but this was not to be his primary task.

Efforts toward obtaining a minister had begun a year and a half before the church's founding in February, 1809. Jedidiah Morse of the Charlestown church had been asked in October, 1807, by the men of the Religious Improvement Society to find a suitable pastor during a visit to New York. After Dr. Morse had spoken with President Timothy Dwight of Yale and other men in New York, the society had turned its attention toward Dr. Griffin.

The following summer, both Dr. Kollock and Dr. Griffin had visited Boston. When both had made indelible impressions upon the evangelical leadership of Massachusetts, they were immediately invited to New England—Dr. Kollock to Park Street Church and Dr. Griffin to the newly established Andover Theological Seminary. The reaction to Griffin's preaching was summed up by Dr. Samuel Spring: "What a *mammoth* of an orator." The Christians had not heard such powerful preaching for many years. Morse wrote President Dwight that all the friends of the seminary and of Park Street Church were united in saying that he must come. He pleaded with Dr. Dwight to use every influence, directly and through the New York clergy, to persuade Griffin.

The appearance of the new seminary at this time resulted in a number of problems for the orthodox Christians in Andover and Boston. William Bartlett, a trustee and benefactor of the seminary, had personally selected Dr. Griffin for the newly endowed chair of Pulpit Eloquence. However, Dr. Morse and the leaders of the Religious Improvement Society wanted him for Park Street Church as an associate with Dr. Kollock. The Andover invitation, therefore, was made as attractive as possible through the generosity of Bartlett, who offered a salary of $1,200, a new house, firewood, moving expenses and $500 for incidentals. He was adamantly opposed to Griffin's acceptance of any official pulpit position. This objection caused Griffin to delay his decision, because if he joined the seminary faculty he would have to have a stated pulpit, and something more than the tiny congregation of students at the Andover chapel. Writing to Morse, Griffin said the Andover offer was totally unacceptable. He enumerated further difficulties in a twofold responsibility: (1) Would he live in Boston or Andover? (2) Must he furnish and maintain two houses? (3) How much time was to be allotted to each position? Relative to his proposed association with Dr. Kollock, he asked whether the new church was to be founded and the sacraments administered on Edwardian principles. If so, would Dr. Kollock conform or would there have to be two different modes of practice in one church?

To spend half his time in Boston and the other half in Andover, as some suggested, seemed impractical to Dr. Griffin. Furthermore, such a practice would be detrimental to church discipline, especially in regard to the sacraments. He said he had to have the necessary freedom to forbid any maladministration of the sacraments. The new congregation would have to make a clear-cut decision involving a thoroughgoing discipline, he said. Over the portals of the meetinghouse, as well as on the foreheads and hearts of the pastors, would have to be written, "Come out from among them and be ye separate." Only men of this kind, he wrote, would succeed. There had to be a visible difference between the old and the new churches, otherwise people would not leave the old for the new.

This particular problem resolved itself the following year when Dr. Kollock decided to not accept the church's invitation to become its first minister.

A second major obstacle was dissolved when Bartlett relaxed his position, enabling Griffin to consider more seriously this letter of call from Park Street Church:

Rev. and Beloved Sir,

The preceding votes of the New Church, in which we cordially united, afford us the satisfaction of addressing you upon the subject of your coming to preach to this church upon such terms as will, we hope, be mutually agreeable, and at the same time consistent with your filling the office of Bartlett professor of Pulpit Eloquence at Andover.

.   .   .   .

We do now, in behalf of this Church, earnestly request you to accept the call expressed in their votes before recited, and promise you in the discharge of your duty all that support, encouragement and obedience in the Lord which is proper, and that the extra expenses of this connection shall be faithfully defrayed by this Church.[1]

Although Dr. Griffin would have preferred to accept the one invitation to become pastor of Park Street Church, he yielded to

[1]Park Street Church, Proceedings of Business Meetings, 1809-34, p. 47.

Andover pressure, particularly to Professor Leonard Woods, who also desperately wanted him at the seminary, and made his final decision to assume both positions. Dr. Woods, the seminary trustees, and Park Street Church, were notified on March 27, 1809.

The following months were busy ones in the life of the new church. The meetinghouse was being erected, and members were enthused over prospects for soon filling the pulpit. But their hopes vanished in September when Dr. Kollock declined the call. This news not only upset the ministerial plans of the church, but also many subscribers who withdrew their support despite work already contracted for. To the infant congregation, this was a most appalling event. Thurston, in an attempt to win Dr. Kollock for Boston, personally visited Savannah, but his trip was in vain.

The church's only remaining hope to secure a resident minister as speedily as possible lay with Professor Griffin, who was just then commencing his first year as a member of the Andover faculty. On September 23, Park Street Church extended him a unanimous call, offering to pay him as high a salary as any Congregational minister in Boston. But he declined. The following evening Dr. Griffin, Tyler and Thurston were appointed a committee to locate a pastor. Their difficult assignment did not end until nearly two years later, and then only by Dr. Griffin's responsive action.

At a church meeting on January 16, 1810, the pastoral committee presented the name of Eliphalet Nott, president of Union College, Schenectady, New York. Dr. Griffin conveyed the call to Dr. Nott, in which he was asked to promise, should he accept the call, not to baptize any children unless one parent was a communicant, and that he not exchange pulpits with any minister denying the Trinity as explained in the Westminster Confession. His salary was set at $1,300 with a house and provision of wood.

Three weeks later Dr. Nott declined the call. Dr. Griffin was instructed to write a second letter, which was also refused. In an April 14 letter to his brother, Dr. Nott told why he declined: (1) He did not wish to live in a city; (2) A friend had written that Park Street Church was divided; (3) He considered himself unfit for the position which required a man of manners and management, a man skilled in the subtleties of metaphysics and

familiar with disputation. He recognized that a theological war-
fare was about to begin in the East for which he had neither
talents nor inclination.

Meanwhile Dr. Morse, who was in South Carolina, wrote to
Rev. Dr. J. M. Mason, recently resigned pastor of the First Associate Reformed Church, New York City, imploring him to consider the Boston pulpit.

During the next six months, calls were extended to Dr. John
Romeyn of the Cedar Street Presbyterian Church, New York City;
to Dr. Gardiner Spring of Andover; and for a third time to Dr.
Nott. Each call was politely declined.

These successive disappointments indicate two religious facts,
one related to Park Street Church and the other to the religious
situation in Boston. As the church deacons well knew, and as
Dr. Griffin often said, there were two great sins of which the
brethren were guilty: pride, and dependence upon man. This
inability to find a minister was a disciplinary measure calculated
to humble the new society. Even after his installation as pastor,
Dr. Griffin, in a letter of September 14, 1811, wrote to his Newark
friend, James Richards:

> But our church is still dead, and still looking to an arm of
> flesh. We have not got enough yet. We shall have to receive
> more scourging before we shall be fit for any work. Of all
> creatures, some of us seemed the most unlikely to be selected
> to make such a stand in Boston.[2]

The second fact related to Park Street Church during these
years was the liberal phalanx intent on destroying this small
orthodox congregation. Dr. Griffin, who corresponded often with
Richards during 1810, told of this opposition:

> You can form no adequate idea of the strength of Satan's
> kingdom in this town and its vicinity. The injury which
> Chauncey, and a few other men, have done to the church
> in this region, is incalculable. Our church has been over-
> whelmed with contempt. The catholicism of Boston is the
> most intolerant bigotry that I ever witnessed, when directed

[2]William B. Sprague, *Memoir of The Rev. Edward D. Griffin, D. D.*, (New
York: Taylor & Dodd, 1839), p. 124.

towards the religion of Christ. It is a fiend which never wears
a smile but when its eye is directed towards the most abominable errors.

.   .   .   .

You have no conception of the falsehoods which are prop-
agated, and the pains which are taken, to prevent people
from coming to our church. But the more they try to prevent,
the more the people will not mind them. Prejudice is fast
wearing away.[3]

Obviously Dr. Nott was not alone in his unwillingness to place
himself amid such a religious tempest, nor were many men willing and able to leave relatively secure pastorates for an infant
flock destined, for a while at least, to remain small and feeble
and to bear patiently the ridicule and scorn of her proud and
opulent foes. As 1810 drew to a close, Dr. Griffin pondered the
future: "What is before us I don't know; but unless God speedily
interposes, it does seem as though the cause must be given up."[4]
The task of finding a pastor seemed insurmountable. Who could
be found to take the job? The young clergyman thought to himself, "If nobody else will, must I come?"[5]

During the first week of February, 1811, two years after the
organization of the church, Dr. Griffin was invited once more to
accept the pastoral call. On March 23 he wrote a letter of reply
which seemed to offer a glimmer of hope:

DEAR BRETHREN,

As I am a member of the Presbytery of Jersey, I am not
permitted by the rules of the Presbyterian Church to consider your call as being in my hands, till it has been submitted by you to the Presbytery. Nor could I be installed,
consistent with the rules of the Presbyterian Church, by any
but the Presbytery, or their Committee, unless I should be
dismissed from the Presbytery to join some other body in this
region. Previously to my taking any steps in relation to your
call, I wish to know whether, in case some body cannot be
formed in this region which I shall be willing to join, and
for which I shall be willing to be dismissed from the Presby-

[3]*Ibid.*, p. 117.
[4]*Ibid.*, p. 118.
[5]*Ibid.*, p. 119.

tery, you are willing to submit the call to the Presbytery, and to have the installation performed by them. I should be gratified by receiving an answer by the next Sabbath after tomorrow. I am, dear brethren, most affectionately yours.[6]

In other communications Dr. Griffin emphasized the importance of reducing the church debt if he would become their pastor. With the first definite hope of securing a minister since September, 1809, a new subscription was begun and $26,500 was raised. The candidate committee of Tyler, Bumstead and Thurston was empowered on April 13 to present their call to the Jersey Presbytery with a request that they convey it to Dr. Griffin.

In the meantime, the people at Andover, fearing that their professor might accept a Park Street call, wrote him on March 28, stressing again his importance to the infant seminary. The school's interests should have first claim to his services, they said, and if he left Andover, the loss might prove irreparable. However, Professor Griffin had obviously reached a definite decision. The responsibilities and duties of the two positions continued to increase, thus demanding more of his time. The impossibility of the situation was now fully recognized. He felt he must go to Park Street for he was more accustomed to the office of the minister than to that of the professor, and having made his choice he could no longer remain on the campus for the seminary's constitution forbade that a professor, receiving his support from an endowment, should ever preach for hire or take the pastoral charge of any church or congregation.

Griffin wrote to Rev. James Richards on April 16, 1811, telling of his decision to go to Park Street and of the seminary students seeking, through Bartlett, to forestall his going. Despite this, his decision remained firm. After being tossed about for two years and kept in a state of restlessness without a home, and crushed with the cares of both Andover and Boston, he had at last found rest.

Dr. Sprague, in commenting upon Park Street's dire need for a pastor, pointed out the significance of Dr. Griffin's acceptance at this time. Considering Boston's religious conditions, and recalling that twenty-six months had passed since twenty-six men

[6]Park Street Church, Proceedings of Business Meetings, 1809-34, p. 85.

50

BRIMSTONE CORNER

and women had founded the church, he said that if Griffin had not accepted, the congregation would have been forced to seriously consider disbanding and selling the meetinghouse.

On May 1, 1811, after having received at least six negative replies to their calls for a resident minister, Park Street Church got Dr. Griffin's affirmative answer.

DEAR BRETHREN,

I have respectfully and seriously considered the call presented to me in your name, by your joint committee, to become your pastor. I have endeavored to pay all that attention to the subject which the importance of it seemed to demand. At length, after mature deliberation, I have thought it my duty to accept the call, and I do hereby declare my acceptance of it. In view of the interesting and tender relation which is to subsist between us, the awful responsibility which must rest upon me, the peculiar difficulties with which I shall be surrounded, and the eternal consequences which are likely to result from this relation, I am constrained to ask your daily prayers, for my support, direction, and success. I shall need your sympathy; I shall need your counsel; I shall need the mantle of your charity to cover many imperfections. God grant that our union may be blessed to our mutual comfort in this life, and be reviewed by us all with great and unceasing pleasure in the world to come.

I am, dear brethren, with great affection, your brother and servant in the Lord.[7]

With Dr. Griffin's dismission by the Jersey Presbytery to the fellowship of the orthodox Congregational churches of greater Boston, the congregation was free to install its first minister. Invitations to participate in an examining council were sent to the churches of Cambridge, Charlestown, Newton, Salem, Beverly, Danvers, Lexington, Dorchester, Milton, Randolph, Weymouth, Dedham, Reading, Braintree, and in Boston, to the Old South Church. Individuals invited were Drs. Leonard Woods and Moses Stuart of Andover Theological Seminary.

At 10 A.M. Wednesday, July 31, 1811, the council, composed of the invited lay and clerical delegates, met in the land office of the state house on Beacon Hill. Rev. William Greenough of

[7]*Ibid.*, p. 90.

Newton was elected moderator; Rev. Williams of Lexington, the scribe; and Rev. Joshua Huntington of Old South Church, assistant scribe. After an opening prayer, the council was presented a letter from the First Presbyterian Church, Newark, New Jersey, dissolving that pastoral relation, and with the letter of dismission from the Jersey Presbytery, recommending Dr. Griffin to the association of orthodox ministers in Boston and vicinity. A communication from the Newark church officers was read, in which they testified to their affection for their former pastor.

Dr. Griffin was then asked to make a confession of his faith, relate his Christian experience, and declare his views and motives for preaching the gospel. Then the council voted for the installation service to take place. These assignments were made: the sermon by Rev. Samuel Worcester of Salem; the consecrating prayer, Dr. Abiel Holmes; the charge to Dr. Griffin, Rev. William Greenough, Second Congregational Church, Newton; the right hand of fellowship, Rev. Jonathan Homer, Newton; prayers, Dr. Morse and Joshua Huntington. At 11:30 A.M. the adjourned council members moved in procession down Park Street to the meetinghouse where the public exercises of formal installation were held before a large assembly.

Dr. Worcester's sermon was based on II Timothy 2:19. He said the foundation of the church, being Jesus Christ, standeth sure, and its bears a twofold inscription: (1) the Lord knows them who are His own; (2) let all who name the name of Christ depart from the practice of sinning. Addressing himself to the new minister, Worcester declared:

> If for this [ministry] you have found it necessary to force yourself away from scenes the most pleasant and endeared, and from Christian friends in many tears, at Newark; from the pleasures of the consecrated shades, and the solicitations of the affectionate sons of the prophets, at Andover; the Master whom you serve will not be unmindful of these painful sacrifices. In his sovereign wisdom he has assigned you to this post, and here you must stand. It is indeed a post of arduous duty, and of vast responsibility.[8]

[8]Samuel Worcester, *The Foundation of God Sure and Sealed* (Boston: Samuel T. Armstrong, 1811), p. 34.

During 1809-11, when Dr. Griffin pastored Park Street Church without having been installed, he lived in a Beacon Street house rented from a William Paine. The church paid annual rent of seven hundred dollars. In addition to this furnished and heated house he was given four hundred dollars for necessary expenses. The church also provided fifty dollars annually for stabling and boarding the horse Dr. Griffin used for transportation between Boston and Andover.

On January 9, 1810, the day before the dedication of the meetinghouse, a daughter, Ellen Marian, was born to Dr. and Mrs. Griffin. Her baptism during the afternoon of March 4, 1810, with that of Edward Griffin Bumstead, were the first two baptisms in the new edifice. The initial observance of the Lord's Supper was on the morning of the same day. Dr. Griffin also performed his first wedding ceremony in January.

Sabbath services during Dr. Griffin's ministry included a morning and afternoon meeting with an evening lecture supported by a freewill offering. The house was often crowded, especially in the evenings, but the doctrines presented were not received well by the visiting public. An occasional Thursday evening meeting was held in the small vestry of the meetinghouse with good attendance.

Communion was celebrated the first Sunday of each month with a preparatory lecture on the preceding Friday, when prospective members met to subscribe to the Articles of Faith. The monthly business meeting was on the Monday following the third Sunday.

These activities and concerns in the first two years of the church's existence reveal what demands were laid upon Dr. Griffin. And his interests were not confined only to the church and the campus. The early nineteenth century saw the creation of numerous religious, educational, humanitarian and evangelistic organizations in New England as a direct result of the Great Revival. The ministers and laymen of Park Street Church were integrally associated with many of these. Dr. Griffin became a key figure in the movements which produced not only Park Street Church but also Andover Theological Seminary and the American Board of Commissioners for Foreign Missions. On June 26, 1810, in the house of Moses Stuart, he spoke passionately for the inauguration of a missionary enterprise which would send Judson, Nott, Newell, Hall and Rice as missionaries.

Since then Park Street Church has been a key institution in the development and advancement of Christian missions, evangelism, and Christian education, both at home and abroad.

4. *The Definitive Years*

The town of Boston was originally built on a peninsula one and three-quarter miles in length, of irregular shape, and connected to the mainland by a mile-long, narrow isthmus. In 1809 its 33,000 inhabitants traversed its eight hundred acres on one hundred streets, lanes and alleys, most of them unimaginatively laid out. The wooded and rolling terrain was topped by three hills: Beacon Hill on the west, Copp's Hill on the north, and Fort Hill on the eastern end of town. The first Boston census, in 1791, reported 2,376 houses. After 1800 however, many of these houses, largely wooden, together with the town farms, slowly disappeared to make way for brick residences and an increasing number of commercial buildings. These changes created new residential sections in the uncrowded north and south ends, and on Beacon Hill.

In the year of Park Street Church's founding, Boston was still governed by the town-meeting concept, although much of its force and vitality had dissipated over the years. Attempts toward a more adequate form of government had been tried throughout the eighteenth century, but not until 1822 did Boston change from town to city government with a mayor, seven executive aldermen and a common council.

In addition to the Congregational, Episcopal, Baptist and Methodist churches in existence during this period, there was one Roman Catholic church in Boston. The Cathedral of the Holy Cross on Franklin Street was dedicated September 29, 1803, by Bishop Carroll of Baltimore. In 1808 Boston was made an episcopal see by Pope Pius VII, and Dr. John Ceverus was consecrated as the first bishop in November, 1810.

The Congregational churchmen of Boston were not the only segment of the population embroiled in controversy in the early years of the nineteenth century. As a result of hostilities between England and France, world trade suffered a serious setback. The United States merchant marine and Boston shipping interests immediately stepped into the gap and began reaping a rich harvest. Ship tonnage in Boston mounted steadily as a result of this sudden expansion of international trade. Financial wealth began pouring into the town. However, with the ensuing retaliation by Great Britain against United States shipping, and the Embargo Act passed by Congress in December, 1807, New England shipping came to an abrupt halt. The citizens of New England quickly objected to these national policies by threatening secession from the Union. Local Federalist protest was reflected in the election of Governor Christopher Gore in 1809 and in numerous town meetings calling for petitions to the state legislature and to President Thomas Jefferson.

As those twenty-six men and women awakened to the dawn of February 27, 1809, they found the entire first page of their local newspaper given over to the text of the Memorial and Remonstrance of the Massachusetts legislature addressed to the Senate and House of Representatives in Washington. Continued political pressure finally resulted in the repeal of the act in 1809, thus enabling the fishing and commercial interests of Boston to revive.

These tensions continued into 1811, when Edward Dorr Griffin commenced his duties as Park Street's first minister. Obstacles of every description—religious, political, economic and social, together with those personal perils of fear, doubt, anxiety and trepidation—seemingly combined with abortive intent to halt the church's development. Even a full-scale war was begun and won to the sound of the booming cannon in Boston Harbor, the marching of the Boston Brigade on the Common, and with the brimstone stored in the cellar of the meetinghouse.[1]

[1]According to Mrs. Hannah Dana, grandmother of Mrs. Erastus Smith, the epithet, "Brimstone Corner," had its origin in this storage of brimstone required in the manufacture of gunpowder. See *Commemorative Exercises at The One Hundredth Anniversary of the Organization of Park Street Church* (Boston: Park Street Centennial Committee, 1909), p. 194.

Dr. Griffin came to New England from successful pastorates in New Hartford, Connecticut, and Newark, New Jersey. In every one of his churches, both before and after his Boston pastorate, his ministry was marked by a strong revivalistic quality. At Park Street Church occasional revival seasons occurred, but not to the degree experienced elsewhere. The mighty deluge of the Spirit's power was not to come until the pastorate of Sereno Dwight. The years 1811-15 were to be years of establishment, of solidifying theological convictions, and of charting directions. The success of those earliest definitive labors was revealed by succeeding events and years. Griffin put Park Street Church on the map.

One of his first tasks was to formulate a strong, clear-cut standard of church order and discipline. Responsibility for examining candidates for church membership was given to the Standing Committee, which carefully reviewed the certificates and Christian credentials of those seeking admission from other churches. The committee having satisfied itself on the candidates' qualifications, their names were then brought before the church on the Sunday before communion, when each name was voted on separately. During the following week, all the candidates subscribed to the Articles of Faith. On the next Sunday, prior to the celebration of the Lord's Supper, the church covenant was read to those to be received "from the world," that is, without certificate. Upon their willing assent they were admitted, followed by those requesting admission by church letter.

This procedure was no mere formality. The church members were expected to keep their vows; whenever any failure occurred, the church quickly made inquiry and initiated disciplinary measures.

In addition to the Standing Committee, other elective posts included those of clerk, treasurer, two auditors, a nine-member Prudential Committee and a sexton.

The spiritual concerns of the pastor and his deacons extended to youth as well as to adults. In a meeting of January 10, 1814, a rule was adopted calling upon "the church to . . . meet with all baptized children four times per year for the purpose of examining their progress in divine knowledge, [thereby ascertaining whether the parents have been faithful] pressing upon them the

obligations resulting from their baptism." These and similar measures, though calculated to bring the faith and order of the membership to a level more in keeping with the heritage of the church,
were not planned to enhance its image. The polity and discipline
of the Congregational churches in Boston had become exceedingly
lax over the years. The strictness of the Reformed standards had
been displaced by an all-inclusive spirit of toleration. The "en-
lightened" clergy had neither taste nor respect for the policies of
Dr. Griffin. Blasts of ridicule and reproach were regularly un-
leashed from the Unitarian camp against the infant church and
its first pastor.

On October 20, 1813, Dr. Griffin preached at the dedication of
the Calvinistic Congregational Society of Sandwich, Massachusetts. This church was formed after the forcible ejection of its
pastor, Rev. Burr, from the original meetinghouse. Burr, having
become a Calvinist, was no longer desired by his parish, and a
new society had been formed by sympathetic members of the
church and society. Dr. Griffin reminded these Christians that
persecutions would come to those living godly lives for Christ's
sake, and that these sufferings could be easily avoided by side-
stepping the support and preaching of pointed doctrines for the
Lord's more mild and beneficent aspects.

This sermon, delivered midway through his Park Street pastorate, clearly reveals that force of conviction which impelled Dr.
Griffin's weekly proclamation of orthodox beliefs from New England pulpits:

> But let any man continually carry about him a full and
> distinct image of God, exhibiting all the truths of His Word,
> all the strictness of His law, all the guilt and danger of sin-
> ners,—carrying reproof to every thing selfish, every thing
> proud, every thing vain, every thing that does not make
> God the supreme object . . . ; and let him moreover be con-
> stituted by his age or office a reprover; and there is not a
> community of worldly men in Christendom who will not be
> offended. . . . This *must* be true or "the carnal mind" is no
> longer "enmity against God."[2]

[2]Edward D. Griffin, *Sermon at Dedication of Meetinghouse at Sandwich,
Massachusetts, October 20, 1813* (Boston: Nathaniel Willis, 1813), p. 9.

In respect to exchanging pulpits, Dr. Griffin absolutely refused to exchange his pulpit with any who taught another gospel. In the face of pressure, even from his own camp, to moderate his rigid stance, he stood unshakable. Some said he would ruin his cause. He was reminded that some in his own church had come out of heretical societies unscathed; therefore, he would be wise to refrain from following over-zealous advice. This interchange of pulpits was carried on to a greater degree in Boston than perhaps anywhere else. In religious circles, failure to exchange was a great discourtesy as well as a disparagement of the clerical community. Dr. Griffin, nevertheless, was willing to suffer social and clerical ostracism in order to shepherd those in his care. He felt that to exchange pulpits with Arminians and Arians was to proclaim the innocence of error and the precedence of peace over truth. A Unitarian minister in Philadelphia wrote to a friend in England that Park Street Church was deeply in debt with half the pews yet unrented and that Dr. Griffin, by not returning the civilities of the other ministers, was largely neglected by them and their congregations.

Dr. Griffin's association with the Harvard College overseers brought him in contact with state government officials, several of whom occasionally attended Sunday services. Their attraction to Park Street Church makes this advice in a liberal literary journal interesting:

> What is the best policy for a layman, wishing the votes of the people, to adopt in regard to his religious profession? The answer in New England is apt to be, that Calvinism is the best aid *to an ambitious man.* Our answer, however, is opposed to this. We believe from theory and from fact, that catholic [liberal] Christianity is better adapted to conciliate the affections of the people as a body, than any form of sectarianism. If this be so, it will follow that catholic Christians are more likely than sectarists to obtain such political situations as shall give them influence and power.[3]

This sort of sniping was bound to affect the church's financial condition. Though many admired the young minister and at-

[3]"Contrast Between Calvinism and Hopkinsianism," *The General Repository and Review,* April, 1813, p. 374.

tended his services, few purchased pews; new members averaged only twenty-three per year. However, Dr. Griffin's power of debate and vigor of presentation continued undiminished. As a staunch Edwardian he preached as the Puritans before him, supporting his sermons with powerful argument and logic, close reasoning, and much utilization of Scripture. His manner was pointed and direct. He did not use euphemisms which would tend to rob words of their full impact. With unusual force, and aided by a six-foot, three-inch physical frame, he arraigned the sinner before the bar of divine justice, and with equal vigor pointed men to a compassionate and redeeming Saviour.

During the winter of 1812-13, Dr. Griffin began a series of Sunday evening lectures which was heard by large crowds and was regarded as an able and eloquent exposition of the Edwardian form of Calvinism. These discourses, later published under the title of *Park Street Lectures*, were primarily devoted to four major doctrines: total depravity, regeneration, election and perseverance. Dr. Griffin said he chose these doctrines because they formed the "great hinges" of the true gospel. Any theological system denying any one of them he declared to be a false gospel. He said they were the necessary parts of the whole system bound together by an inviolable connection of premise and consequence. Using masterful apologetic, supported and saturated with hundreds of Scripture texts and laced with powerful logic and argument, Dr. Griffin performed an outstanding service for the orthodox cause in eastern Massachusetts. It was perhaps the high point of his entire Boston ministry.

While busily engaged with his pastoral and ministerial duties, Dr. Griffin was also an important figure in the burgeoning missionary enterprise. Perhaps the most famous missionary sermon of this period was the one he preached before the 1805 meeting of the General Assembly of the Presbyterian Church. Speaking from Colossians 1:16 on "The Kingdom of Christ," he reminded his audience that the earth was made by Christ in order that through the events of history His mediatorial work for the glory of the Father and for the salvation of mankind might be accomplished. Therefore, he said, no man was licensed to set up on this ground, sacred to the Redeemer, any interest other than that which bore a

direct relation to His royal cause. He upbraided those who left
the conversion of the heathen wholly to God, and those others
who timidly pleaded insufficient funds:

> But in the awful hour when you, and I, and all the pagan
> nations, shall be called from our graves to stand before the
> bar of Christ, what comparison will those [earthly] objects
> bear to the salvation of a single soul? Eternal mercy! let not
> the blood of heathen millions, in that hour, be found in our
> skirts! . . . I pronounce the conversion of a single pagan of
> more value than all the wealth that ever omnipotence pro-
> duced.[4]

The Haystack prayer group at Williams College republished this
missionary address as one of its first projects.

Since the early days of the nineteenth century were difficult
both politically and economically, it was not until 1812 that the
first missionaries were ordained and sent out by the American
Board. This historic ordination service took place on February 6
in the Tabernacle Church, Salem, Massachusetts, where Samuel
Skelton and Francis Higginson ministered in 1629, and Roger
Williams in 1633. The five young men ordained were Adoniram
Judson, Jr., Samuel Newell, Samuel Nott, Gordon Hall and Luther
Rice. Dr. Griffin, who represented Park Street Church at this meet-
ing, invited Judson to become his assistant in Boston, but the offer
was politely refused.

Although these first missionaries set sail for India with much
excitement and hope, they only possessed sufficient funds to sustain them for a few months. The American Board treasury being
nearly depleted, appeals were made to the Christian public for
financial help. On Sunday evening, February 16, Dr. Griffin
preached a missionary sermon at Park Street Church designed to
raise funds for the board. A collection of $339.65 was received
and forwarded immediately to the missionary society. In addition
to this offering, American Board accounts show the receipt of
$1,075.17 from the Boston Foreign Mission Society, $525 of which
was "received by the hand of the Rev. Dr. Griffin." During the

---

[4]Edward Dorr Griffin, *The Kingdom of Christ: A Missionary Sermon*
(Philadelphia: Jane Aitken, 1805), p. 29.

first half century of its existence, the church gave eight of its members to the American Board for missionary service.

The church's fidelity to missions was matched by its interest in Christian education. The women were as zealous as the men in promoting the organization of benevolent societies to financially assist young men in their ministerial education. The Corban Society, founded in 1813, was one of the earliest of such organizations. Among its first officers were Mrs. Dorcas Homes and Miss Elizabeth Haskins of Park Street Church. A more significant beginning was made in the autumn of 1815 with the formation of the American Education Society. Incorporated on December 6, 1816, its purpose was to aid pious young men in their educational preparation for the gospel ministry.

As with missions, Dr. Griffin always gave stellar leadership to the cause of Christian education. Williams College owes its existence to its former stalwart president, who, in lean times, restored the school to health and strength. Speaking before an American Education Society audience in Boston in 1825, he thundered these verbal bolts which reveal the passionate level of his convictions. Lashing out at those who felt no particular compulsion to contribute, he said:

> If he could part with his blood and life for our salvation, shall we think it much to give our paltry pelf for the salvation of his members? And consider that every cent we call our own came from his hands—came marked with the price of blood. . . . For what did he give it to us to demand it again? What but to try us by an experiment the most decisive? And if under these solemn circumstances we will not return to him the bloodmarked coin, what an awful exhibition it will be of ingratitude, idolatry, and rebellion. Show me the tribute money. Whose is this blood and superscription? A voice from heaven answers, Christ's. I charge you then by the living God, Render unto Christ the things that are Christ's.[5]

Dr. Griffin's hammering affirmations of divine truth, though markedly beneficial to his congregation, failed to produce that high level of holiness necessary to a spiritually dynamic church.

[5]Edward Dorr Griffin, *An Address Delivered Before The American Education Society, May 23, 1825* (Boston: Ezra Lincoln, 1825), p. 3.

Periods of revival like those he had witnessed in his New Hartford and Newark churches did not come. A revival cloud, the size
of a man's hand, did appear in early 1812. The latter part of
February, he instituted a conference exclusively for persons under
serious impressions; approximately thirty attended these inquiry
sessions, but only five indicated interest in becoming Christians.
Over the next eighteen months, a total of ninety-one persons received instruction in these conference meetings. Dr. Griffin noted
a greater solemnity in the Sabbath services, but there was no significant break. Disappointment followed hope as the small cloud
disappeared beyond the horizon. Candidly expressing his feelings,
he unburdened himself to his friend, James Richards, in a letter of
August 23, 1813:

> Boston folks will be Boston folks still. They will not re-
> trench a habit, nor lose a nap at church, to save their lives.
> Had I known as much as I now do, I never would have left
> the Presbyterian world; and if my conscience would suffer
> me, I would enter it again as soon as I could. . . . We are
> in peace, but a peace attended with more stupidity than
> comfort.[6]

Seven months later, he wrote again of the need for spiritual
renewal: "We all remain as cold and hard as rocks." Speaking
powerfully and pointedly on the weakness of the church, he declared in a sermon:

> But the moment you bring out religion in its own naked
> nature, as waging an eternal war with selfishness; the mo-
> ment you disturb their security and awaken fears for their
> own dear selves;—the moment you uncover a God that lays
> their Dagon on its face; you perceive that these smooth
> Christians have the heart of a Jew still; and unless restrained
> by social affections or some apparent interest, they will rise
> with the spirit of the scribe and Pharisee.
>
>   .   .   .   .
>
> Private Christians are afraid to have the whole counsel of
> God declared in the most pointed form, lest it should drive
> people from the sanctuary. They are afraid to talk them-

[6]William B. Sprague, *Memoir of the Rev. Edward D. Griffin, D.D.* (New
York: Taylor & Dodd, 1839), p. 129.

selves to their fellowmen in the manner most calculated to impress their hearts. They are afraid to reprove sins in their brethren and to exercise the faithful discipline of the Church. They are afraid to take any thorough measures to promote religion, lest some should scoff and others complain.[7]

This type of forceful and sometimes excoriating preaching, combined with financial problems, eventually led to the resignation of the church's first minister. On the one hand, the regularly attending nonmembers, who were the best source for recruiting communicants, were exceedingly reluctant to join a church having such an outspoken minister; thus many pews remained unsold while others were returned to the trustees. On the other hand, the political and economic condition of the times was not advantageous to fiscal stability. Dr. Griffin came to Park Street Church at a fixed salary of $2,100, but seldom did he receive his quarterly payment on time. Salary receipts bearing his signature show he was paid in amounts varying from $25 to $400. As early as April, 1812, having been the installed minister less than a year, his salary was already in arrears by nearly $1,000. The treasurer's report shows the solicitation of a subscription to cover this item.

In a meeting of the society on December 6, 1813, this letter from Dr. Griffin, telling of his financial plight, was read:

But having spent all that I could command of my own stock . . . and having not enough left to carry me through another week, I had no other way but to make this direct application to you. . . . I have repeatedly offered to go to boarding, but this my friends would not allow. I well know that my preaching is not acceptable, and that I do not succeed to draw together a congregation to increase your strength. And I see little prospect of succeeding better for the future. To cast myself longer, therefore, as a burden on a few friends, is very distressing to my feelings.

Commending them again for their liberality, he nevertheless called for added sacrifice in order to buttress the church's lingering life. He informed them of his readiness to resign at an hour's notice; however, should they wish him to remain, he said he could

[7]Edward Dorr Griffin, "Christian Boldness," *The American Pulpit* (Edinburg: T. & T. Clark, 1852), pp. 226-28.

only do so with a punctual payment of his salary at the beginning of each quarter according to contract. He said a better means than the yearly subscription should be devised, nor should the salary be provided from differing sources, some of which served to meet other debts, but from one stable source.

A committee chosen to study the problem reported on December 20, 1813. But their recommendations were not well received by the society. Numerous complaints were made concerning the yearly subscription and a suggested additional assessment. In the light of these grievances, the society postponed further action until its annual meeting in April. Passage of time, they felt, would produce greater harmony.

Not until nearly six months later did Dr. Griffin learn of the society's adverse reaction to his communication of the previous December. Deeply hurt by their attitude, he conveyed his feelings to the entire church and congregation on April 26, 1814:

> It was never known to me till yesterday that my communication made to you on the sixth of December last had been deemed improper. I made it in the sincerity of my heart without dreaming of giving offence. Considering however the sensations which have been excited, I regret that it was made, and wish you to dismiss the subject, and let everything remain as to my salary as though nothing of this nature had been done.

In a letter of May 3 the committee reflected the mind of many in the congregation who believed that Dr. Griffin's salary troubles were self-initiated. His ministry was directly related to the numbers of pews sold, and because of his type of preaching, even the orthodox in the town were hesitant to purchase or rent seats. Meanwhile, the annual deficit had climbed to a figure between $700-$1,000. The letter stated further:

> The experiment has been made, and although other Societies, whose ministers have been acceptable, have met with no difficulty in their support, yet we very much fear our embarrassments will continue to increase, by the departure of many of those who at present belong to the society. . . .
> We have also extended our inquiries among those attached to evangelical sentiments out of our society, and this

we felt bound to do, that a correct opinion might be formed
by our prospect of increased strength from the families most
likely to come among us, and have found not only no prospect of addition, but that they had come to the conclusion
not to join us, and even contemplate forming a new Church
and building, a new House for public worship (to do which
they are fully able) that they may sit under the preaching
and receive the parochial services of a minister more acceptable to them.

The society's disenchantment with Dr. Griffin was mirrored by
its reluctance in November, 1814, to wipe out a salary deficit of
$600. A committee appointed to call on the members of the so-
ciety reported that only $302 had been pledged or contributed.
These continuing crises plus the society's unwillingness to reach a
satisfactory solution prompted Dr. Griffin's resignation on April
12, 1815.

> After much solemn deliberation and prayer, I have con-
> sidered it my duty to request you to consent to a dissolution
> of my pastoral relation to you, with a view to my acceptance
> of the Call from Newark, which was lately laid before the
> Congregation. My reason for this application is a failure, as
> I conceive, of a rational prospect of support; but I consent
> to wave [sic] all details.

The Second Presbyterian Church of Newark, New Jersey, which
extended the call to Dr. Griffin, was an offshoot from his former
charge in that city. The renewal of old friendships and the personal fellowship in the gospel ministry with his beloved colleague,
James Richards, seemed a pleasant prospect to the weary, departing pastor.

Prior to the calling of the council, the church and society voted
to pay Dr. Griffin's salary through May, the money to be raised
by voluntary subscription. On April 27, 1815, eight of the nine
invited churches responded to the call for an ecclesiastical convocation. These were from Charlestown, Beverly, South Reading,
Salem, Danvers, Dorchester, Milton and Braintree. (Joshua Huntington of Old South Church was out of town.) The council, moderated by Dr. Morse, having examined all the pertinent documents
relative to dismission, voted for the dissolution of the pastoral re-

lationship. Trusting that their action was consonant with the divine will, Dr. Griffin was commended to the brethren in Newark, and prayer was offered that Park Street Church might in good time acquire another pastor of God's own choosing.

The significant beginnings and failures of this first pastorate are reviewed in these summary conclusions:

1. Dr. Griffin did establish and give direction to the infant church. Though weak and often in distress, the first shock of battle was courageously borne under his leadership.

2. His insistent demands for purity of doctrine and for an active church discipline created a singular image for Park Street Church which was to be reflected in the organizing principles of other new churches.

3. Dr. Griffin's self-effacing acceptance of an unwanted pulpit in 1811 kept the church alive and honored God before those who waited for the enterprise to collapse.

4. He was unable to gather a large pew-holding society, so in this sense he had comparatively little success. However, the house was so crowded for some time that in order to secure seats the members had to put locks on their pew doors. But few were willing to contribute even a dollar.

5. Dr. Griffin restored and amplified the sound of evangelical preaching in Congregational churches long accustomed to the smooth and insipid pap of an apostate clergy.

6. Foundations were laid not only in doctrine, discipline and discourse, but in the areas of benevolence and Christian education. The church's influence on the city, the nation and the heathen world during the next several decades was principally due to the impressions it received from Dr. Griffin.

Upon his departure, the financial condition began to show immediate improvement. During the following twenty-eight months while the church remained without a minister, income from pew taxes alone exceeded the 1815 figure by $800. Although this was a good forecast for the years ahead, a more serious problem persisted. "This desire to our idols did not wholly leave us. . . . We had to learn more perfectly that hard lesson that the Holy Spirit is the author and finisher of this work."

As Park Street Church prepared to enter its second decade of

Christian service, it looked for a leader having different manners and a more gentle temperament. In Sereno Edwards Dwight it found such a man, but he was not to arrive on the scene for nearly two and a half years.

5. Church Discipline

Dr. Griffin had used the New Testament pattern and Calvin's teachings in establishing a system of discipline designed to govern the character of the church's membership, to instruct and correct the weak, and restore or punish flagrant behavior of immoral persons. The sanctity, peace and orderliness of the Park Street religious society required such a system. During Dr. Griffin's ministry, steps were taken to draw up rules for regulating disciplinary procedures. To supervise and purify the church rolls, a committee was formed on May 22, 1815, whose duties included the investigation of why dismissed members had not joined elsewhere, why those no longer attending regularly had been careless in not removing their letters and why more regular members were not attending monthly prayer services.

The general procedure for public discipline entailed these steps: (1) Upon initial complaint, the church appointed a committee to investigate the charges. (2) The committee reported its findings to the deacons. (3) The defendant was asked to appear before the deacons to answer the complaint, being given time and opportunity to prepare a defense. Both sides could introduce witnesses. (4) After the hearings, the deacons read their findings to the church and sent a copy to the defendant.

In all cases the church proceeded with dignity and caution, carefully examining and seeking corroboration for each charge and countercharge. Sometimes the investigations continued for several months; one case lasted two years.

The minutes of the 1810-80 business meetings reveal many causes requiring disciplinary action, including drunkenness, dishonesty, theft, fornification, absence from the church's stated meetings, lying, assault, profanity, Sabbath breaking, worldliness (theater attendance, card playing), apostasy, adultery, and one instance of wife desertion. Moral and spiritual failures recurring most often were: absence from the services, thirteen cases; fornication, twelve cases; dishonesty, ten cases; drunkenness, seven cases; apostasy, six cases; worldliness, six cases.

Sixty-eight persons are individually mentioned in the minutes, and eleven other cases are referred to as a whole. Of the sixty-eight names given, forty-one were men and twenty-seven women. The most common female offense was fornication (eight), while among male members, dishonesty in business and failure in church attendance ranked highest (eight each). The most cases investigated during any single period were from July, 1828, to December, 1829, when fourteen persons appeared before Pastor Edward Beecher and his deacon board.

One early case was based on charges of drunkenness and dishonesty against Amasa Fisk in June, 1813. The board decided non-Christians were not acceptable witnesses in such an investigation. Fisk was told to appear to answer the complaints but, as often happened, he failed to do so. However, he sent a written confession admitting to excessive drinking, although not to the degree stated in the charge. The dishonesty complaint against Fisk was for selling his pew under fraud. It was not his to sell since he had not fully paid for it, the title still being held by Deacon Tyler. His confession, though admitting fraud, sounded hollow to the deacons. On July 23, 1813, they concluded:

> It is the opinion of the Church that the honour of religion requires that he should be cut off from our communion. . . . Resolved unanimously that Amasa Fisk be, and he hereby is, in the name and by the authority of the Lord Jesus Christ, excommunicated from this church.

In cases of fornication, the church sometimes suspended the guilty for one year, hoping to restore them to full fellowship upon sincere confession. The story of Mrs. Margaret Kneeland is an example of this kind of discipline. On March 7, 1814, she wrote the board, confessing to a criminal and grievous sin, "understood to be the sin of ante-nuptial fornication." During her twelve-month suspension from the communion of the church, the deacons were faithful in visiting her. She was restored to church fellowship in May, 1815, upon evidence of her sincere contrition. On the other hand, several failed to show satisfactory penitence and were excommunicated.

Church records reveal the discipline of only one person having an official capacity: Elnathan Duren, the first president and choirmaster of the Park Street Singing Society. In September, 1828, he was charged with habitual intemperance over a period of eight years and was excommunicated from the fellowship of the church as a result of his failure to show satisfactory repentance. Notice of this action was read publicly before the entire church.

The longest case on record concerned one Joseph Jenkins who on December 22, 1841, was put out of the church on grounds of general dishonesty and fraud. A year and a half later Jenkins requested reconsideration of his dismissal, but it was not granted. In August, 1843, a second request was made and denied. Two weeks later he asked the church to convene an ecclesiastical council. Though unwilling to do so, the church agreed, only to discover that Jenkins disapproved of the letter sent to convene the council. His behavior was so argumentative and his manner so objectionable that it was obvious he was interested only in badgering the discipline committee. On October 4 the church ceased further action.

An amusing case involved Mrs. Tamer Carey. In 1846 a complaint of unchristian conduct was leveled against her by four women. These witnesses stated to the church that Mrs. Carey was guilty of the most abusive language in that she had "wished they were all to the Devil," and "wished they were in the Cistern." Furthermore, she had called them "Cats," and had said at various times, "Get out of my way, you Curse"; "shut that door, you Curse"; and that she "would fight them out of the house." The church quickly decided to excommunicate Mrs. Carey.

In connection with the 1855 case of Sylvester P. Gilbert, found guilty of illicit intercourse with females, this note was made by the committee: "His first deviation from the path of duty was neglect of secret prayer."

The sentiments of the nineteenth century evangelical church regarding hypocrisy are revealed in the action taken against John H. Tobey in 1878. Although he was also guilty of embezzlement, the church made a special point of his hypocritical behavior:

> That during the time covered by the foregoing specifications, John H. Tobey was guilty of the sin of gross hypocrisy in that while continuing in these heinous sins, he taught a Sunday School class, led prayer meetings, exhorted, and in all possible ways assumed to be and placed himself before the world and the church as a true Christian and as a man consecrated to the service of God.

This guilt alone was sufficient to dismiss him from the fellowship of the congregation. To avoid worse scandal, the other offenses were not presented for action.

After 1880 specific cases of discipline do not appear in the church minutes. Deacon board proceedings on February 6, 1947, mention the case of an immoral female member, but such notations were then the exception. During the twentieth century disciplinary matters have been handled by the diaconate who simply remove the name of the offending member from the membership roll for such reasons as nonattendance, nonsupport, and failure to abide by covenant obligations.

6. Strengthening the Inner Man

The years 1817 and 1826 marked the commencement and the conclusion of the pastorate of Sereno Edwards Dwight, second pastor of Park Street Church. Equally as important as the direction afforded the young church by Dr. Griffin was the necessary strengthening Dwight gave its inner spiritual life. This was accomplished by a direct and purposeful involvement in the establishment of missions abroad and of local churches at home, in the creation of benevolent and educational societies, and by virtue of the first great revival in the history of Park Street Church.

The church's inability to locate a pastor before Dr. Griffin's acceptance was again experienced upon his departure. During the remainder of 1815 and throughout the following year, the pastoral committee of Tyler, Bumstead and Parker made several unsuccessful attempts to find a minister. The events which finally led to Dwight's coming to Park Street Church had their commencement in the annual meeting of March 4, 1817, when a letter was received from George Odiorne and twenty other persons. They desired the ministry of Dwight, a Christian believer of less than two years, who had received his license to preach just six months earlier, and at that time was serving as the thirteenth chaplain of the United States Senate. Receiving the general recommendation of the members present, he was invited to supply the pulpit eight Sundays; on the following May 19 he was chosen by a 33-5 vote to become the pastor at a salary of $2,000. The church notified the congregation (pew proprietors) of its action and requested concurrence. Upon their approval, a joint committee was formed to extend the formal call. Dwight's letter of acceptance was dated July 20, 1817:

> I hope, Gentlemen, that in thus accepting the invitation you have presented me, I do not act from confidence in my own strength; that I feel the solemn responsibility of the Pastoral Office, and of the terrible nature of the account I must soon give, if unfaithful; and that I am conscious, that without the guidance and blessing of the Holy Spirit, constantly sought and found, I can do nothing.

Plans for forming an ecclesiastical council were immediately activated. Invitations were sent to fifteen Congregational churches as well as to Dr. and Mrs. Lyman Beecher, Litchfield, Connecticut, and to Dr. and Mrs. Nathaniel Taylor of New Haven. Dr. Taylor's preaching at the First Church during a revival in 1815 had brought Dwight to faith in Christ.

The ordaining council met in Concert Hall on September 3, 1817, at 8 A.M., under the leadership of Dr. Abiel Holmes. The pertinent letters of call and the candidate's qualifications for the gospel ministry were carefully examined. This was followed by Dr. Taylor's testimony concerning Dwight's character. The council then voted to proceed with the ordination and made the following assignments: introductory prayer, Dr. Taylor; sermon, Dr. Beecher; consecrating prayer, Rev. Doth Dana; charge to the pastor, Dr. Spring; and the fellowship of the churches extended by Rev. Joshua Huntington.

The ordination sermon preached by Dr. Lyman Beecher in Park Street Church was, in the estimation of his son Charles, one of his most important. The forty-two-year-old pastor from Litchfield, Connecticut, had been viewing the spread of Arianism and Unitarianism in New England with great alarm. Given his first opportunity to preach in Boston, he revised a sermon delivered at the East Hampton Presbyterian Church, Long Island, New York, on his 1810 departure from that parish. Using Psalm 19:7-10 as his text, he preached on the subject, "The Bible A Code of Laws." "My mind had been heating, heating, heating," he wrote; "now I had a chance to strike."[1]

[1]Charles Beecher (ed.), *Autobiography and Correspondence of Lyman Beecher, D.D.* (New York: Harper & Bros., 1864), I, 351.

Dr. Beecher began by discussing the nature of moral government and the influence of law upon accountable creatures with
faculties of understanding, conscience and choice. He said the
sacred Scriptures contained that system of divine laws best suited
for God's glory and man's redemption, and that it was the pastor-
elect's duty to explain and enforce those laws. Speaking more directly to thirty-one-year-old Dwight, he declared:

> That you may understand the Scriptures, examine them for
> yourself. Receive no opinions on trust; and allow no man to
> dictate what you shall believe.
>
> Dare to think for yourself; but do not imagine that inde-
> pendence can compensate for indolence, or ignorance, or
> heresy, or hatred of the truth; or that, to be independent, you
> must of course despise antiquity, and differ from the vast ma-
> jority of the wise, and great and good.
>
> .   .   .   .
>
> Set your heart upon the great blessing of a revival of re-
> ligion. Desire it speedily and constantly. Pray for it without
> ceasing, and stir up the members of your church to concen-
> trate, on this point, the whole importunity of the prayer of
> faith. And live, and preach, and pray, and act, in such a man-
> ner, as shall lay the best foundation to expect the blessing.[2]

One feature of this service was the ordination of five missionary
candidates, examined by the American Board the previous evening in the vestry of the church. After a brief intermission following Dwight's ordination, the council reassembled to set apart these
men to missionary service: Elisha P. Swift, John Nichols, Allen
Graves, Levi Parsons and Daniel Sabin Butterick.

From its founding in February, 1809, to the ordination of
Dwight—a period of eight and a half years—Park Street Church
had had a resident pastor for only forty-four months.

The first ministers of Park Street Church were official keepers
of the church records. The resignation of Dr. Griffin had required
the appointment of an interim clerk, John E. Tyler, who wrote
this note on the day of ordination:

> The deeply interesting solemnities of this day having been

[2]Lyman Beecher, *The Bible A Code of Laws* (Andover, Mass.: Flagg &
Gould, 1818), pp. 344-45.

auspiciously closed, the subscriber, with a humble prayer and strong faith, that this church will ere long be watered, its borders enlarged, its stakes strengthened, and its rights guarded, by her Great Head, who has this day given us a Pastor, as I trust, a *scribe well instructed* in the school of Christ, cheerfully resigns his office as Clerk *ad interim*.

Tyler's humble faith was well rewarded by the events of the next nine years. The church and congregation were immediately blessed by an increase in membership and improvement in the financial condition.

Due to the increased demands of the growing membership, two additional deacons, Jeremiah Evarts and John C. Proctor, were elected in May, 1819, to enlarge the diaconate to four. With the large influx of members following the revival of 1824, the number of deacons was again enlarged. Other committees functioning during this period were a nine-member Standing Committee to assist the deacons; a five-man auditing committee; a committee of six to collect the contributions at the Sunday evening lectures; a committee to rent pews and cellar space; and a committee to aid the pastor in attending to inquiries.

In order to preserve silence and order in the Puritan meeting-houses of New England, tithingmen were employed. They prodded the drowsy, awakened the sleeping, and rapped the heads of noisy, squirming youngsters. None were permitted to linger about the doors of the meetinghouse or sit on its fences on the Sabbath. Two such constables were appointed by Park Street Church in 1812 to maintain order—in the galleries especially. In 1823, three were chosen, and by 1830, six were required.

The hour and frequency of the communion service were matters which underwent change during these early years. One year after the founding of the church, the following rules regarding the sacraments were formulated: (1) the congregation is not to be dismissed before communion; (2) a general invitation to participate is to be extended from the pulpit to all those in good standing at Park Street Church or sister churches; (3) at year's end, nonmembers having regularly attended the communion service at Park Street Church must apply for admission to membership if they wish to enjoy this privilege; (4) the communion service is to be celebrated the first Sabbath in March, June, September and December; (5) a benevolence offering is to be taken for the poor.

In 1819, forty-nine female members of the church petitioned for a more frequent remembrance of the Lord's Supper in the light of the general declension of religion and as a token of their constant love for the Saviour. The petition was granted with the church voting to have the sacrament the first Sabbath of each month. Fourteen years later the rule was changed to provide for a bimonthly celebration, which has continued until now. In 1824 the hour of the service was changed from the morning to the afternoon meeting, and in later years to the evening meeting. In 1934 it was returned to the forenoon service. At present Park Street Church celebrates the Lord's Supper bimonthly during the Sunday morning service. Not until about 1908 did the church change over to the use of individual communion cups. The gift of a communion service by two church families helped to encourage this alteration. Church records for the year 1865 show the purchase of twelve and a half gallons of communion wine for $40.23, and thirty-six loaves of bread for $6.

The weekly prayer meeting of Park Street Church, originally held on Monday evenings, was moved to Friday in 1825. This change was undoubtedly due to the conflict with the monthly concert which was a city-wide missionary gathering held at the church one Monday evening a month.

The primary task of the Prudential Committee was to help strengthen the financial resources of the indebted church and society. As early as March, 1816, some consideration had been given to the possibility of erecting tombs beneath the sanctuary of the meetinghouse. During the next several years the subject was discussed from time to time, but no specific action was taken until 1822 when the committee recommended that the church and society petition the city for authorization to build such tombs.

As this was not an uncommon practice by religious societies of the day, and since it would provide much needed revenue, the proprietors of the church addressed the city fathers on January 11, 1823:

The petition of the Subscribers, a Committee of the Proprietors of Park Street Church respectfully represents:

That the cellar under their Church adjoins the Common Street Burying Ground; is large and deep, and a very suitable place for the erection of tombs; and

That while it will be very convenient to your petitioners to make use of a place, which, by the consent of almost all Christian nations, is appropriated as a repository of the dead, there is no reason whatever to apprehend any evil to the public.

Your petitioners therefore ask permission to erect tombs under Park Street Church, subject to such provisions and limitations as your honorable bodies shall seem expedient and proper.[3]

Two days later, Mayor John Phillips, with the Board of Aldermen concurring, passed the following order:

Ordered: that the prayer of said petition be granted under the same restrictions and limitations as that granted to Saint Paul's Church and that no tomb be appropriated to the interment of strangers or any person in consideration of payment therefor.

The Common Council concurred with the order, but added this amendment:

Provided that the only entrance into the cemetery under Park Street Church shall be through the Granary Burying Ground at the Northeast side of the house, that the cellar be dug as much deeper as possible without injury to the foundation of the building, and that the petitioners shall be restrained from building more tombs under their church than one range on each side.

With a final stipulation that the tombs be constructed under the direction of the Common Council, the church was given its go-ahead order on February 17, 1823.

The first seventeen tombs were built along the northeast side of the cellar during the summer and fall of 1824. Each tomb was twelve feet six inches long, five feet wide, and seven feet from

[3]Petition of Committee of Proprietors to City of Boston, 1823, Park Street Church.

the floor to the arch. Its front wall was twelve inches thick with
the side walls eight inches in diameter; the arch covering the
tomb was also eight inches thick. The space between the rear
walls of these tombs and the north wall of the cellar was twenty-
two inches wide in order to permit an adequate brick water-
course. The floor of each tomb was made either of brick or flat
stones twelve inches below the surface of the earthen cellar. The
entrance into each tomb was four and one-half feet high and two
feet wide. The doors were of iron, not less than a half inch thick,
hanging on hinges, and the frames were made of iron or stone.

In December, 1827, the Prudential Committee erected eleven
more tombs, which were ranged along the southwest side of the
cellar, and in 1830, nine additional tombs beginning about six
feet northwest of the front of the tombs at the east end and
extending to the northwest corner of the vestry wall. This made
a total of thirty-seven tombs with a capacity of 148 bodies. A
single tomb cost $400, and a half tomb, $200. Treasurer's records
show the sale of thirty tombs for $13,000 as of September, 1830.

In 1846 a member of the family of Silas Aiken, fifth pastor of
Park Street Church, died. At that time Nathaniel Willis turned
the deed to his tomb over to the society for purposes stated by
Deacon Odiorne:

> When the Church alienated their right to the cellar of this
> house for the purpose of a Cemetery, they reserved to them-
> selves the right of only one tomb and that for the interment of
> the poor of the Church, nor to this day does the Church pos-
> sess any right of sepulchre for their Pastor or any of his de-
> scendents [sic] beneath these walls, nor have they realized
> their destitution of such privilege until the present bereave-
> ment of Divine Providence. Considering therefore that in
> large cities every Church ought to be provided with a respect-
> able place of interment for their deceased Pastors and their
> children and wives, our worthy and beloved Brother Deacon
> Willis has requested me in his name and upon the conditions
> hereinafter named to present this his deed of a tomb in Park
> Street Cemetery to the acceptance of this Church and to be
> by them appropriated and used exclusively as a sepulchre for
> the ministers of Christ who have been Pastors of Park Street

Church and also for such of their wives and children as may
need interment within the City of Boston.[4]

A marble tablet, bearing this inscription, was placed on this tomb:

No. 3
Pastor's Tomb
Presented to Park Street Church by
Deacon Nathaniel Willis
1846

The missionary spirit engendered by Dr. Griffin reached a high
point during his successor's pastorate. A major contributing factor
was the monthly concert, a missionary meeting designed to present missionary information, to encourage increased participation
by the members, and to unite in prevailing prayer. These meetings had their backgrounds in the quarterly concerts in Great
Britain and eighteenth century colonial America. The more frequent monthly concert was originated by the English Baptists of
Nottingham in 1784. Aided by the support of various evangelical
agencies, the practice gained an ever wider acceptance, and in
1816 became an established feature of church life.

In February, 1816, Park Street invited the Old South Church
to unite in a monthly concert to be held on the first Monday evening of each month under the direction of Pastor Dwight, who was
well suited for the leadership of these meetings due to his professional knowledge of world geography. Though at first declining, Old South finally did join Park Street. In 1819 when the
Essex Street Church was formed, the three churches met regularly
in this union service which continued until 1857, when each
congregation began an independent missionary program. The
concerts at Park Street continued well beyond the close of the
Civil War. A notice of February 28, 1870, shows a change in the
time to the Friday evening following the first Sabbath of every
month.

Although Park Street Church was active in the support of the
American Board of Commissioners for Foreign Missions, largely
through the work of the local Women's Auxiliary Society, a
new and higher plateau of missionary commitment was reached

[4]Park Street Church, Proceedings of Business Meetings, 1834-54, p. 231.

with their direct involvement in the establishment of mission stations at opposite ends of the world.

Organized Protestant missionary work on the Sandwich (Hawaiian) Islands began in 1820, forty years after their discovery by Captain James Cook. The animistic nature of the native religion and the low moral state of the inhabitants, aggravated by the debauchery of white traders, made the islands a fertile field for the entrance of the gospel.

The story begins in 1809 with the arrival in New Haven of a seventeen-year-old Hawaiian orphan named Henry Obookiah, an escapee from the tribal wars then raging in his homeland, during which his parents had been killed. Found weeping on the Yale campus, he was befriended by Rev. Edwin W. Dwight, first principal of the Cornwall School, who cared for and tutored him. Shortly thereafter he was received into the home of Samuel J. Mills in Torringford, Connecticut. The younger Mills proposed to Gordon Hall that Obookiah, who had recently been converted, be returned to his native land accompanied by a Christian mission, but on February 17, 1818, the young islander died. Sufficient interest in a Sandwich Island mission had been generated, however, to stir a number of ministerial students and laymen to apply for missionary service. William E. Strong has written that this desire for a Pacific-based mission provided the backdrop for the organization of the American Board.

Two of the earliest volunteers were Andover Seminary students Hiram Bingham and Asa Thurston, graduates of Middlebury and Yale Colleges, respectively. These young men were ordained to the Christian ministry on September 29, 1819, by the Litchfield County Consocation at Goshen, Connecticut, with a view to missionary evangelism in the islands. In addition to these men, the history-making party included Samuel Whitney of Brantford, Connecticut, mechanic and teacher; Thomas Holman of Cooperstown, New York, physician; Samuel Ruggles of Brookfield, Connecticut, catechist and teacher; Elisha Loomis of Middlesex, New York, printer and teacher; Daniel Chamberlain of Brookfield, Massachusetts, agriculturalist; their wives and five Chamberlain children. In addition to these were three Hawaiian students from

Park Street Church around 1900.

Taken from a painting of Park Street Church as it appeared soon after construction (1810-16)—*The Bostonian Society.*

Billy Graham, Cliff Barrows and Dr. Ockenga at the opening service of the great revival of January 1950.

Dr. Ockenga with missionaries during the annual Park Street Missionary Conference.

The outside of Park Street Church bedecked with flags from many nations during a missionary conference.

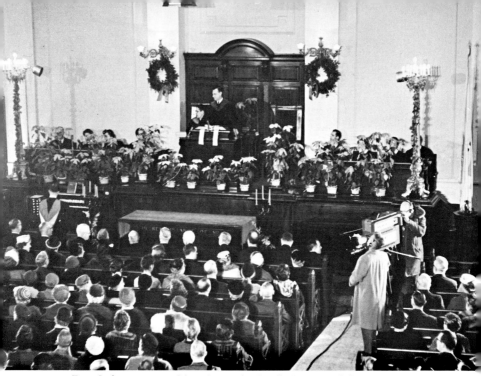

Dr. Ockenga preaching from the Park Street pulpit on the nation-wide telecast of NBC's "Today" show, occasioned by PSC's 150th anniversary.

The choir sings for the "Today" show service.

Dr. and Mrs. Ockenga, with son John and eldest daughter Starr, commemorate 25 years of ministry at Park Street Church (1961).

Dr. Ockenga in his study, which overlooks Boston's historic Granary Burial Ground.

Edward D. Griffin
1811-15

Sereno E. Dwight
1817-26

Edward Beecher
1826-30

Joel H. Linsley
1832-35

PARK STREET MINISTERS

Silas Aiken
1837-48

Andrew Leete Stone
1849-66

William H. H. Murray
1868-74

John L. Withrow
1876-87, 1898-1907

PARK STREET MINISTERS

David Gregg
1887-90

Isaac J. Lansing
1893-97

Arcturus Z. Conrad
1905-37

Harold John Ockenga
1936 —

PARK STREET MINISTERS

the Cornwall School: Thomas Hopu, William Tenui and John Honuri.

The postponement of the original sailing date of October 16 led to the decision to form the missionaries into a church of Christ. Thus, on the Friday evening of October 15, 1819, in the Park Street meetinghouse, seven couples and three native Hawaiian Christians united to constitute the Sandwich Islands Church. Rev. Hiram Bingham preached from II Timothy 3:16-17, on the theme: "It is the great end of the Bible to promote benevolent action." This was followed by the instructions of the Prudential Committee of the American Board and the charge delivered by Dr. Samuel Worcester, secretary of the committee. The next morning at ten o'clock, Rev. Asa Thurston spoke the farewell message to another large audience at Park Street Church. Thomas Hopu gave a brief gospel address, calling on the unsaved to receive Jesus Christ; he then engaged in a ten-minute dialogue in his native tongue with five Hawaiian youths recently arrived from the islands, who were seated in the pews before him. The benedictory prayer was offered by Rev. Pliny Fisk, missionary candidate to the Near East. At the conclusion of the regular Sabbath afternoon service on October 17, the Lord's Supper was administered to the missionary party and the more than five hundred others assembled from the orthodox churches of the city. Missionary offerings received in the Friday and Saturday services amounted to two hundred dollars.

The vessel arrangements being completed, a brief dockside service was held at 10 A.M. October 23, with remarks by Dr. Worcester and Thomas Hopu. A barge, the "Independence 74," conveyed the missionaries to the brig "Thaddeus," which, after an overnight layover in the harbor, put out to sea the next day. The 18,000-mile voyage around Cape Horn required 163 days; land was sighted on March 30, 1820.

As the result of a reaction against idolatry which took place just prior to 1820, and the hospitable reception given the missionaries by the government and the royal family, the Hawaiian Church enjoyed a happy beginning. Powerful movings of the Holy Spirit produced awakenings in the years 1836-38 under the dynamic preaching of Rev. Titus Coan, ordained in Park Street

Church on August 4, 1833. His church at Hilo received 5,000 members in one year during the revival. By 1839 the entire Bible had been translated. After twelve years of missionary labors, nine hundred schools with an enrollment of 50,000 pupils, had been established on a number of the islands. The total population of the Sandwich Islands in 1820 was 130,000; that of Hawaii was 85,000. The American Board withdrew from Hawaii in 1870 and transferred its responsibility to the Hawaiian Evangelical Association.

Having bade farewell to the Sandwich Islands Church, the evangelical churches of Boston turned their attention to the Near East. Ever since Dr. Griffin's suggestion for a mission to Jerusalem, the American Board and the Park Street and Old South churches had planned and prayed for its realization. The monthly concerts of the two churches emphasized the need for such a mission. Special gifts were contributed toward the purchase of a printing press and for the assistance of students preparing for missionary service.

By the fall of 1819 the American Board was prepared to enter this new field. Its two pioneer missionaries were Pliny Fisk and Levi Parsons. Fisk had been engaged by the Savannah Missionary Society as their representative in Palestine as early as January, 1818, and was highly recommended by Dr. Kollock and Lowell Mason of the society to assist Parsons in the founding of the Near East Mission.

Services similar to those for the Sandwich Island missionaries were held on November 1. At an afternoon gathering in the Park Street meetinghouse, Parsons spoke from Hosea 3:4-5 on the "Dereliction and the Restoration of the Jews." That evening, Fisk preached to an overflow audience in Old South Church from Acts 20:22, on "The Holy Land, a Field for Missionary Enterprise." Commissioning instructions were then delivered by the board's secretary, Dr. Samuel Worcester of the Salem Tabernacle. A collection received at this service amounted to $293.31. At the regularly scheduled monthly concert at Park Street Church the following day, final farewells were said, and the contributions which had been made for the mission during the previous year were presented. The missionary couple sailed from Boston harbor on November 4, 1819, on the "Sally-Anne" bound for Smyrna, Malta and Jerusalem.

William Henry Harrison Murray, seventh pastor of Park Street Church, recounted in a sermon delivered in January, 1872, that 180 missionaries received their parting instructions in Park Street Church during the first two generations of its history.

The first quarter of the nineteenth century was marked by a proliferation of humanitarian and benevolent societies, many of them generated by evangelical lay leadership. It was natural for Park Street Church, having some of the more prominent church laymen of the day, to be a part of this burgeoning scene. In the nine years of Dwight's ministry alone, the men of Park Street Church were among those active in the founding and establishing of several organizations whose benevolent purposes were to bear nationwide influence in the years ahead.

The American Society for Educating Pious Youth for the Gospel Ministry

Impressed with the dire and increasing need for gospel ministers on the ever expanding frontier, eight young Bostonians met several times in the summer of 1815 to consider forming an association geared to the education of men for the ministry. With the mounting of interest and the adoption of a constitution during the autumn months, the formal organization of The American Society for Educating Pious Youth for the Gospel Ministry took place in Park Street Church on December 7, 1815. The importance of this organization, which changed its name in 1819 to the American Education Society, and in 1894 to the Congregational Education Society, is seen in figures given by Dr. Eliphalet Pearson in his founding address. He reported that in nine Western states and territories having a population of 1,078,815, there were but 116 ministers. A similar imbalance existed in the Southern and middle states. Of the 8,500,000 persons living in the United States and the territories in 1816, a total of 6,500,000 had no educated ministry. The American Education Society was to play a significant role in correcting this situation. In its first two years of existence, a total of 105 young men were given financial aid. At the founding meeting on December 7, Deacon John E. Tyler was elected auditor. The society, being largely benevolent in nature, required large sums of money to maintain its operation. Park Street Church was foremost among the churches of Boston in contributing to this cause. The women of the church provided a Dwight scholarship of $1,000. Other individuals contributed another $1,000 known as the Park Street Scholarship. During the ministry of Silas Aiken, the society's treasury was nearly depleted. It was given a new lease on life through the efforts of Park Street Church in sparking the evangelical community. An annual day of prayer for colleges was inaugurated as a regular feature of church life in 1826. Thus, by supplying dedicated Christian leadership, thousands of dollars and earnest prayer, Park Street was faithful to the educational facet of the Christian mission.

The Society for The Moral and Religious Instruction of The Poor

The Society for The Moral and Religious Instruction of The Poor, or as it was popularly called, The Moral and Religious Society, was founded in 1816 for the religious instruction of the poor within the town of Boston. It became the forerunner of the local Sabbath school movement. Among the society's founders were Sereno Dwight, William Thurston, Henry Homes and John C. Proctor from Park Street Church. Rev. Joshua Huntington of Old South Church became its first president.

During the first year, the undenominational society gathered together five hundred children in its two schools on Mason and School streets. A year after its founding, the Moral and Religious Society offered to contribute all necessary supplies to any religious society or group of individuals desirous of forming a school of their own and providing their own teachers. In 1818 William Thurston, a charter member of Park Street Church, became superintendent of the Mason Street School.

The Maternal Association

The first maternal association in Boston was formed by six women from Park Street and Old South churches on July 31,

1816, in Miss Perry's schoolroom on Newbury Street. The purpose of The Maternal Association was to devise and adopt measures to assist mothers in performing their maternal duties and responsibilities.

This initial union of churches was dissolved in 1824 so each church could form its own association. The Maternal Association of Park Street Church was organized with forty-one members on January 6, 1825, at the house of Henry Homes on Central Court. The monthly meetings were used to read pertinent books and discuss relevant topics, followed by prayer for the mothers and their children. The society also published its own *Mothers Magazine*. Subjects presented for discussion were: (1) Dancing—a vain and frivolous pomp wholly irreconcilable and inconsistent with genuine consecration to God. (2) How far is it safe and right for parents to allow their children to leave their regular place of worship on the Sabbath to hear preachers more suited to their taste? (3) Causes and preventives of lying. (4) How shall the Sabbath be made a delight?

From 1825 to 1843, ninety-eight mothers signed the association's constitution, and 153 children were enrolled. The records indicate many conversions of children, with several entering the gospel ministry.

The Prison Discipline Society

Louis Dwight, son of Henry W. Dwight and son-in-law of Nathaniel Willis, founded the Prison Discipline Society under whose auspices the life of America's prison population was greatly improved.

A graduate of Yale College and a member of Park Street Church, Dwight became an agent for the American Tract Society in 1820 and for the American Education Society in 1823. During his travels for these organizations, he became interested in prison life and conditions. Assisted by the American Bible Society, he began the first distribution of the Scriptures to the men behind bars in 1824. This ultimately led to the founding of the Prison Discipline Society on June 30, 1825, by Dwight, who served as its secretary for thirty years.

The society's purpose was to oversee the construction of prisons to see that they were secure, well lighted, ventilated and clean; to provide for moral instruction; to separate youths from the hardened criminals; and to restrain improper indulgences.

The American Temperance Society

Previous to a meeting early in 1826, several evangelical churchmen of Boston had been considering the evils of intemperance and the importance of further efforts to restrain them. Concerned more with the abuse of drinking than with total abstinence, the American Temperance Society was formed on February 13, 1826, in the vestry of Park Street Church with George Odiorne serving as moderator. After adopting a constitution, Rev. Justin Edwards, for many years the pastor of the Andover Church, was elected president, and Samuel Hubbard, noted jurist and member of Park Street, was elected vice-president. Some years afterward, on June 25, 1829, the male members of the church and congregation organized the Park Street Auxiliary Temperance Society with pastor Edward Beecher as president and Jeremiah Evarts as vice-president.

At the close of the Sunday service on September 7, 1817, Pastor Dwight received a note requesting that a series of prayer meetings be held each Monday evening (except on the monthly concert night) for the purpose of a revival of religion and for the outpouring of the Holy Spirit. Several months later the *Boston Recorder* reminded its readers that two generations had passed since Boston had seen its last full-scale revival. It called upon ministers and churches to come before God "with weeping and with mourning, with girding in sackcloth and sitting in ashes," until righteousness would reign again throughout New England. An intensifying spirit of prayer began to engulf Park Street Church and her sister congregations. Days of fasting, self-humiliation and prayer prepared the people for the revival that was soon to bless the city.

In May, 1822, Congregational ministers in Boston convened to consider the multitudes of non-Christians in the city. Dwight recommended that the situation be made a special matter of prayer in all the churches. By the new year it was evident that the Holy Spirit was working in many hearts. The volume of prayer in Park Street Church continued to grow as the first signs of spiritual conviction were manifested in the lives of three young women. The deacons held a special meeting for Christians only, at which many confessed their sins one to another. News of this outbreak quickly spread to other praying churches, who then asked Park Street members to come and relate the wonderful works of God. A number of laymen visited these churches and explained the method used: (1) Provide an exhortation (evangelistic) service for unbelievers. (2) At the same time gather the Christians together for prayer for the salvation of those being exhorted. Old South, Essex Street and the Charlestown churches adopted the same measures, and the revival expanded to their churches.

The growing harvest required the services of additional ministers. Rev. W. Hawes of Glastonbury, Connecticut, was the first to be invited from outside the city. He was soon followed by Dr. Edward Payson of Portland, Maine; Lyman Beecher of Litchfield, Connecticut; and Dr. Nathaniel Taylor of New Haven.

Dr. Beecher, in a letter of April 16, 1823, to his son Edward, described the state of the revival in its early stages:

> There is unquestionably a great and auspicious change going on in Boston in respect to evangelical doctrine and piety. The orthodox have for years been delving in their Sabbath-schools and other evangelical efforts, and their zeal, and strength, and momentum, as to preparing the way for a revival are noble, and they are reaping their reward.
>
> .   .   .   .
>
> The revival is progressing steadily, but rather slowly; about six a week in Mr. Dwight's inquiry meeting are found to hope. I set up a Sabbath eve lecture in Park Street last Sabbath evening, which was filled, pews and alleys, to overflowing, with Unitarians of all sorts, as well as others. The solemnity was profound, and the effect of the sermon good.[5]

This being the first great revival in Boston since the days of George Whitefield, the Christians of the city found themselves

[5]Charles Beecher (ed.), *Autobiography and Correspondence of Lyman Beecher, D.D.* (New York: Harper & Bros., 1864), I, 517-19.

engaged in religion to an extent not seen since that earlier awakening. For example, the Old South Church was opened for a stated weekly lecture for the first time in eighty years. Dr. Beecher wrote that the meetinghouse was crammed, with many Unitarians present.

Union inquiry meetings for the use of all the churches were held as well as meetings in private houses. As the number of inquirers increased to several hundred, larger halls were found— Academy Hall on Broomfield Lane, and Pantheon Hall near Boylston Market. Each individual was personally addressed by either a minister or a layman. Bible classes were established by the pastors for the youth of their congregations, with Bible memorization and catechetical instruction.

In addition to the public lectures held during the week in the various churches, separate meetings for men and women were provided for persons not ordinarily attending orthodox services. There were also neighborhood meetings, district meetings conducted by laymen to attract the attention of the general public, and daily prayer meetings every morning at 5 A.M. General intercessions continued around the clock even by those engaged in business.

In a letter of April 24, 1823, Dr. Beecher called upon Nathaniel Taylor to take over his responsibilities in Boston since he had to return to his parish—especially his Sunday evening lecture at Park Street Church and the Tuesday evening lecture at Old South Church. These lectures had to be continued, he wrote, in order that the many Unitarians who attended might continue to hear and see Calvinism in purity and not in caricature.

Six days later Dr. Beecher wrote his son Edward that Park Street had written to the Litchfield Church requesting to keep him three or four weeks longer. In the meantime Dr. Taylor had agreed to the call from the revival scene. Dr. Beecher's letter of May 1 suggested to Dr. Taylor that his sermons, at this point in the campaign, must not be of the pugnacious or controversial variety, but of a quality of exposition calculated to prevent objections. The sermons must have a threefold aim: to remove misapprehension and prejudice concerning Calvinist doctrines; to commend these doctrines powerfully to the conscience; and to extend a clear understanding of the nature of true religion.

Although the churches had been praying and hoping for such a revival, they were not too well prepared to handle its various demands. Qualified workers were lacking. The evangelical churches of Boston being exceeding few, the supply of Christian ministers and laymen was insufficient for the proper management of the meetings. This situation could be remedied only with the assistance of Christian workers from outside the city. This explains the urgent appeal of Lyman Beecher to Nathaniel Taylor and that of Park Street Church to the Litchfield society. In similar vein Deacon Jeremiah Evarts wrote to Dr. Gardiner Spring on July 1, 1823, informing him of God's gracious visitation upon the churches and of the desperate need for added laborers. The situation had been made all the more critical by Rev. Dwight's need to take a leave of absence for health reasons. Evarts wrote:

> He has been zealously employed for more than six months in extraordinary labors from house to house, and in private social meetings, so that we should rather be surprised that his strength should hold out so long rather than that he should be compelled to suspend his labors awhile.[6]

He then asked Dr. Spring, in behalf of Dwight, who was too fatigued to write, whether he could spend some of his summer in Boston:

> The services of peculiar importance are a sermon in Park Street Church, on Sabbath evening, and two addresses weekly, to heads of families, collected in private houses; one of women, on Wednesday afternoon, and one of men, on Friday evening. These meetings are now suspended; but they were very useful, and would be again.[7]

In spite of the hardship brought on by a lack of able help, many lives were changed, families were reunited, and the churches enlarged. Pastor Dwight's special interest in the youth of the church and his years of faithful teaching in their own Bible class bore

[6]Letter of Jeremiah Evarts to Dr. Gardiner Spring, July 1, 1823, in the Evarts Letterbook, January, 1820-August, 1826, in Evarts Family Papers, Yale University Library.
[7]*Ibid.*

good fruit during the revival years. More than a dozen young men formed a private association to promote their mutual spiritual welfare.

Total additions to the four participating Congregational churches as a direct result of this 1823-24 revival numbered 348: 120 to Park Street Church, 101 to Old South Church, 62 to Essex Street, and 65 to Charlestown.

By 1825 the revival fires had diminished; nevertheless, many continued in a spirit of prayer and expectancy. The awakening served to whet ministerial appetites for a fresh outpouring of the Spirit's power upon the city. Persistent prayer by all the churches throughout the remaining years of that decade resulted in a renewed shower of revival blessing. In 1826 the infant Hanover Street Church experienced such a gracious moving of the Holy Spirit that it aroused the liberal clergy once more to hostile action. In order to prevent their people from attending orthodox preaching, a number of the Unitarian churches opened their meeting-houses for Sunday evening lectures. Lyman Beecher, the newly installed minister at Hanover Street, recalled the reaction which followed the admission of seventy members into his church:

> There was an intense malignant enragement for a time. Showers of lies were rained about us every day. The Unitarians with all their principles of toleration, were as really a persecuting power while they had the ascendancy as ever existed. Wives and daughters were forbidden to attend our meetings; the whole weight of political, literary, and social influence was turned against us, and the lash of ridicule laid without stint.[8]

This hostility was not peculiar to the Hanover Street congregation alone but was felt by all her sister churches.

The renewal and refreshment of church life at Park Street was mirrored in numerous ways, all of which bore the sanctifying marks of the Holy Spirit. One such evidence of growth occurred during the ministry of Edward Beecher in April, 1829, and concerned the Friday night prayer service. A committee which was formed to discuss ways of making the meeting more beneficial,

[8]Charles Beecher (ed.), *Autobiography and Correspondence of Lyman Beecher, D.D.* (New York: Harper & Bros., 1865), II, 77.

reported the following: (1) to promote the spiritual knowledge and holiness of each church member; to foster general unity in sentiments, feelings and practice among all members; to pray for the manifestation of the Spirit in the local church and society, in the church at large and in the world; (2) to encourage personal Bible study at home by assigning subjects at each service; (3) to inspire participation in prayer, discussion, and Scripture exposition; (4) to give opportunity to tell members of the state of Park Street Church or the cause of Christ generally, and of persons in need of sympathy, prayer or counsel.

The revival of the 1820's was a grand spectacle, a significant movement of sanctifying power. The evangelical churches of Boston and vicinity needed such an awakening to strengthen and and enlarge their borders, to increase their influence in a community long oblivious to the doctrines of grace and the regenerating power of God, and to multiply their number by the founding of new churches.

During the colonial period prior to the Revolutionary War, the New England landscape was marked by a relatively small number of meetinghouses. Population figures plus Congregationalism's almost complete domination of the ecclesiastical scene left little need for church organization on a grander scale. With the sundering of this monolithic denominational structure, the landscape took on a different complexion by the proliferation of church building construction. The rapid growth of cities and towns together with the evangelistic impulse to form new congregations further accelerated the need for church extension. Those Boston churches which Park Street Church helped to found came into being as a direct result of the spirit of prevailing prayer and revival of that time.

The Essex Street (Union) Church

The initial band of Christians who were later formed into the Essex Street Church met in 1818 for services in Boylston Hall in the south end of town. On January 27, 1819, they were organized into a church; land was purchased at the corner of Essex and Chauncy streets, and Rev. James Sabine of St. Johns, Newfoundland, was installed as pastor.

Due to differences of opinion between Sabine and a deacon, Nathan Parker, who had contributed heavily toward the purchase of the lot and the erection of the meetinghouse, a division occurred in 1822. The Sabine majority had to move from the meeting house as a result of an ecclesiastical council's unfavorable decision. Preserving the Essex Street name, they returned to their former meeting place in Boylston Hall.

After the formal separation of the two groups on March 28, 1822, the twelve male minority members made application to Park Street and Old South for assistance in saving the meetinghouse. A generous subscription was raised by these two churches and a thorough reorganization was instituted under the name of the Union Church on June 10, 1822. In order to strengthen the new assembly, these nine members of Park Street Church requested the transfer of their letters: Andrew Bradshaw, Aaron Woodman, John W. Rogers, Daniel Noyes, Gilman Prichard, David Hale, Jr., Ezra Haskel, Laura Hale and Martha Rogers. The following March, Rev. Samuel Green became their first pastor.

The Sabine group continued to experience difficulties as they changed denominational affiliation twice in seven years—to Presbyterian in 1823, and to Episcopalian in 1829.

The Hanover (Bowdoin Street) Church

The Hanover Church, a direct product of the 1823-24 revival, was formed as an expression of gratitude to God and to further extend evangelical Christianity in the city of Boston.

During the winter of 1825 several male members of the three orthodox Congregational churches met to discuss plans for a proposed new church in the north part of the city. On May 12, a lot having been obtained on Hanover Street and the edifice already begun, the building committee solicited the three congregations for joint cooperation in gathering a church for the meetinghouse.

Samuel Hubbard, John C. Proctor and Henry Homes were appointed as a Park Street committee. They met with representatives of the other churches and, in line with similar actions taken among the other congregations, requested twenty-two members of Park Street Church to become organized with others from the Old South and Union Churches into a new religious society. Those recommended were: Josiah and Sarah Colburn, Elizabeth B. Colburn, Lemuel P. Grosvenor, Ezra Palmer, Peter and Isabel Meston, Newton and Lucretia Willey, Jacob and Martha H. Bancroft, Thomas A. Davis, Dexter Gilbert, Rufus Anderson, William G. and Sarah Lambert, Amos H. Haskell, Charles Willey, Julius A. Palmer, John Bennett, Isaac H. Parker and William R. Lovejoy.

These individuals together with six from Old South Church and five from the Union Church were organized into the Hanover Church by a council in the Park Street vestry on July 18, 1825. The meetinghouse was dedicated March 1, 1826, with Moses Stuart delivering the dedicatory sermon. Three weeks later Lyman Beecher was installed as pastor.

Due to a fire on February 1, 1830, which destroyed the edifice, a more convenient lot on Bowdoin Street was purchased and a second meetinghouse erected. Thereafter it was called the Bowdoin Street Church. Dr. Beecher preached the sermon of dedication on June 16, 1831.

The Church of Liberia

In the autumn of 1825 Horace Sessions, an agent for the American Colonization Society, contacted the orthodox leaders of Boston about the possibility of organizing a small group of Negroes, who were soon to embark for the African colony of Liberia, into a church of Christ. Park Street Church opened its vestry to an ecclesiastical council on December 28, 1825. That same evening thirteen Negroes were formed into a church, with two being chosen deacons. Sereno Dwight delivered a ninety-minute discourse from Psalm 68:31.

The demands of the revival upon the physical energies of Dwight increased the strain upon his health. Though in a good state physically upon arriving in Boston, he had been slowly deteriorating due to the multiplied labors and anxieties of his office. In a letter to his congregation during the summer of 1824, he told them of the serious condition of his health. Since the first of that year he had been unable to devote himself to study; he had not written an original sermon during the past three months. Suffering from a severe case of chronic indigestion, he was living by the constant aid of medicine. Two extended journeys of over one thousand miles each by horseback and train gave only a little relief. His physicians suggested a complete rest for at least one year. He had to either resign or employ a colleague. Placing his thoughts candidly on paper, he indicated a distaste for resignation. The preaching service each Sunday had been effective in reaching many with the gospel and in producing many new members. The peaceful, flourishing state of both the church and the congregation was a source of great delight from which he did not want to separate himself. The cumulative influence of seven years of ministry would be weakened, he said, by the usual difficulties involved in finding a new minister. He felt it unlikely that he would ever be so eligibly and happily situated elsewhere. Despite these reasons, he nevertheless proposed to resign because of the inevitable problems and hardship with which the church would be confronted in the face of a lengthy absence.

The church and congregation were strongly opposed to Dwight's resignation and conveyed to him their desire for him to remain and to take whatever time was necessary for recuperation.

His lengthy reply of July 25, in which he thanked them for their generous grant of a leave, concluded with this typical exhortation to the church and congregation:

> Be present, all of you, at the weekly meeting for prayer; and come to it regularly from the closet. In all your deliberations, let every personal and private feeling and end give way to the purity and peace of the Church.
>
> Take peculiar care of the children and youths of the parish; and as far as possible provide for them the requisite instruction in the Bible class,[9] and the catechism.[10]

Dwight toured Europe during his forced absence, hoping to return with a fresh enduement of energy. However, his hopes were not to be realized; for within six months of his return, he contracted a new ailment which ultimately removed him from his

[9]With reference to the origins of the Sabbath School movement in Boston and Park Street Church's involvement in it, William T. Dwight has noted the establishment of a Bible class for Park Street youth by Sereno E. Dwight, the first such class in Boston. See Preface to *Select Discourses of Sereno Edwards Dwight, D.D., with a Memoir of His Life* (Boston: Crocker & Brewster, 1851), p. xli.

[10]Letter of Sereno E. Dwight to Park Street Church, July 25, 1824.

pulpit. In January, 1826, he suddenly found himself unable to control and project his voice while preaching in the large meeting-house. This voice injury had its roots in a fever of the lungs suffered some fourteen years earlier and now complicated by an adverse reaction of medicines. Realizing he could no longer impose on the generosity and patience of the church, he felt compelled to address them on March 11 concerning the dissolution of their relationship:

> Notwithstanding my own reluctance, however, this subject is forced upon my attention by the circumstances in which I now find myself. On the last Sabbath in January in consequence of unusual exertion in speaking which I knew not how to avoid, I was too much injured, that every subsequent attempt to speak from the desk, as all who have heard me must have perceived, has been attended with extreme difficulty and embarrassment, and has led me to apprehend that a continuance of such attempts at present would probably render the injury permanent.
>
> This evil as well as my former ill health have arisen from the uncommon size of the Church in which I preach and the corresponding numbers of the congregation. The size of the church, one of the largest and perhaps the loftiest in the union, renders the labours of the Sabbath, when I am in good health, exhausting to my strength and when in feeble health, overpowering; whilst the pastoral duties of the parish are to say the least exceedingly laborious.

The church voted to observe the following Friday as a day of prayer and fasting for guidance. The vestry was opened for services at 11 a.m. and 3 p.m., but by this late date the unhappy conclusion was unavoidable. The church had no other alternative but to call for a dismissing council, which met on April 10, 1826, under the chairmanship of Dr. Moses Stuart and dissolved the existing relationship. At a church meeting two days later, the council's action was unanimously approved. As a token of their esteem and affection for their departing pastor, it was voted to give a gift of $500 for moving expenses. Deacon Henry Hill was put in charge of the book containing the records of births, deaths, and marriages, and the book of the Articles of Faith. A committee of nine men was chosen to supply the pulpit and to find another pastor.

Dwight, though not a distinguished pulpiteer as was his predecessor, nevertheless possessed and exemplified qualities of character necessary to the strengthening of Park Street Church in the second decade of its history. He was a man with great common sense, impartial in his actions, and always honorable in his bearing. From his youth he pursued holiness and the ways of moral excellence. Not awed by his lofty position nor spoiled by pride, he was a pastor to all his people and especially to the children, for whom he cherished God's highest.

No mere professor of religion, his pulpit ministry was well suited to his day. Preaching always to the conscience, his sermons were pointed, direct and practical. He was never harsh or overly sentimental in manner but was bold to present the truth in a most searching way.

On the occasion of his death in 1850, Andrew Stone, then pastor of Park Street Church, recalled Dwight's ministry:

> Many surviving members of the church testify their strong appreciation of his services.
>
> They well remember his faithful preaching; his attractive and heavenly conversation; his most acceptable and useful pastoral visits; his earnest, personal, private appeals to their hearts and consciences; and his successful labours as a minister of Christ.
>
> Especially do they remember and speak of his comprehensive views, his animating addresses; and his earnest prayers, at the monthly concert for the conversion of the world, and his most effective services in revivals of religion.[11]

As clearly revealed in these remembrances by his own congregation, the two most significant features of Dwight's ministry were the inauguration of the monthly concert, which became an immeasurable boon to global missionary effort, and the grand spiritual awakening which sparked a reversal in the trend toward acceptance of Unitarian preaching by the common people, and paved the way for the formation of strong evangelical churches in this and later decades.

[11]Letter of Andrew L. Stone and Louis Dwight to Rev. William T. Dwight, December 6, 1850, Park Street Church.

7. Continuous Revival

A unique feature of the revival period was its continuing recurrence every three or four years over the decade beginning in 1823. Swells of revival appeared in 1826-27 and again in 1831-32. Boston's orthodox community was kept busy counseling inquirers, praying for the penitent, and shepherding the increasing numbers of persons being regularly admitted to the churches. A dormant orthodoxy had revived at Old South Church under Rev. Joshua Huntington and Rev. Benjamin B. Wisner. The Hanover Church, led by its dynamic new minister, Lyman Beecher, was reaping a large harvest. But Park Street Church, in the midst of the stirring, was without a leader. It was imperative that a successor to Sereno Dwight be found as soon as possible. The needs of an enlarged congregation and the mutual support of the city's brotherhood required the forces of evangelicalism to remain at full complement. The lengthy intervals of past years had to be avoided. For this reason the membership of the pulpit committee was triple the usual number.

Soon after Lyman Beecher came to the Hanover Church, he encouraged his son Edward, then a tutor at Yale, to be prepared to accept the Park Street pulpit should a call be forthcoming. At one time Beecher envisioned hopes of Edward being used of God to promote revivals in the nation's colleges, and he hoped his daughter Catherine would play a similar role on female campuses. The plan was for Edward to finish Yale and then go on to Andover Seminary for theological training in preparation for such a career. The vacant Park Street pulpit and the founding of Hanover Church changed these plans.

Shortly after Dwight's separation from Park Street Church, Catherine Beecher wrote to her brother:

> I hope Providence will make your way plain so that you may at last be led as a fellow labourer with Papa to that Peculiarly interesting and desolated field. The Lord I think is raising a standard there and calling his children to gather round it, and with the moral influences which he may enable such men as Papa and you to exert, we may hope for great things in Boston.[1]

While Beecher busied himself with personal visitations in behalf of his son, the Park Street pastoral committee presented the name of Justin Edwards of Andover for its pulpit. The church having approved his selection, a subcommittee personally extended the call on July 22, 1826. Five weeks elapsed before the reply was received declining the opportunity. (Sixteen months later Edwards accepted the call to Boston's Salem Street Church, which Edward Beecher was to pastor beginning in 1844.)

By midsummer Dr. Beecher was able to write this promising note:

> There is, I find, an earnest desire at Park Street to have you supply them. As things now stand there is no impediment, but a manifest providential indication that you should come. And my advice and my request now is that you will do it without fail.[2]

Edward's reply informed his father of an imminent invitation to become associated with the Dartmouth College faculty. In response to his son's request for advice on this new development, Dr. Beecher counseled that by no means should he consent to the Dartmouth invitation. He informed him of the decision of the Park Street deacons to invite him to supply their pulpit four Sabbaths during the fall. The prospects of a call appeared excellent, and he would be assured of the decided support of nearly all the influential members such as Evarts, Proctor and Hubbard. He

[1]Letter of Catherine Beecher to Edward Beecher, April, 1826, in Beecher Family Collection, Yale University Library.
[2]Charles Beecher (ed.), *Autobiography and Correspondence of Lyman Beecher, D.D.* (New York: Harper & Bros., 1865), II, 61.

further advised his son to preach written sermons on subjects requiring his mental effort.

In another letter written about the same time, he spoke again of the productive influence they could have in the recuperative process going on in Boston:

> And when I consider the similarity of our minds, and views, and systems of action, I can not but feel as if the concentration of our resources in a system of preaching and action would give additional momentum to our individual power.
>
> You were pleased to say once that nothing brought out your mental vigor and energized your soul like my society. The effect of your society, for obvious reasons, is the same on my mind; and if it please God to place us where the action and reaction of intellectual power may be habitually experienced by us both, the public results may be great and good.[3]

In early November Jeremiah Evarts, Park Street's pastoral committee chairman, announced to Edward Beecher his election as pastor. Having been well prepared for this moment, the twenty-three-year-old Yale tutor required little time to formulate his affirmative decision. That young Edward was a chip off the old block is clear by his ambitious plans for Boston:

> As for the importance of the stand in Boston, as the center of extended and powerful action, I have never stood in such a place before and do not believe that there is, all things considered, such another place perhaps on earth. It is here that New England is to be regenerated, the enemy driven out of the temple which it has usurped and polluted, the college to be rescued, the public sentiments to be revolutionized and restored to evangelical tone, and all this with reference to the resurrection of New England to an undivided and renovated effort for the extension of religious and moral influence throughout the land and throughout the world.[4]

Before entering his ministry or even being ordained, young Beecher had to settle personal doctrinal problems. Correspondence between father and son during November and December

[3]*Ibid.,* p. 69.
[4]Harold John Ockenga, *Boston at the Crossroads* (Boston, 1950), p. 15.

reveals serious doubts by Edward concerning the proper mode of baptism, as well as infant baptism. Impressed with the validity of the Baptist interpretation and faced with his impending ordination into the Congregational ministry, his conscientious and idealistic nature kept him from beginning his pastorate without resolving the difficulty. In no biblical instance was immersion the certain mode of baptism, wrote Dr. Beecher, nor had the application of baptism to infants been revoked; only the covenant seal had been changed.

In a letter of December 4, Edward reflected on the recent course of events which had deterred him from a thorough theological education and now was threatening to delay his ordination:

> My mind has been troubled as to the mode of baptism . . . . I cannot administer this ordinance until I am satisfied that I can conscientiously adhere to the present mode.
>
> I have read or heard all the arguments which can satisfy Dr. Dwight and such men, and I know the common arguments of our denomination; but my mind refuses to act, and my conscience is unsatisfied until I can survey the field so as to satisfy myself.[5]

Concerning the possible postponement of the ordination and his son's mental unrest, Dr. Beecher wrote on December 7:

> I will take care of the business of the delay of time, if need be. I shall not mention to anyone the occasion of delay—it is unnecessary; and, as publicity could do no good and might do harm, I should advise you not to communicate unless quite confidentially.
>
> There is no cause for alarm or solicitude. Your present state of mind is occasioned not by any perceived cause for change of views, but from a tender conscience, and the necessity imposed upon you of grasping, condensing, and weighing circumstantial evidence, scattered over a vast field, in so short a time and under such serious responsibilities. There is only one thing you will have occasion to watch and pray against, and that is the morbid sensibility of what may be termed nervous conscience, by which I mean a conscience made preternaturally sensitive and fearful. This I have reason to believe

[5]Letter of Edward Beecher to Lyman Beecher, December 4, 1826, Beecher Collection.

has worried many a man till he became a Baptist through excess of conscience.[6]

Swayed by his father's counsel and recognizing the impossibility of fully settling his mind under the circumstances, Edward Beecher for the time being passively acquiesced to the Congregational way. The seriousness with which he personally viewed the doctrine is revealed in the publication of his volume in 1849 entitled *Baptism with Reference to Its Import and Modes.* In this work he said the fundamental idea in baptism is purification. Where this underlying concept is maintained, the mode becomes relatively unimportant. The Baptists, he wrote, are incorrect in holding to an exclusive method.

The ordaining council composed of representatives from twenty-two churches met in the lower vestry on December 26, 1826, with Rev. William Jenks of the Green Street Church as moderator. Satisfied with the presentations of the young minister, the council voted to proceed with his ordination at ten o'clock the following day. Dr. Beecher delivered the sermon.

At a church meeting on December 2, during the discussion of the upcoming ordination service and, more specifically, the ordination dinner, the following resolution was adopted:

> Whereas many ministers of the Gospel and Christians as well as other respectable members of the community are at the present time adopting measures to suppress the crying sin of intemperance which is so mournfully prevalent throughout our country; and whereas this church views with much satisfaction the spirit which is thus manifested, and deem it a solemn duty to give the sanction of their opinion, and to contribute their influence to promote so praiseworthy an object: Therefore, voted; that the committee of arrangements be requested to dispense with the provision of ardent spirits in their preparations for the ordination dinner.[7]

The "measures" referred to were those of the newly formed American Temperance Society in which a number of Park Street laymen were members. In April of the following year a committee, appointed to determine how Park Street Church could best support the work of this society, reported:

[6]Beecher, *Autobiography* . . . , II, 86.
[7]Park Street Church, Proceedings of Business Meetings, 1809-34, p. 217.

That whilst all admit and deplore the evils of intemperance, yet the reformation of persons given up to intemperate habits, has in general been found to be hopeless.

That our object therefore should be to prevent entirely the formation of such habits by arraying public opinion against the use of ardent spirits in any quantity, as an article of drink, as both useless and injurious.

And that to the church of Christ is committed the duty of regulating and enlightening the public opinion by the exhibition of truth and by example.

In view of the above-mentioned considerations, we would submit for consideration the following resolution: Resolved, that we as a church feel ourselves required by the spirit of the Gospel, to abstain entirely from the use of ardent spirits except as an article of medicine, and also to exert all our influence to restrain others from a habit so pernicious.[8]

The committee's report and resolution were easily adopted.

The church's Examining Committee, before whom all prospective candidates for admission now appeared, was kept busy during the revival years. Many inquirers who had confessed faith in Christ applied to this committee, which carefully examined the doctrinal understanding of the candidates—especially with regard to election, sovereignty and human depravity—and inquired about personal habits of Christian devotion and communion. The committee then indicated its conclusion on each individual by these designations: very favorable, favorable, approved, deferred and doubtful.

Samples of committee findings are recorded in the minutes of their meetings:

Abigail Lord. Has had doubts and fears in regard to the true state of heart; but hopes her heart has been changed. Among what she considers evidences of a change, are a great interest in prayer, and a delight in the Scriptures, a desire to live a holy life, a love for Christians. Deferred.

.   .   .   .

Mr. David B. Spencer, Staniford Street, from the Third Congregational Church in New Haven, made a profession of religion in Northampton twenty-two years ago. There was a

[8]*Ibid.*, p. 229.

revival about that time, but his first impressions were produced by reading the life of David Brainerd. Had deep convictions of sin; and many dark hours. The Saviour afterwards
appeared very precious.

Attends daily to secret prayer, and hopes he desires to be
wholly devoted to God. Believes in everlasting punishment,
the divinity of the Saviour and the Holy Spirit, the total
depravity of the heart, the atonement, and regeneration by
the Spirit of God. Had some difficulties respecting Solomon's
Song.[9]

This last item caused the committee to defer action on Mr. Spencer. A month later this entry appears: "His difficulties in regard
to the inspiration of Solomon's Song have been relieved. He now
considers that book divinely inspired, and that it forms a part of
the canon of Scripture. Approved."

The high level of piety and Christian concern is further revealed
by the appointment of a committee in the winter of 1827 to consider those measures best suited for the advancement of the
church's spiritual interests. Reporting on February 7, it recommended that the Friday meetings in the vestry, being so well attended by strangers as well as members, must not be changed;
that since some desired a meeting exclusively for the local membership, Monday evenings be set aside for prayer and mutual
edification; that neighborhood meetings be begun for devotional
exercises; and that disciplinary measures be maintained and im-
plemented whenever required by members' irregularities.

As the spirit of revival continued to dominate the orthodox
scene, the city's evangelical forces were emboldened to new
ventures of faith. Although the number of orthodox Congregational churches had risen to five, certain leaders felt the time was
ripe for the formation of additional new churches, especially in
those parts of the city where an orthodox vacuum existed. On
March 21, 1827, members from these five churches, having met in
the Hanover Church vestry to discuss the matter, resolved to erect
two meetinghouses, one in the north end of the city, to be called
Salem Street Church, and one in the south end to be known as
the Pine Street Church. A sum of $20,000 was subscribed in this

[9]Park Street Church, Records of Examining Committee, 1828-34, pp. 26,
37.

meeting toward the construction of these two houses; this figure
was soon raised to $30,000. During the following summer a letter,
similar to this one to Park Street Church, was sent to the participating congregations:

> The subscribers address you in the name of two several
> companies of believers principally members of the evangelical
> churches in Boston who propose to be constituted into two
> new churches to occupy the houses for public worship now
> building the one at the South part of the city and the other at
> the North. We respectfully request your attendance by your
> pastor and a delegate in a council for the organization of said
> churches to meet on Saturday next at three o'clock P.M. in
> Park Street lower vestry. The churches invited are Old
> South, Park Street, Union, Hanover, and Green Street in Bos-
> ton, the first in Cambridge, the second in Dorchester, and the
> first in Charlestown.[10]

Two days before, the following Park Street members had requested recommendations and dismission in order to become
charter members of the Salem Street Church: John C. Proctor,
Nancy Proctor, William Adams, Betsey C. Adams, Daniel Safford,
Sarah Safford, Charles W. Homer, Adeline D. Homer, Benjamin
Kingsbury, Marcia Howland, Rebecca B. Ramick, Lucy Gilpat-
rick, Betsey Stevens.

A similar request led to the dismissal of these members to the
Pine Street Church: Marcus Whiting, Eunice N. Whiting, Nathan
Barrett, John Gamell, Jr., John Robinson, Jr., Josiah F. Bumstead,
Lucy D. Bumstead, Catherine S. Killen.

Both churches were organized September 1, 1827, with the right
hand of fellowship being extended on the following day. The
Salem Street Church (corner of Bennett Street) received a total
of ninety-seven members from her sister churches, thirteen from
Park Street and seventy-seven from the two-year-old Hanover
Church. The edifice was dedicated on January 1, 1828, with Rev.
Justin Edwards of Andover, Massachusetts, as the first pastor. The
Pine Street Church (corner of Washington Street) was constituted
with forty-five members, eight of these from Park Street Church.
The meetinghouse was dedicated Christmas Day, 1827. Its first

[10]Park Street Church, Proceedings . . . , p. 285.

minister, Dr. Thomas H. Skinner, was forced to leave after four months because of ill health. He was succeeded by Dr. John Brown of Cazenovia, New York. The church later changed its name to the Berkeley Street Church.

This decade of revival also witnessed the arrival of Charles Grandison Finney to Boston in the autumn of 1831. Having been invited by the Congregational churches upon the recommendation of Dr. Wisner, who had attended his Providence, Rhode Island, campaign, the evangelist soon discovered that Boston audiences were somewhat different than those in the West. He began by preaching in the different orthodox churches on the Sabbath and in Park Street Church on weekday evenings. Considerable interest was created and large numbers attended his services. He soon perceived "a peculiar type of religion," which seemed to inhibit that freedom and strength of faith which he had witnessed throughout New York. Dr. Beecher had cautioned him that his *modus operandi* would require adjustment in Boston, that he would have to pursue a different course of instruction and begin at the foundation. Nothing must be taken for granted.

Finney announced, therefore, that he would preach a series of weekday sermons designed especially for Christians. To his dismay, the people found his searching sermons most unpalatable. Never before had he seen Christians shrink back from his plain, pointed preaching. But these Christians were not accustomed to it, and the attendance at Park Street became less and less, especially on those evenings when he preached to professed Christians.

In a few weeks, however, as evangelist and audience adjusted to each other, Finney noticed an improved attitude and a greater acceptance and appreciation of his ministry.

Having spent several weeks in constant labor among the churches, and being somewhat fatigued by a decade of evangelistic effort without any prolonged rest, Finney consented to fill the Essex Street pulpit in the absence of Rev. Green who was in Europe for reasons of health. In April, 1832, the evangelist left Boston to become the minister of the Second Free Presbyterian Church in New York City.

For more than a year before concluding his ministry at Park

Street, Edward Beecher was opposed by certain influential members because of his inadequate pulpit ministry. Having been weaned and fed on the ministrations of Griffin, Dwight and the Andover men, a growing number of his congregation were unsatisfied with Beecher's homiletical efforts. His lack of theological training and a number of doctrinal doubts did not produce the type of preaching to which Park Street had become accustomed. His father strongly recommended that he write out his sermons with considerable care and thought in order to assure a maturity of style and orthodoxy of content sufficient to the church's tastes.

However, this inability to fill the pulpit acceptably had its roots in yet deeper causes. Beecher's life and writings reveal a highly sensitive and inquisitive mind unsatisfied with pat answers, particularly in the area of doctrine. This trait explains his problem regarding baptism. It explains the controversial nature of his several more important works. To this searching, ever restless mind, came a new "revelation" in 1827,[11] a new mode by which to overhaul the unbending God of the Puritans (and of Park Street Church) and make Him more sympathetic to the principles of human right and honor—an idea greatly embraced during the nineteenth century. He "became satisfied"[12] that original sin and human depravity and regeneration could not be upheld on the doctrine of the fall of the race in Adam, but that they could be so supported on the ground of the soul's preexistence, a theory both honorable to God and beneficial to mankind.

The impact of this revelation upon his personal life and ministry is revealed in this illuminating passage:

> Mercy now seems to be no mercy, and he who once delighted to speak of the love of Christ is obliged to close his lips in silence, for the original wrong of giving man such a [depraved] nature seems so great that no subsequent acts can atone for the deed. In this state of mind, he who once delighted to pray kneels and rises again, because he cannot sincerely worship the only God whom he sees. . . . He feels as if he could not be bribed by the offer of all the honors of

[11]Edward Beecher, *History of Opinions on The Scriptural Doctrine of Retribution* (New York: D. Appleton & Co., 1878), p. 294.
[12]*Ibid.*

the universe to pretend to worship or praise a God whose character he cannot defend.[13]

This sort of mental posture was hardly conducive to preparation of sermons of the type demanded by Park Street Church. The nature of this revelation is described in these words:

> The transition in my own case was as if, when I had been groping in some vast cathedral, in the gloom of midnight, vainly striving to comprehend its parts and relations, suddenly before the vast arched window of the nave a glorious sun had suddenly burst forth, filling the whole structure with its radiance, and showing in perfect harmony the proportions and beauties of its parts.[14]

Although Beecher kept his findings hidden from public view for a number of years and determined to continue his Park Street ministry in a discreet, orthodox manner, his searching mind, not unlike that of his admired friend, William Ellery Channing, was all the more open to further "resolutions" of problems associated with Calvinistic doctrine. It is questionable how he intended to maintain his clerical honesty in attempting to compose sermons with a fully orthodox content while no longer supporting such essential tenets of Calvinism as the universal sovereignty of an inscrutable God and the depravity of man.

Whether or not Dr. Beecher was aware of his son's revelation is not known. In writing to Catherine on December 1, 1829, with regard to Edward's difficulties, he recorded only these reasons:

> That Edward is not to have the support of his principal men I am confident. That he will have their real and secret, but most efficient opposition, is my full belief. I am not prepared to doubt the intentional rectitude of one of them; but I cannot resist the evidence that defective preaching, etc., is only the ostensible, while personal dislike, and a fixed, determined purpose to get him dismissed, is the real cause. They are not willing he should succeed. They have no pleasure in his manifest improvement. They are afraid he will succeed, and, but for my letter, matters would have been brought to a crisis, in my judgment, in a few weeks.

[13]Edward Beecher, *The Conflict of Ages* (Boston: Phillips, Sampson & Co., 1853), pp. 190-91.
[14]*Ibid.*, p. 191.

It is important, however, to his reputation, and to his usefulness to the Church, and to his safety and health, and to
Park Street, and the general cause here, that, if possible, he
stand it through; and, unless something new occurs, I think
he has got by the pinch and will rise; and if he may have
health, and write as I can advise and he execute, they may do
what they please then.[15]

The attitude of a significant number of church members was
stated in a letter of Ebenezer Parker written March 22, 1830:

I presume you are aware that I was not one of those individuals in Park Street Church who was either in favor of
or who assisted in your settlement over that society, nor was
I one who was so violently opposed, as some of our church
and society were, and while I was always satisfied that your
invitation to settle in Park Street was not the unbiased wish
of the Church, yet encouraged as you were to believe yourself
qualified for the situation and able to perform the duties required I cannot see that you were to be blamed for accepting
the Call. Notwithstanding I did not agree with my brethren
who invited you. Yet I hoped I might be satisfied with you
as a preacher; I listened to your discourses for a considerable
length of time with a real desire of being pleased and edified,
but after a considerable time had elapsed, I became convinced I was not benefited by your preaching.

For a long time I have felt very unhappy in view of your
settlement in Park Street, and when I consider some of the
great sacrifices some of us have made that we might have
not only an able ministry, but a minister in whom we could
be united and happy and keep together our families I feel my
unhappiness increased, and when I take into consideration
days that are past when we not only had an able ministry but
when efforts were made to introduce occasionally men of the
most brilliant talents my unhappiness is not abated. If I had
felt as though there was any prospect of my profiting under
your preaching I should have called on you and conversed
with you freely in relation to the difficulties in my mind.

At length, however, I came to the conclusion that I had
better leave rather than do or say anything which should have
a tendency to disturb the Church or in any way injure your

[15]Beecher, *Autobiography* . . . , II, 211.

feelings, in short that however great the sacrifice of property and feelings I had better make the sacrifice myself.

I communicated this feeling to a number of the brethren who were the most instrumental in placing you in Park Street Church and found they were no better satisfied than myself and all appeared to think that something must be done. Accordingly conversation was had with your Father, who requested that nothing should be said to you, that he would manage the affair and that if it should appear you were not in the right place some other place should be found for you.

After a further length of time, there appeared to be a pretty general dissatisfaction with your preaching among the principal members of the Church and a meeting was held in which I had no hand in calling, but at which I was invited to consult with regard to what course should be pursued. All, I believe twelve or fifteen in number, expressed not only their decided dissatisfaction but expressed also their full belief that no better state of things could be expected six months hence, should your ministry be continued.

At the earnest request of your Father again nothing was done and we have reason to believe the same state of feelings still exist and I am authorized to say that some of those who were the most anxious for your settlement are now the most dissatisfied.

Indeed I do not hesitate to state it as my belief that a great portion of both Church and Society are entirely uninterested in your preaching. I have contended all along that it was not doing justice to you to keep you ignorant or to conceal it from you especially as we have reason to believe your Father has concealed from you what we suppose he would feel bound to communicate.

We suppose so from the fact that you write your friends as I understand that all things are quiet in Park Street now, and also from the fact that your prayers and other performances seem to carry with them the idea of permanency as respects your situation, whereas you could not feel so if you really knew the feelings of the Church towards you.

It is in kindness therefore that I make this communication to you and if you doubt all, inquire of whom you please in our church save of very few individuals and you will find it so as I cannot doubt you wish to be useful, so I cannot doubt that on hearing from some other source the truth of what I have now communicated you will be able readily to perceive the path of duty. No man I think can wish to remain where they cannot give satisfaction and be useful; indeed I think I owe it to you to say, that it is the opinion of some of your best friends that you ought frankly to say to the Church that in accepting their call you took upon yourself more than you are able to sustain. I have no ill will towards you at all, and hope you will not construe anything in this letter as unkind, ungenerous, or unchristian, feeling as I do, my mind is fully made up as to the course it will be my duty to pursue.[16]

Upon his arrival in Boston, Lyman Beecher had looked upon New England orthodoxy as the key to the salvation of the nation. By 1830 he had changed his mind. Writing to Catherine he revealed his hopes for the future:

But if I go [to Cincinnati], it will be part of my plan that *you* go, and another that Edward, and probably all my sons and all my daughters who are willing to go. . . . If we gain the West, all is safe; if we lose it, all is lost.[17]

Concerning Edward's problems at Park Street Church, he wrote:

Edward is well, though rather worn down by his long effort to rise in the face of opposition, which, however, he has achieved, and now writes, and has long since, so that if any grumble, it is manifest that they are unreasonable and unwilling to be pleased.[18]

The whole issue was brought to a head when Edward Beecher was invited to become the first president of the newly established Illinois College at Jacksonville, Illinois. This call not only fit into Dr. Beecher's plans, it gave Edward a new field of service.

In informing his son William of this new development, Dr. Beecher wrote on September 3, 1830: "But there are many and great things in favor of his going, and nothing very inviting in his remaining where he is."

[16]Letter of Ebenezer Parker to Edward Beecher, March 22, 1830, Park Street Church.
[17]Beecher, *Autobiography* . . . , II, 224.
[18]*Ibid.*, p. 225.

Seven weeks later, Edward Beecher resigned his pulpit. Although he recognized the influence of Park Street Church upon the civil and religious institutions of New England, he looked upon the regions of the West as an area of even greater usefulness:

> Believing then that this nation was raised up in the providence of God to affect the destinies of the world I am persuaded that nothing can be more important than to establish and perpetuate throughout all that immense region those institutions which we received from our fathers as heaven's richest gift and which have made New England the glory of all lands.

He then spoke of the vision of the college's founders to establish a system of common schools and other institutions of learning throughout Illinois and to inaugurate a program of colonization to induce intelligent and pious families from New England to emigrate and to assist in the implementation of this pioneer plan. Referring again to his Boston ministry, he said: "I am convinced that there is a prospect of doing more to promote the glory of God and the general good in the field thus opened before me than in the field which I now occupy."

According to his request, an ecclesiastical council was convened on October 28, 1830, and the pastoral relation was dissolved. On November 1, Lyman Beecher wrote to his son William of Edward's final Sabbath at Park Street Church:

> Edward was dismissed on Thursday—all things pleasant; many presents from individuals—$500 by the church; and yesterday, under his farewell sermon, a great many tears were shed.
>
> Public sentiment is doing justice to him and to his friends, and to others. But all things in Park Street are quiet, and they want me to supply them for three months to come, which probably I shall do.[19]

The closely knit family ties which bound father and son undoubtedly proved a comfort to young Edward in his personal and pastoral relationships with Park Street Church. The older and more experienced minister was well suited to guide his son and

[19]*Ibid.*, p. 236.

to protect him from those errors common to the novice. However, Lyman Beecher's hand was too much in evidence. Had Edward been encouraged to secure a thorough theological education, the doctrinal and intellectual problems which plagued him might have been avoided, and the preparation and delivery of his sermons would undoubtedly have met with greater approval by those who heard him regularly. Dr. Beecher's strong desire to always have his children about him—though not unnatural—was not suited to their best interests, especially those of his sons.

As for Park Street Church, its leaders had soon lost any hopes that Edward would pattern his sermons after those of his father. Had they looked more to the Stem of Jesse than to the stock of Beecher in their quest for a candidate, their disappointments could have been entirely averted.

The revivalistic atmosphere of Boston's orthodox churches proved a boon to the newly ordained and inexperienced minister with its pervasive influence toward the development of personal piety and the opportunity to engage in the best methods of evangelism. The significance of Beecher's four years at Park Street Church rests not so much on what he was able to accomplish but rather on the natural outcome of revival power and momentum.

8. Sacred Music and Sabbath Education

Closely associated with the early history of Park Street Church were two important movements, which since then have had enduring significance for America's Protestant churches: the development of sacred music education and the rise of Sabbath schools. The vision and talents of a number of the church's laymen were used in the often unappreciated task of introducing novel methods of singing and teaching for the improvement of the church's worship and witness.

The music in the colonial Puritan churches was a fairly dismal and monotonous affair. The confusing versification of the Psalms, ministerial inability to set the tunes, the irregularity of rhythm, and the absence of guiding notes combined to keep hymnody on a low level. The Psalms were usually read aloud line by line by a deacon and sung by the standing congregation. The length of many of the songs sorely taxed the patience and the stamina of the worshipers, especially the young. In the eighteenth century, the new practice of singing by note, or rule, came into vogue, although in the face of dire prophecies as to their evil origin and design. Many feared that, as a result, musical instruments would be introduced into the services. Alice Morse Earle quotes one writer who in 1723 saw the shadow of the antichrist over this new scheme: "Truly I have a great jealousy that if we begin to *sing* by rule, the next thing will be to *pray* by rule and *preach* by rule and then comes popery."[1]

As the century progressed however, the new way found more and more advocates. This led to the eventual establishment of the

[1] *The Sabbath in Puritan New England* (New York: Charles Scribner's Sons, 1893), p. 208, quoting the *New England Chronicle*, 1723.

New England singing schools, which provided instruction in reading music as well as a much needed recreational outlet in an age of little entertainment. Thus "taught singers" were much in demand by choirmasters in the nineteenth century. The rapid increase of these musical societies, whether independent or church-related, played a major role in raising the standard of sacred music.

One of the more famous church-associated groups was the Park Street Singing Society formed in the house of Caleb Bingham on January 17, 1810, one week after the dedication of the meeting-house. Several months before the completion of the edifice several individuals met together in order to provide the new church with a higher type of music conducive to the increase of devotional feelings, the elevation of religious affections, and the cultivation of a taste for "scientific music." Their aim was to introduce tunes of a more sacred quality and the plain and solemn music of the masters in place of the light, fuguing melodies common to the churches of the day.

The advances made by this society found ready acceptance:

> The singing of the choir at the dedication of Park-street Church, . . . and on the Sabbath and other public occasions for many years, will be among the last things forgotten by those who were performers or hearers.[2]

The music at the new church was of such high caliber that it attracted large numbers of Bostonians to the services, where many of them heard the orthodox preaching of Dr. Griffin.

After the dedication service on January 10, 1810, this nucleus of singers met in the "singing seats" of the new sanctuary on Tuesday, January 16, to officially organize. A committee of Benjamin Reed, Elnathan Duren and Asa Duren was chosen to draw up society regulations and to report the next day. Their report was quickly approved and accepted as the constitution of the Park Street Singing Society.

Candidates for admission were carefully examined, and impressed with the importance of their duty. Evidences of strife among the singers were quickly investigated, and troublesome

[2]Nathaniel D. Gould, *Church Music in America* (Boston: A. N. Johnson, 1853), p. 74.

members were disciplined. Withdrawal from the society without previous notification was considered a grave offense. The constitution also called for the pastor to occasionally visit practice sessions to set forth the importance of their labors.

The first officers, elected at the organizational meeting, were Elnathan Duren, president and choirmaster; Benjamin Reed, first vice-president; Asa Duren, second vice-president; Benjamin F. Waters, third vice-president; and John Bingham, secretary (and treasurer in December, 1812). Under the direction of Elnathan Duren, a well-known musician, the choir soon grew to about fifty and in a short time achieved a wide reputation. Duren had a native talent and notable skill in teaching; his leadership was capable of moving the choir at will with the utmost precision and facility. He continued as president and director until October, 1818, when he was excommunicated from the membership of Park Street Church because of habitual intemperance. In 1820 John Bingham became president, and Deacon Nathaniel D. Gould was chosen choirmaster.

Weekly rehearsals emphasized much drill on syllabic enunciation and singing with understanding. The music for the morning worship services was of a plain, choral style; that for the evening lectures was of a higher, more advanced type. The singing seats were located in the gallery at the rear of the auditorium in order to not distract from the platform ministry. During choir selections, the audience rose and faced the singers. In connection with the singing society, the church voted in February, 1810, to establish, at its own expense, a singing school for the training of promising singers.

By the spring of 1812 the choral society needed reorganization due to deaths and failures in administration. New officers were chosen with choirmaster Duren reelected president. The roster of singers now included forty-four men and thirty-three women; each was required to sign the constitution before taking his seat for the first time.

The unanimous acceptance of the society's selections led to the institution of a second society in Boston—independent of any church—for further improvements in the science of sacred music. On April 26, 1815, the Handel and Haydn Society, America's

oldest oratorio society, was founded in the house of Elnathan
Duren. Many of its charter members were associated with the
Park Street Singing Society. Nathaniel D. Gould observed: "This
choir was an important nucleus to the Handel and Haydn Society at its formation, and took a prominent part in its performances."[3]

Choir records reveal a low period of activity and interest commencing in the summer of 1815 with various attempts being made
to revive the society. A committee recommended another school
for the training of prospective members on the order of the
earlier one which had ceased functioning. In 1817 such a school
was begun by action of the Park Street congregation and placed
under the direction of a Mr. Bailey. The church and congregation,
having been requested to assist the choir financially, voted to contribute an annual sum of one hundred fifty dollars. However,
four years later the problems of the singing society had not been
resolved. A committee of inquiry reported the causes for the
decline: failure to be punctual at the Sabbath services; laxity in
admission procedures; and the abominable habit of some members to be present on the Sabbath after having been absent during
rehearsal—this was found to be especially true of the female section. The church acted upon this report by dissolving the society
on January 24, 1821, and selecting seven men with the authority
to constitute a new organization.

Even after its reorganization the Park Street Singing Society
remained in this somewhat lethargic condition until the arrival of
Lowell Mason, who immediately reawakened interest in the choir
and introduced new measures in music for the benefit of the entire city. Although a native of Medfield, Massachusetts, Mason was
living in Savannah, Georgia, working as a bank employee. He was
for many years a prominent figure in Southern Presbyterian circles, being organist and superintendent of the Sabbath school at
the First Presbyterian Church of Savannah. Hearing of his musical work in the South, a committee of churchmen invited him to
Boston to establish singing schools and to elevate church music
generally throughout the city.

Mason arrived in Boston in 1827. Continuing his employment

as a teller in the American Bank, he opened several private and church-related schools of music, both vocal and instrumental. His charming, quiet manner together with his natural ability brought scores of students to his classes. In October of that year Park Street Church voted to permit him the use of its vestry for one of his singing schools. Demands on his time were also made by a number of the churches. At a meeting of the Prudential Committee on October 27, 1828, William T. Eustis, the chairman of the Singing Committee, recommended hiring Mason as choirmaster and organist. An invitation was made and accepted at a yearly salary of $400. The contract was for one year beginning January 1, 1829, with all the related expenses to be borne by the organist, except for blowing the organ.

On the first day of January, Mason appeared before the Examining Committee as a candidate for church membership. The committee's records show this entry:

> Mr. Lowell Mason, from the First Presbyterian Church in Savannah. It is about fifteen or sixteen years since he professed religion. About sixteen years ago he went from this part of the country to Savannah, where he was under the preaching of Rev. Dr. Kollock. He became serious and disposed to pray; saw something of the character of God, and felt himself to be a sinner. The Saviour appeared precious to him. He joined the church there about six months afterwards.
>
> His principal evidence now is a growing conformity to the precepts of the gospel, and obedience to the will of God. Believes in total depravity; that if we are saved it must be through the mercy of God in Christ; that we are induced by the Spirit of God to turn to God; believes in sovereignty, and election, and the Trinity; the inspiration of the Scriptures.
>
> Had considerable conversation with Mr. Mason in regard to his experience and belief. Approved.

The following month Mason was received by letter into the church; at the same time his wife's letter was transferred from the Independent Presbyterian Church of Savannah. They remained members of Park Street Church until April 18, 1834.

The music department at Park Street improved decidedly as

Mason's concepts were put into practice. He strongly emphasized the importance of the words in sacred music, saying that sentiments had to accompany emotion, and the tune had to be connected with articulate language. Mason stated the purpose of church music: to attract and fix the attention, to excite and express religious emotions and, through its union with language, to excite and express religious sentiments. Church music was not to be an interlude, a temporary expedient. Neither was it a preparation for worship; proper psalmody was to be worship.

Believing that the best use of psalmody in public worship was by persons having a musical sense and a spirit of responsibility, he objected to the "universal and promiscuous chorus of the congregation." He taught that a choir should lead in music, directed by a competent master and accompanied by an organ rather than by other instruments.

The awakened interest in music generated by Mason was responsible for the following resolutions adopted by Park Street Church on October 16, 1829:

> Resolved that this Church approves the method universally adopted by the Congregational Churches of New England of conducting the Singing by a Select Choir and that in addition to the performances of such a Choir it is desirable that the ancient responsive mode of singing should be occasionally introduced as soon as it may be deemed practicable and expedient.
>
> Resolved that this Church considers it the duty of such individual members of the Church as are capable of being useful in the department to devote themselves to the cultivation of sacred music as a religious duty and to make such personal exertions and sacrifices as may be required to raise the character of church music to the Scriptural Standard.

A further significant action arising from this overhaul of the music department was the purchase of an organ. This was a rather bold move so early in the nineteenth century due to the centuries-old stigma attached to the church use of organs in England and America. By 1800 there were approximately twenty organs in New England, mostly in Episcopal churches. Private homes had very few musical instruments of any kind. In the entire town of Boston with its six thousand families there were no more than fifty privately owned pianos. The first instruments permitted in New England churches were the violin cello and the bass viol. The Park Street choir in its early years was accompanied by an orchestra consisting of a flute, a violin cello and a bassoon.

The organ was purchased for two thousand dollars, half the cost being covered by a subscription and the remaining half loaned by William Eustis. An annual sum of twenty-five dollars was required to hire a competent organ blower. Later organs were installed in 1885, 1910 and 1961.

Ever since Mason's arrival in Boston, the Hanover (Bowdoin Street) Church had made several attempts to woo him away from Park Street. These proved successful in 1831, though not without some hard feeling between the concerned parties. Mason, who had contracted his services through the year 1831, requested a release from his pledge. The superior accommodation of the singing seats, a larger organ, and the prospect of introducing his own hymnal into the church were the reasons given for seeking a dismissal.

When Mason learned of the church's refusal to release him, he became quite indignant, and as a result the choir suffered from lack of leadership. The choirmaster no longer met with the singers for rehearsal, having directed the sexton not to open the vestry on the customary practice evenings. To avoid the complete collapse of the choir and any prolonged bitterness, the church finally released Mason from any further obligation. Ten years later, during the years 1839-40, when the church was without an organist, Mason again conducted the music, though on a temporary basis, as he was still engaged at Bowdoin Street. Of this period of service he wrote as follows to William Eustis:

> Received also for upwards of two years past the kindest treatment and attention from the Park Street choir, Committee, and Congregation, which has made an impression on my mind not to be forgotten, and for which I desire ever to be grateful.

For sixty years Mason was a dominant personality in the areas of the philosophy and instruction of church and school music. The Doctor of Music degree awarded him in 1855 by New York University was the first award of its kind ever conferred by an American college.

In addition to his compilation and production of tune books and hymnals, Mason is especially remembered by the nation's churches as a prolific composer of hymns, many of which are still in use: "Work For The Night Is Coming," "Safely Through Another Week," "From Greenland's Icy Mountains" and "My Faith Looks Up to Thee." The lyrics of this last hymn were by Ray Palmer, who confessed Christ as a youth in Park Street Church, and later entered the Congregational ministry.

Problems confronting the Singing Committee in later years revolved around (1) congregational singing, and (2) the quartet and choir. A poll taken among Congregational churches in the Boston area by *The Congregationalist and Boston Recorder* in 1869 showed almost no churches permitting congregational singing without the leadership of a trained quartet. Apart from this professional assistance the singing was apt to degenerate into a lifeless exercise. The poll showed that at Park Street Church the singing was done by a quartet with the congregation uniting in the closing hymn of the service. The subject of congregational singing was often discussed by the society and its committees; however, the majority felt that such singing could not be satisfactorily adopted. In 1870, during the pastorate of William Henry Harrison Murray, quartet singing was deleted entirely from the worship service and greater emphasis placed on audience participation. In the century since then the singing at Park Street Church, other than that of the congregation, has been performed by a choir at one time, by a quartet at another time, and today by a duet. More recently a choir has once again been formed.

Over the years the music committees of the church have attempted to achieve the highest type of sacred music. Large sums of money have been expended to secure consecrated Christian musicians and to provide them with the best tools available. Unfortunately however, the meetinghouse architects allotted no space for a choir. In the context of 1809 this is understandable, but as a result the church has suffered musically ever since.

The Sabbath school idea as worked out in the years following the Revolutionary War was as much a work of benevolence as it was of religion. The purpose of the Society for The Moral and Religious Instruction of The Poor was not only to provide religious training, but also to teach the three R's, especially among Boston's poorer youth. Two schools were opened in existing town schoolhouses. The one on Mason Street was opened on May 11, 1817, with three hundred thirty-six children; the second, on School Street, began its classes on June 15, 1817, with one hundred sixty-four students. Park Street men present at the society's organizational meeting were: Josiah Bumstead, Elnathan Duren, Henry Homes, John C. Proctor, William Thurston and Aaron Woodbury.

Thurston was chosen superintendent of the Mason Street School. The society's first annual report states that not one-fourth of the three hundred thirty-six students in Mason Street could read words of one syllable when admitted, and most did not know the alphabet.

It is difficult to ascertain the date of Park Street's first Sabbath school, due largely to its involvement with the Mason Street School, which it helped support with funds and personnel. A Sabbath school in the modern sense was not instituted in Park Street Church until the close of 1829. An early historical report tells of the custom prior to this date:

> Previously to the year 1830 there was no Sabbath School which might be considered as strictly belonging to this Society—perhaps a majority of the children connected with us and who attended any Sabbath School were accustomed to attend the school in Mason Street, but this school was never under the special supervision of this Church or its pastor but was, as most of the schools were in the City at that time, a "local" school, not connected with any particular religious society but under the charge of a board of managers selected from the several Evangelical Congregational societies in the City.[4]

Any organized religious instruction of Congregational youngsters was carried on outside the province of the local church on a

[4]Historical Report on Various Topics Made Before the Annual Meeting, 1845, Park Street Church.

benevolent and philanthropic level. The concept of a church-sponsored Sabbath school operated by its members was most objectionable in the first twenty or thirty years of the nineteenth century. Those opposing the idea did so on the grounds that the children's religious education was their parents' sole prerogative, that Sabbath school attendance would foster pride in the students, and that participation in such a school would profane the holy day designed for rest. Not until 1830 was the Sabbath school movement fully accepted as a desirable part of church responsibility, and it was much later before the churches were ready to financially support their own schools.

Albert Matthews lists the Sabbath schools that were in existence in Boston during this early period:

West Church, Congregational	1812
Christ Church, Episcopal	1815
Third Baptist Church	1816
Second Baptist Church	1816
First Baptist Church	1816
First African Baptist Church	1816
Mason Street School	1817
School Street School	1817[5]

He then lists Park Street Church under the date of 1817, which is a confusion of location and auspices. It may be stated that Park Street Church helped to found, through its association with the Moral and Religious Society, the first orthodox Congregational Sabbath school.

A forerunner of a locally sponsored school at Park Street was the catechism class for young people over the age of fourteen formed in October, 1822. Undoubtedly Pastor Dwight's concern for the religious education of children was responsible for this venture. Under the direction of Rev. H. Wilbur, the class met every other Wednesday evening in the church vestry to study the Scriptures, using Wilbur's *Biblical Catechism*. Within six months the class had grown in size from the original forty members to two hundred and fifty. Church records dated May, 1824, show authorization to grant fifty dollars to Rev. Wilbur for his services.

[5]Albert Matthews, *Early Sunday Schools in Boston* (Reprint from the publications of The Colonial Society of Massachusetts, Vol. XXI; Cambridge: John Wilson & Son, 1919), p. 284.

In the fall of 1829 the church began a Sabbath school more strictly parochial and under its direct supervision. Pulpit notices announced the new school, encouraging parents to bring their children, and those attending Mason Street to support their own church school.

The initial meeting of the Park Street Church Sabbath School was held December 13, 1829. The superintendent was Joseph Jenkins. Teachers included Nathaniel Willis, Andrew Ellison, Benjamin Bennett, Mrs. William T. Eustis, Mrs. Beecher and Miss Polly Barker. The following Sunday Rev. Dwight made the first address to the school. The same day a two-dollar donation was received for the formation of a library. A generation later this library contained five hundred titles on a variety of subjects.

The school's development and growth in the ensuing years prompted the organization of branch schools in other parts of Boston. The first mission school sponsored by Park Street was founded by two of its women, Miss Sylvia Dana (Mrs. Erastus Smith) and Miss Lizzie Gilbert (Mrs. Henry Frost), in March, 1855. A room was made available to them by the city in a schoolhouse in Haymarket Place. Beginning with two children, the enrollment soon increased to two hundred, with most coming from the poorer population. The growth in numbers necessitated continual changes in location for the first two years, but in 1857 the mission found a large room on Mason Street where it continued for fifteen years until its merger with the Old Colony Mission on Tyler Street. Another mission school supported by Park Street Church, in the years after the Civil War, was Eliot Chapel, which also was united with the independent Old Colony School. Other branch schools with which the church was associated during the nineteenth century were the Cross Street School in Dorchester and the Revere Street (Negro) School. In 1887 thirty Park Street members were teaching in Chinese Sabbath schools.

The fears and forebodings which encompassed the Sabbath school movement in Park Street Church were soon dissipated by its success and its proven value. After a quarter of a century of Sabbath school history, the average attendance was one hundred fifty pupils, half of whom were under sixteen years of age. In recalling the early years of the experiment, it was said:

We think there can be no reasonable doubt of the wisdom of instituting this school, inasmuch as every revival of religion which has been experienced by us as a society has been largely shared in by its members and in some instances the greater number of hopeful converts were members of the Sabbath School, who during the season of their anxiety and interest for the salvation of their souls came under the immediate and personal influence of the pastor and the members of the church.

9. The Antislavery Upheaval

The name of Beecher is linked historically to the fall of slave power in America, and it was during the pastorate of Edward Beecher that Park Street Church provided a platform for one of the most famous voices to be heard in behalf of the Negro. During the second phase of the antislavery movement after 1830, Boston became the focal point for antislavery sentiment, though the Beechers were destined to carry on their social and religious labors elsewhere. Joel Harvey Linsley, the fourth pastor of Park Street Church, was brought face to face with problems which were to plague the Congregational clergy of Boston and vicinity for many years.

The time lapse between the departure of Beecher and the arrival of Linsley was a long twenty-six months. Some of the more prominent men who supplied the pulpit during this interim were Lyman Beecher, Edward Beecher, Calvin E. Stowe (husband of Harriet Beecher Stowe), Edwards Amasa Park, Leonard Woods and Parsons Cooke. In the meantime letters of invitation were sent out by the pastoral candidate committee to a number of clergymen: in February, 1831, a call was given to Dr. Joel Hawes of Hartford, Connecticut, and declined; in January, 1832, the name of Rev. Ichabod S. Spencer of Northampton, Massachusetts, was presented to the church, but the invitation was refused; in September, a second call was extended to Dr. Hawes with the same result.

One week after being notified of this second refusal of Dr. Hawes, the church voted unanimously to invite another Hartford minister, Rev. Joel Harvey Linsley, of the South Congregational

Church, at an annual salary of two thousand dollars. He accepted
on October 26, 1832, and was installed on December 5 with Dr.
Moses Stuart delivering the sermon.

The interest created by the church's previous pastors in the
benevolent and charitable societies of the evangelical church continued to be encouraged and supported by its new minister. Records pertaining to Linsley's pastorate, though scarce, show his
concern for the ongoing of the church in the following:

1. His appreciation of the value of the Sabbath school is revealed in his statement in 1828 while still in Hartford:

> The Sabbath School Institution, as an auxiliary in educa-
> tion, does not need the author's feeble praise: It is above all
> praise; and the subjects of its benign instructions are be-
> coming its living letters of commendation, "known and read
> of all men."[1]

2. The wide-ranging benevolent interests of the church are indicated by its method of collecting annual contributions. Each
month except August and September was associated with a specific benevolent agency to which the church pledged annual support. This arrangement originated in a joint committee of several
orthodox Congregational churches in 1834 and was as follows:

January	Foreign missions
February	American Education Society
March	Home and City missions
April	Home and City missions
May	Tract society
June	Sabbath schools
July	Africans
August	Miscellaneous
September	Miscellaneous
October	Seaman's Friend Society
November	Bible society
December	Prison Discipline Society

The Prudential Committee was responsible for visiting each
church member to solicit "a generous and general contribution."

3. The fifth church to be formed in Boston with the aid of Park

[1]Joel Harvey Linsley, *Lectures on the Relations and Duties of the Middle
Aged* (Hartford: D. F. Robinson & Co., 1828), p. 96.

Street members was Central Congregational Church. A number
of evangelical men from several churches banded together to
initiate the organization of a new society on May 11, 1835, in the
vestry of the Bowdoin Street Church. Of the sixty-three charter
members, twelve transferred from Park Street Church: William
Bates, John Benson, William Beck, Elizabeth Beck, Edward Haskell, Edward Knight, Mary Ann Knight, Jeremiah Peabody, Catherine Peabody, Daniel Safford, Ann Eliza Safford, Ruth H. Safford.

During its first six years, services were held under the name of
the Franklin Street Church in an unused theater. With the erection of its meetinghouse on Winter Street, the society changed its
location on December 24, 1841, and also its name. The first pastor,
William M. Rogers, was installed on August 6, 1835.

4. Another important advance was made by Park Street Church
in 1835. On January 29 the pew proprietors heard a church report regarding a proposed petition to the state legislature for an
act of incorporation. Suggested bylaws and a form of indenture
conveying the meetinghouse to the corporation were also read.
The recommendations of the church were readily adopted, and
a committee composed of Henry Hill, George Odiorne and Francis
Watts was chosen to unite with the church in the presentation of
the petition. On March 24, 1835, the House of Representatives
approved the incorporating act; three days later, the Senate having
concurred, the bill creating the Park Street Congregational Society
was enacted. The legislature's action was approved by the new
society on April 16, 1835.

The conveyance of the meetinghouse deed was made by the
church to the society on August 18, 1835; however, the original
trusts regarding the choice of ministers remained unchanged:

> That whenever and as often as a pastor of the said Church
> and Society is to be chosen, the said Church shall have the
> exclusive right to nominate the same, and shall propose the
> person so nominated to the said Society for its concurrence;
> and if upon such nomination the said Society concur, and not
> otherwise, a call shall be presented by the said Church and
> Society jointly, the amount of the salary of the pastor so
> chosen to be determined by the said Society only.[2]

[2]Registry of Deeds, Suffolk County, Boston, Massachusetts, Libro 395,
Folio 177.

Indelibly stamped upon Park Street's history during the years
1829-35 are two paradoxical events which, because of their sur-
passing significance, have found a place in the history of the nation: the first major public address by William Lloyd Garrison
against the evil of slavery, and the introduction to the public of
the patriotic hymn "America."

Upon his graduation from Harvard College in 1829, Samuel
Francis Smith entered Andover Theological Seminary. In February, 1831, while looking through a German tune book lent him
by Lowell Mason, he noticed a piece of music, to which he soon
wrote five verses. One verse was deleted later. The composition
was forgotten by the young student when he returned the book to
Mason.

With the approach of Independence Day that year, a number
of Boston's churchmen, disturbed by the frivolous manner in
which the day had been celebrated in the past, planned a more ap-
propriate program for observing the holiday. On July 4, 1831, the
Boston Sabbath School Union sponsored the following program
at Park Street Church:

Selection	Juvenile Choir
Scripture Reading	
Selection	Choir
Prayer	Dr. Lyman Beecher
Selection: "America"	Choir
Address to Children	Dr. Benjamin Wisner
Selection	Choir
Benediction[3]	

The rendition of "America" by the choir under Mason's direction
was the first public performance of the hymn. Its author, who
later became a notable Baptist clergyman, did not know of its
inclusion in the program and was surprised to learn of its use.

Even as the children sang "sweet freedom's song," loud and
enraged voices were decrying the ugly servitude of the Negro
slave. Mortal tongues began to awaken and give strength and
volume to the sound which in ensuing years was to be prolonged
throughout the land, after it was given an early impulse by William Lloyd Garrison within the hall of Park Street Church.

[3]Exercises of Celebration of American Independence, July 4, 1831, Park
Street Church, by permission of the Harvard College Library.

The Massachusetts colony had remained a party to the slave trade until the passage of the state's Bill of Rights in 1781 at which time about two thousand slaves were freed and slavery was abolished. Bostonian sentiment toward slavery in the South during the next half century, though mildly deprecating on ethical grounds, at the same time was generally permissive. Although the prevailing consensus was one of inaction, it is a mistake to infer, as does William L. Garrison, Jr., that the entire community was silent until the famous abolitionist appeared on the scene.[4] In 1823 the Baptist and orthodox Congregational churches of Boston had inaugurated a lecture series on the subject of antislavery. Given annually on the Fourth of July in the Park Street Church auditorium, the first was delivered by Louis Dwight. The concluding message in this series was given by Garrison in 1829. Park Street Church, therefore, was in the forefront of a movement designed to hasten abolition, but in a peaceful and wise manner. It is a "worn-out falsehood" therefore, to charge the evangelical churches especially with a noncommittal attitude toward the slave issue. Dr. Leonard W. Bacon has written: "The early years of the Park Street Church were years of widespread, earnest and effective antislavery effort."[5]

William Lloyd Garrison was born in Newburyport, Massachusetts, on December 10, 1805, of a devout Baptist mother who early acquainted her son with the struggles of the Baptists for religious freedom in the previous century, and instilled in him the Puritan virtues of morality, conviction and energetic will. Before his Boston speech he worked as a journalist for several New England newspapers which printed his articles on Negro colonization. The Boston chapter of the American Colonization Society, attracted by Garrison's forthright and enthusiastic writings, invited him as their speaker for the 1829 lecture in the Park Street antislavery series.

Although Garrison is known as the fighting leader of the abolitionist cause, his speech in Park Street Church on July 4, 1829, was in behalf of colonization, for as yet he had not changed his

[4]William Lloyd Garrison (the younger), *Boston Anti-Slavery Days* (The Bostonian Society Pubns., Vol. II; Boston: Old State House, 1905), p. 84.
[5]Leonard W. Bacon, "A Forgotten Glory of Park Street Church," *The Congregationalist and Christian World,* July 9, 1904, p. 52.

convictions. He believed that by moral suasion, with the support of the church, a network of colonization societies could be established to finish the task.

Independence Day, 1829, turned out to be a hectic day for the twenty-three-year-old newspaperman. In a letter written June 27 to his friend Jacob Horton, he requested a loan of eight dollars to pay due bills, one of them being for failure to appear for the May militia muster; as a result, he had been summoned to appear in police court on July 4. The same letter mentions his forthcoming appearance in Park Street Church:

> My address for the Fourth is almost completed; and on the whole, I am tolerably well satisfied with the composition. The delivery will occupy me, probably, a little over an hour—too long, to be sure, for the patience of the audience, but not for the subject. . . . Its complexion is sombre, and its animadversions severe. The assembly bids fair to be overwhelming. My very knees knock together at the thought of speaking before so large a concourse. What then, will be my feelings in the pulpit? . . .
>
> Rev. Mr. Pierpont . . . has promised to write an original ode for that day; and says he shall take a seat in some corner of Park-Street Church to hear the address—a thing that he has not done for many years.[6]

Rev. John Pierpont of the Hollis Street Church wrote this hymn especially for the occasion; it was sung that afternoon under the direction of Lowell Mason and in many antislavery meetings thereafter:

> Hearest thou, O God, those chains,
> Clanking on Freedom's plains,
>   By Christians wrought!
> Them who these chains have worn,
> Christians from home have torn,
> Christians have hither borne,
>   Christians have bought!
>
> Cast down, great God, the fanes
> That, to unhallowed gains,
>   Round us have risen—

[6]Letter of William Lloyd Garrison to Jacob Horton, June 27, 1829, by courtesy of the trustees of the Boston Public Library.

> Temples whose priesthood pore
> Moses and Jesus o'er,
> Then bolt the black man's door,
> The poor man's prison![7]

The meeting began at four o'clock. A local newspaper described the guest speaker as being of youthful appearance and "habited in a suit of black, with his neck bare, and a broad linen collar spread over that of his coat." The lecture, entitled "Dangers to the Nation," covered four broad propositions: (1) The slaves are entitled to the prayers and charities of the American people, and their claims for redress should be heard. (2) It is the duty of the free states to assist in the overthrow of slavery. (3) There is no justification in law or in religion to perpetuate slavery. (4) The colored man must be freed and permitted an education.

Speaking of a method which he would categorically renounce six weeks later, he said:

> I answer, the emancipation of all the slaves of this genera-
> tion is most assuredly out of the question. The fabric, which
> now towers above the Alps, must be taken away brick by
> brick, and foot by foot. . . . Years may elapse . . . but the
> work will go on. . . . The victory will be obtained, worth the
> desperate struggle of a thousand years.[8]

Upon completing his address, which was well received, Garrison moved to Baltimore to continue his writings in the pages of the *Genius of Universal Emancipation* in conjunction with his Quaker friend, Benjamin Lundy. His partnership with the gradualist Lundy soon came to an abrupt end as Garrison's views underwent a radical change. This change came from his belief that slavery was a sin, and like all sin, it had to be removed immediately. The revivalist emphasis on immediate repentance by the sinner was transferred to the slave issue. This abolitionist scheme also arose from a disbelief in the ability and the capacity of colonization societies to attain their goal. Lyman Beecher vigorously protested to his one-time parishioner: "Oh, Garrison, you can't

[7][Garrison children], *William Lloyd Garrison, 1805-1879, The Story of His Life* (New York: Century Co., 1885), I, 126.
[8]William Lloyd Garrison, *Dangers to the Nation* ("Old South Leaflets," Vol. VIII; Boston: Directors of the Old South Work, Old South Meeting-house, n. d.), p. 9.

reason that way! Great economic and political questions can't be solved so simply. You must take into account what is expedient as well as what is right."[9]

Having returned to Boston in 1830 to establish *The Liberator*, Garrison recalled his Park Street lecture in the very first issue:

> In Park-Street Church, on the Fourth of July, 1829, in an address on slavery, I unreflectingly assented to the popular but pernicious doctrine of *gradual* abolition. I seize this opportunity to make a full and unequivocal recantation, and thus publicly to ask pardon of my God, of my country, and of my brethren the poor slaves, for having uttered a sentiment so full of timidity, injustice and absurdity. A similar recantation, from my pen, was published in the "Genius of Universal Emancipation" at Baltimore, in September, 1829. My conscience is now satisfied.[10]

The abolitionist editor suddenly found himself adrift from many who had been his associates eighteen months earlier. Seeking for support, he turned to Jeremiah Evarts who, as secretary of the American Board, had spoken and written much in behalf of the plight of the Indians. But he found little response. The managers of the American Board and most of the orthodox clergy were hostile to this new side of the antislavery movement. Many feared that excitement over the slavery issue would quench the spirit of revival then very much in evidence, and that it would divide the churches, so recently torn, and divert them from primary spiritual concerns. They felt the time was not ripe for abolitionist agitation.

Although Boston citizens were generally sympathetic to the principle of freedom for the Negro, their Anglo-Saxon prejudices refused permission to non-Caucasian persons to enter the churches unless they were willing to accept the "nigger pew." From the testimony of Oliver Johnson, an orthodox author of that day, it appears that Park Street Church was not excluded from such prejudice. Johnson, a frequent attendant at the Bowdoin Street Church, tells of a Negro who, through a commercial transaction with a white person in 1830, became owner of a pew on the central aisle of Park Street Church. Soon afterward he occupied the

[9]Lyman Beecher Stowe, *Saints, Sinners, and Beechers* (Indianapolis: Bobbs-Merrill Co., 1934), p. 60.
[10]*The Liberator*, January 1, 1831, p. 1.

pew on Sunday with his family. Although permitted to remain
that day, the church trustees informed him that it would be impossible for him to hold the pew. "His appearance and that of
his family in that fashionable house of worship was accounted by
all Boston as an outrage scarcely less flagrant than would have
been the use of a pew as a pigpen."[11] In a church business meeting immediately after this incident, the following motion was
moved and adopted:

> The Prudential Committee is requested to consider the
> expediency of so altering the deeds of pews as to prevent
> coloured persons procuring deeds of the same and report at
> an adjourned meeting of the church.[12]

One week later the committee reported proposed alterations
which, after being reviewed by legal authorities, were adopted by
the church and inserted into a new pew deed. Thereafter all ap-
plications for pew deeds were cleared through the Prudential
Committee.

During the years of Linsley's pastorate, the city and its churches
were in ferment and agitation. Three weeks after the pastor's departure from Park Street Church, Garrison was seized by a mob
of leading citizens and hustled through the downtown streets on
the end of a rope. Fear that the abolition movement might cause
bloodshed and the ruin of the entire antislavery cause led many
to refuse cooperation with the Garrison forces even though basically sympathetic with their goals. The clergy was afraid to assume a positive stance for immediatism while their people looked
on with disfavor.

The prevailing mood of the orthodox Congregational churches
of Massachusetts is revealed by the *Pastoral Letter* of June, 1837,
which was sent throughout the state by authorization of the General Association. Its purpose was twofold: to encourage the closing of all churches to antislavery lecturers other than their own
ministers, which would supposedly remove the churches from the
arena of debate; and to discourage attendance at the lectures of
the Grimké sisters.

Angelina and Sarah Grimké, having left their Episcopalian

---

[11]Oliver Johnson, *William Lloyd Garrison and His Times* (London: Sampson, Low, Marston, Searle & Rivington, 1882), p. 100.
[12]Park Street Church, Proceedings of Business Meetings, 1809-34, p. 451.

home in Charleston, South Carolina, in 1837, joined the ranks of the antislavery movement in the North. Moving to Philadelphia, they became converts to Quakerism and soon established themselves as energetic writers and lecturers in the tempestuous world of antislavery societies. Their tour through Massachusetts at the invitation of the Massachusetts Antislavery Society, and their initial success prompted the *Pastoral Letter.* John Greenleaf Whittier, who had heard Garrison's Independence Day speech at Park Street Church and was sympathetic to the great abolitionist, was incensed by this action of the General Association. His pen poured forth his scorn:

> So this is all—the utmost reach
> > Of priestly power the mind to fetter!
> When laymen think, when women preach,
> > A "war of words"—a "Pastoral Letter!"
> Now, shame upon ye, parish Popes!
> > Was it thus with those, your predecessors,
> Who sealed with rocks, and fire, and ropes
> > Their loving-kindness to transgressors?
>
> A "Pastoral Letter," grave and dull!
> > Alas! in hoof and horns and features,
> How different is your Brookfield bull
> > From him who thunders from St. Peter's!
> Your pastoral rights and powers from harm,
> > Think ye, can words alone preserve them?
> Your wiser fathers taught the arm
> > And sword of temporal power to serve them.
>
> .   .   .   .
>
> But ye who scorn the thrilling tale
> > Of Carolina's high-souled daughters,
> Which echoes here the mournful wail
> > Of sorrow from Edisto's waters,
> Close while ye may the public ear,
> > With malice vex, with slander wound them;
> The pure and good shall throng to hear,
> > And tried and manly hearts surround them.
>
> O, ever may the Power which led
> > Their way to such a fiery trial,

And strengthened womanhood to tread
   The winepress of such self-denial,
Be round them in an evil land,
   With wisdom and with strength from heaven,
With Miriam's voice and Judith's hand,
   And Deborah's song, for triumph given.

And what are ye who strive with God
   Against the ark of his salvation,
Moved by the breath of prayer abroad,
   With blessings for a dying nation?
What, but the stubble and the hay
   To perish, even as flax consuming,
With all that bars his glorious way,
   Before the brightness of his coming?[13]

Park Street Church did not follow the recommendations of the
Letter too closely, for throughout the 1830's the meetinghouse was
made available to such groups as the New England Antislavery
Society and the Boston branch of the American Colonization Society. This indicated a neutral course, which was quite reprehen-
sible to the abolitionist. The only auditorium that was certain to
be open to antislavery meetings after 1837 was Willard Sears'
Marlborough Chapel; most other landlords feared to open their
halls lest they suffer reprisal or property damage.

Austin Phelps, in an article for *The Congregationalist,* divided
the community in three classes in relation to antislavery reform:
resistants (proslavery); destructives (abolitionists); and reform-
ers (gradualists). Park Street Church, along with the majority
of the New England churches, was numbered with this third class.
The New England orthodox mind turned from immediate abolition to the more peaceful method espoused by the later antislavery
societies. Among the reasons behind this posture of gradualism
was the fact that the abolitionist cause drew many who were
hostile to biblical Christianity. Many evangelicals found it impossible to join hands in a common cause with those who scoffed
at the divine Christ and ridiculed His church.

---

[13]*Poems* (Boston: Sanborn, Carter & Bazin, 1857), pp. 155-58.

10. Drawbacks to Prosperity

Sixteen months after Linsley's installation, he suffered severe hoarseness and injury to his voice, necessitating several weeks of rest. In December, 1834, an additional six-month leave was granted, but his health never returned sufficiently to allow him to continue his labors. The following July he requested the dissolution of his pastoral relationship, which was effected on September 9, 1835.

Linsley was a good man, simple, spiritual and gracious. His health hindered him from any sort of an extended progressive program. Nevertheless, through his preaching and his charitable spirit, he helped to sustain the kind of church life his predecessors had established. He was a choice servant of Christ in a troublous hour in Boston's history.

The recurring problem of a lengthy interim between pastorates again plagued the church. During this year-and-a-half period, calls were extended to Dr. Edwards Amasa Park of Andover Seminary and to Dr. Mark Tucker of Troy, New York. Neither man accepted. In a church meeting on January 23, 1837, the candidate committee reported its difficulty in locating a suitable minister. After continued prayer and the consideration of several names, a unanimous preference was indicated for Rev. Silas Aiken of the Congregational Church of Amherst, New Hampshire, who accepted the position.

Aiken's years at Park Street were to be highlighted by a diligent though unsuccessful effort to place the society on a sound fiscal basis in relation to the sale and taxation of pews, to the church's current operation exclusive of a deficit, and to major repairs and

alterations in the edifice. The financial panic of 1837 and the un-
foreseen increase in alteration expenditures created almost in-
superable obstacles.

Even before Linsley's coming, the trustees had been aware of
the need for extensive repairs, especially to the steeple. There
was even some talk about raising the meetinghouse floor to make
a more commodious lower vestry. In November, 1832, the treasurer was authorized to borrow not more than six thousand dollars
to pay off outstanding debts and to cover the cost of steeple repairs, which were made the following year. Fourteen years later,
as a result of a fierce gale, the steeple swayed badly and was pro-
nounced dangerous. The central timber of the spire was found
to incline eleven inches from the perpendicular toward the northeast. Investigation revealed considerable decay in the upper portion of the spire. A design was prepared calling for the dismantling of the spire down to the bell deck, at which point a permanent square dome was to be placed upon a section of brickwork.
Fortunately for the beauty of the edifice, the society, on a motion
from Louis Dwight, approved an alternate plan.

Three feet of the upper portion of the spire was strengthened
and secured with braces and bolts. Twenty-two supporting timbers required replacement. The entire roofing of all the offsets
above the bell deck were recoppered. New sashes were installed.
These extensive steeple repairs, though costing $4,520.98, did
serve to strengthen and preserve the spire.

The congregation's financial problem was underscored by the
fact that general operating expenses annually exceeded receipts
by approximately one thousand dollars. This table for 1837 indicates the usual expenditures recurring annually during this
period:

Minister's salary		$2,200
Sexton's salary		200
Singers' salaries		
Mrs. Allen	$300	
Mrs. Webster	200	
Blowing organ	30	
Other	70	600
Insurance Premium		83

Interest on Bond	420
Wood and Coal	120
Oil	60
Collecting taxes	30
Incidentals	187
	$3,900

Faced with a mounting debt and a perennial deficit, the society, on December 19, 1837, was confronted by two alternatives, both of which required a large measure of faith and daring: remodel the facilities of the meetinghouse, or raze it altogether and build elsewhere. For the past five years there had been talk of major alterations on the meetinghouse to make it more serviceable and more attractive to potential buyers of pews. Due to the high pulpit and pews, the sanctuary was considered by many to be uncomfortable and unattractive. As in the style of eighteenth century New England churches, the mahogany pulpit had been erected high above the pews, accessible by a flight of winding stairs on either side. During the pastorates of Griffin and Dwight, the church had no vestry apart from a small room over the front entrance of the church. During and after the revival of 1823-24, the need for more adequate accommodations became evident; the new Sabbath school also needed classrooms. A cellar was dug under the sanctuary alongside the tombs to make a lower vestry, but this proved unsuitable because the room was damp and dismal.

Plans and estimates for both proposals were presented. After further investigation, a recommendation was made to remain at the present location and institute major alterations. A sum of $10,500 was immediately subscribed.

Although a few of the more elderly opposed the plan, the need for a larger vestry was felt by the majority. The alterations included the erection of a new floor twelve feet above the original one, leaving space below for a more adequate vestry and four smaller rooms. At the same time the building's outer walls were increased in height, as is clearly visible today by the character of the brickwork above the side windows and by the juncture of the front roof cornices at the tower windows. This entire project was largely the brainchild of Deacon Daniel Safford, under whose superintendence it was successfully completed during the summer of 1838. *The New England Gazetteer* of 1841 describes the meetinghouse as 106 feet long and 82 feet wide, with a 20-foot vestibule. The main floor supported 134 pews (144 prior to alteration) and the galleries, 50. The basement (vestry) was described as "commodious with halls and rooms."

The extensive alterations to the building's interior, where the platform and galleries were remodeled and the pews displaced, required an appraisement of the privately owned pews both before and after the remodeling. The subscribers, in making their pledges, agreed to the following: to accept both pew appraisals as indicating true value, to receive pews in repayment of their pledge, and to invest the appraisement of their old pews in pews of the altered house.

On September 6 the Building Committee reported spending $24,496.81 for interior alterations plus exterior sanding, painting and repair. Since this figure exceeded original estimates by more than $10,000, the committee suggested that the treasurer be authorized to pay scrip and that a new appraisal be made (exclusive of the minister's pew, pews on each side of the pulpit, and the three short pews at each end of the singing seats in the front gallery) in order to arrive at a valuation of $51,000, taxes on which would produce sufficient revenue to help reduce the debt and pay current expenses. These suggestions were accepted, the appraisal was made, and the pews were placed on sale at public auction. Three years later, having borrowed an additional $15,000, and with ninety-two pews valued at $21,300 still unsold, a 2½ percent supplemental tax was added to the 7 percent existing rate, which tax was to be removed whenever the debt had decreased to $10,000. In an effort to sell the remaining pews, the Prudential Committee was given authority to set its own terms and conditions of sale.

Several hundreds of dollars were added annually to the treasury by renting the newly constructed basement rooms. Rates ranged from $125-$200 annually. Even the coalbin was used on occasion. Tenants were usually private music teachers; in 1838 the rooms were used by physicians and their medical students. The auditorium was also made available to the public according to a special table of fees.

Although the church and society used many means to establish a sound fiscal structure—with Pastor Aiken even proposing a temporary cutback in his salary—the treasurer's yearly reports revealed only continuing deficits. A special finance committee was chosen in 1846 to study the entire fiscal situation and to report a plan whereby receipts would equal expenditures. On April 7 this committee reported that of the 184 pews in the newly altered house, only 80 had been sold or rented. With a total pew valuation of $51,000, the regular tax rate of 7 percent should have produced $3,570, sufficient to meet current expenses; however, in 1840-46 this minimum tax figure had never been reached. The yearly deficit in receipts fell from a low of $122 in 1841 to a high of $1,224 five years later. The committee's picture of worsening conditions was mirrored by the fact that an ever increasing number of proprietors were relinquishing their pews to the society. Whereas in 1844 five pews had been surrendered, by 1846, nineteen had been turned back.

What caused this decline in public interest and financial health of the Park Street Church and Society? The special committee offered these reasons: (1) the society made a serious error in failing to make a stronger drive to sell pews immediately after the repairs and remodeling; (2) the policy of allowing the proprietors to surrender pews, though innocuous in normal times, proved harmful; (3) the erection of two new and attractive Congregational meetinghouses (the Central Church and the more recently opened Mount Vernon Church) exerted an influence prejudicial to their interests; (4) the 2½ percent pew tax tended to lessen the number of regular worshipers who, not being pew proprietors or official members, resented paying off the debt; income from this extra tax fell short of the required amount by a total of $369 in its first year of trial; (5) families moving from the city; (6) the death of prominent members; (7) the formation of the Central and Mount Vernon churches was aided by Park Street laymen who left to become charter members.

The committee's solution to the problem: the one hundred four unoccupied pews would be made financially productive when the

Sabbath services were made attractive enough to draw paying worshipers. The society should give serious consideration to the settlement of a colleague for Pastor Aiken. Not only would this extend the influence of Park Street Church spiritually and temporally, it would also promote and strengthen the cause of Christ by multiplying the means of salvation. The additional salary would be paid from the rental and sale of the presently unoccupied pews. Comparing Park Street with its newest sister churches whose pews were fully occupied, the committee believed that its society had many attractive features peculiar to itself which, with the additional pastor, would lead many to purchase or rent pews. Should the income necessary for the support of an assistant not be forthcoming, the committee believed that the proprietors would not object to an increased tax rate in order to produce an income commensurate with that of the Central and Mount Vernon Churches.

	Pews	Value	Tax Rate	Tax Income
Park Street Church	184	$51,000	7%	$3570
Central Church	162	70,000	6%	4200
Mount Vernon Church	182	60,000	7%	4200

The society accepted the report and passed on its action to the church for concurrence, which it received within two weeks. A joint committee from the church and the society extended two invitations in its search for an assistant pastor. In July, 1846, a call was made to Rev. Charles Wadsworth of Troy, New York. A year later the church recommended Henry Ward Beecher, pastor of the Second Presbyterian Church, Indianapolis, Indiana. Both men declined. Park Street was not to have an assistant minister until the present century, nor was the society to emerge from its financial doldrums for many years to come.

Despite these pecuniary problems the church maintained its faithful support of evangelical missions and charities. The benevolence report of 1846 showed total contributions of four thousand dollars—from a membership of 537 persons.

The spirit of evangelism, which characterized the church during the first generation of its history, produced another revival in Boston in 1841-42 and an additional strong, orthodox Congrega-

tional church. Largely through the efforts and evangelistic zeal
of Deacon Daniel Safford and Pastor Aiken, evangelist Edward
Norris Kirk, who was then holding meetings in New York City,
was invited to Park Street Church in the spring of 1840. The
nine-day campaign began on Saturday evening, June 27, with
Dr. Kirk preaching on the text, "Prepare to meet thy God." The
two daily services, afternoon and evening, were soon attended
by overflow crowds, the people filling the aisles and the pulpit
stairs. Many were turned away due to lack of space. The success of the meetings and the eagerness with which the audiences
received Kirk's simple gospel preaching dictated a return engagement the following autumn.

Unable to unite all the orthodox churches in a joint sponsorship of the second campaign, Park Street Church again opened its
doors, and for "many successive weeks" the meetinghouse was
once more thronged with eager listeners, many of whom were
from Unitarian churches. Prayer meetings preceded and followed
each preaching service. The deacons met daily for intercessory
prayer during the entire campaign. Many inquirers went to the
Safford residence nearby, seeking personal counsel from Safford
or his houseguest, Dr. Kirk. One evening soon after the meetings
had been concluded, the church heard the testimony of seventy-
one persons professing their newfound faith in Jesus Christ. As a
result of the revival, one hundred one new members were added.

A year later, early in the autumn of 1841, Dr. Kirk was invited
by Park Street Church a third time. During this visit pastors and
laymen from several orthodox churches met to consider establishing a new religious society and inviting Dr. Kirk as its first
minister. The official call to the evangelist was accepted the
following May. With a charter membership of forty-seven persons, twenty-five men and twenty-two women, the New Congregational Church was organized in the Park Street vestry on Wednesday, June 1, 1842. Fear that the new church might draw away
members from other nearby churches—especially Park Street, and
thereby add to its financial difficulties—reduced to only three persons the number that sought transfers. These were Daniel and
Eliza Ann Safford and George F. Homer.

The original meetinghouse on Somerset Court (Ashburton

Place) was dedicated January 4, 1844. A year after the church's organization, it was renamed Mount Vernon Congregational Church, this name being given by Dr. Kirk simply because of its pleasant and euphonius sound. This first pastorate continued for thirty-two years, with the church assuming a foremost place in Boston's evangelical life soon after its founding.

J. C. Pollock remarks that the New Congregational Church was established by "Bostonians unsatisfied with the rigid doctrinal exclusiveness of Park Street."[1] The foregoing record substantiates the fallacy of this statement. Furthermore, in Pauline Holmes' history of Mount Vernon Church she observes: "To the Reverend Silas Aiken and to Daniel Safford of the Park Street Church, more perhaps than to any others, was due the formation of Mount Vernon Church."[2]

In the first thirty-three years of its history, Park Street relinquished seventy members in order to help found seven orthodox Congregational churches in Boston. Whereas in 1809 there were but two orthodox churches, by 1842 this number had increased to fourteen: Old South, Park Street Church, Essex Street, Bowdoin Street, Green Street, South Boston, Pine Street, Salem Street, Central Church, East Boston, Mariners' Chapel, Marlborough Chapel (Free Church), Garden Street, and Mount Vernon Church. Total membership of the churches approximated 5,000 persons. The Unitarian congregations also numbered fourteen in this same decade.

The entire number of persons received into the Park Street membership from its formation until March, 1845, was 1,234—385 males and 849 females. The largest annual additions were made in 1823 (108); 1842 (102); 1840 (81); and 1827 (74)—all revival years. The greatest number received on one occasion was fifty-two in July, 1842. The smallest addition in any year was five in 1836.

The fourth decade of the church's history was a difficult one due to persistent financial pressures. Though the church continued to enlarge its influence and witness, the pastor's ministry was hindered by this oppressive burden. The ceaseless efforts to

[1]J. C. Pollock, *Moody* (New York: Macmillan Co., 1963), p. 12.
[2]Pauline Holmes, *One Hundred Years of Mount Vernon Church, 1842-1942* (Boston: Mount Vernon Church, 1942), p. 1.

stabilize the treasury and the wearisome committee labor involved, to which Pastor Aiken gave himself unstintingly, finally proved too much. His health became impaired. This, combined with the church's inability to locate a colleague, led him to resign in May, 1848.

Although a spirit of harmony and goodwill existed in the church throughout Aiken's pastorate, apparently there was a slight breakdown at the close. This lack of unity is reflected in certain votes of confidence cast during the spring of 1848, which indicated the church's desire for a dissolution of the pastoral relationship. Undoubtedly the church and society were moved to register these votes more by discouragement over the course of events than by feelings of bitterness against Aiken. Although his appearance was rather rough and he was bold in his convictions, Aiken was a humble, modest man who was never known to make "an injurious or unkind remark."

His letter of resignation reveals the causes for the problems then confronting the church and congregation:

> I deem it my duty to make to you a communication concerning my pastoral relation. It is now more than eleven years since I entered the work of the ministry among you. . . . During the former half of the period, or the first six years, the addition to the church by profession and transfer of relation, considerably exceed those of any equal portion of time since its formation in 1809 and the condition of the society was in the main satisfactory and promising. In regard to the latter half of the above period, as you need not be informed, there have been serious drawbacks upon our prosperity. Besides the prevailing religious declension affecting all the churches of this region, other causes of depression beyond my control, have been in operation. New and inviting places of worship have been opened in the central portion of the city; not a few of our most valued members have been removed by death, and a large number of families have been leaving the city for a residence in the surrounding country. From this last cause the drain upon us has been constant and severe and all of them have conspired naturally to diminish the income and bring the finances of the society into an unsatisfactory state. Under the labors and anxieties conse-

quent in part upon such a condition of things, my health has
suffered, at times severely.

The letter went on to mention the matter of a colleague pastor.
After two years of failure, the colleague committee was dis-
charged on March 13, 1848, with everyone recognizing the im-
practicability of the plan.

To this letter the church replied on June 30, expressing its
"undiminished respect and esteem, . . . [its] confidence in your
Christian and ministerial character, and your pastoral wisdom
and fidelity."

On the afternoon of July 12, 1848, an ecclesiastical council convened to terminate the pastoral relationship. Having completed
its task, it rendered an unusual conciliar testimonial to Aiken's
ministry which indicates that the church and congregation might
have been hasty in accepting their pastor's resignation so readily.
Had the colleague committee been more diligent and more whole-
hearted in their search, and had the society been more patient
with its minister and not so willing to place the blame on his
sagging shoulders, the church may have overcome its difficulties
and his ministry might have continued for many years with that
characteristic success which was experienced in his other pastorates. In thirty-four years of pastoral ministry in Amherst, Boston,
and Rutland, Vermont, eight hundred and ninety members were
added to the churches. He experienced revival in each church.
Dr. Kirk, who was brought to Boston by Park Street Church, said
later of his fellow minister:

> Dr. Aiken was a man of great integrity of purpose, a high
> sense of ministerial responsibility, of great candor and chari-
> table disposition, very regardful of others' rights, of more
> than ordinary humility. He was a man of solid acquirements,
> of firm principle, of thorough devotedness to the cause of
> Christ, of great simplicity.

Unfortunately Park Street was not sufficiently resourceful to
hold on to such a choice servant of Jesus Christ.

11. *Landmarks of Achievement*

Andrew Leete Stone was installed as Park Street's sixth pastor on January 25, 1849. On the same date seventeen years later the pastoral relationship ended. Between these dates the congregation restored its membership losses, balanced the budget for the first time in its history, sold or rented a greater number of pews than ever before, and markedly increased benevolence contributions. The success of this achievement is the more remarkable when seen in the context of a nation preparing for war and of a pastor's ministry being interrupted by a nine-month tour of duty as chaplain in the Union Army.

The comparative speed with which a successor was found for Silas Aiken was an omen of brighter days. Exactly five months after his departure for Vermont the seven-man candidate committee presented the name of Rev. Andrew Leete Stone of the South Congregational Church, Middletown, Connecticut. Just before Christmas, 1848, the call from the church and society was personally extended to Stone. On January 3 he replied by letter, informing the church of his usefulness in Middletown and that there was no reason for halting his ministry. However, he went on to state:

> But the peculiar providences which have led to the action which you communicate, the importance and interest of the field of labor thus presented, together with the great degree of unanimity with which I am invited to its charge, leave me, I am convinced, no right to decline your overtures.

The examining council having met on January 25 and approving Stone's ministerial qualifications, the formal installation service was convened that same evening at seven o'clock with Edward Norris Kirk delivering the sermon.

The most pressing problem facing the new minister was the society's finances, and he gave this his fullest energies and attention. Its removal was largely dependent upon the society's willingness to endure a greater tax burden. Recognizing their recent failures in sacrificial stewardship, the pew proprietors were ready now to bear the additional assessments necessary to pecuniary health. (By the time of the annual meeting in 1864, pew taxes had risen to 20 percent of their assessed value.) Even before the first tax increase, the treasurer's reports began showing definite signs of improvement. The Sabbath audiences grew. The society added fourteen new members in 1852. The debt balance began to drop. Deficits were erased. Pew income increased. By 1851, a total of 168 pews had been either sold or rented. Of the 184 pews in the sanctuary, pewholders possessed 109 by 1854. After a decade of labor under Pastor Stone, only 63 pews remained unsold. Every available pew was held and financially productive, whereas in 1846, less than 100 were occupied. At the close of Stone's Park Street ministry, 123 pews had been purchased. These increased sales and taxes doubled the society's receipts. The loans dating back to Aiken's pastorate were refinanced and gradually liquidated.

A further indication of the society's improved financial condition was Stone's regular salary increases. Beginning with a yearly salary of $2,000, his income was raised to $3,000 in 1852 and to $4,000 five years later. In 1854 the society advanced him $2,000 to purchase a private residence in Roxbury. The goodwill existing between Stone and his people was evident also in their generosity in permitting special leaves of extended absences required by continued labor and faltering health.

With the doubling of revenues, benevolence contributions began to show commensurate gains. The steady growth in benevolences is revealed in these figures:

1850	$ 4,900.00
1851	6,237.23
1852	5,593.63
1853	8,133.80

1854	7,838.75
1855	8,211.76
1856	9,137.37
1857	10,035.98
1858	8,169.47

The monthly concerts continued to play an important role in the presentation of missionary work and in the support of evangelical effort throughout the world. A well-known mission project of the American Board during the mid-nineteenth century was the acquisition of a sailing vessel, the "Morning Star," for $12,000, much of which was raised through the offerings of Sunday school children. This first missionary ship was dedicated at a farewell service for the crew and its passengers on December 2, 1856, at Park Street Church. Among those who sailed to Micronesia on the maiden voyage were Mr. and Mrs. Hiram Bingham, Jr., missionaries to the Marshall Islands.

Pastor Stone's missionary heart is reflected in this "Plea for The Monthly Concert":

> I believe there is nothing that we can do for our Christian growth, no influence under which we can sit for our personal quickening and enlarging, no service which we can render to the Master and the great scheme which he carries on his heart, in any one hour of all the month, at once so profitable to us, so fruitful for human good, so grateful to Christ, as this attendance upon the meeting for missionary intercession.

In the early fall of 1856, Stone invited the Mount Vernon and Pine Street churches to unite with Park Street in an evangelistic endeavor under the leadership of Charles G. Finney. When his proposal was declined, he suggested to his own congregation that they sponsor the meetings. Finney was invited, and the meetings were begun in February, 1857, at Park Street Church.

Many years before, the famous evangelist had discovered that Boston was unlike the cities and towns of New York and the West. Bostonians, though highly intelligent, were religiously backward and unsettled. Biblical truths found no ready acceptance, and Finney had attributed this to Unitarian influences which tended toward religious skepticism. Although the churches were doctrinally straight, Christian practice was out of balance. Thus, in the early sermons of this campaign, Finney preached searchingly to the Christians. He upbraided them for their excessive formalism which robbed the church of that necessary free spirit with which to pray and seek the lost. He said, "Everything must be done in a certain way. The Holy Spirit is grieved by their yielding to such a bondage."[1]

At the close of the first service, Pastor Stone confided to the evangelist his own personal need of such a message:

> Brother Finney, I wish to have you understand that I need to have this preaching as much as any member of this church. I have been very much dissatisfied with my religious state for a long time; and have sent for you on my own account, and for the sake of my own soul, as well as for the sake of the souls of the people.[2]

Finney then goes on to relate that after several lengthy conversations, "he seemed thoroughly to give his heart to God," and publicly testified one evening "that he had been that day converted."[3]

The penetrating and powerful messages of the evangelist resulted in many conversions. The oncoming of spring required his return to Oberlin, but prior to leaving Boston tentative plans were laid for a continuation of the meetings in the autumn.

The winter of 1857-58 was a notable period of revival not only in Boston but throughout the entire North. The famous prayer-meeting movement of 1857 enlisted the supplications of laymen from Boston to the frontier for the outpouring of God's Spirit upon America and the regions beyond. During the Finney campaign a businessmen's prayer service was established in the Old South Church. These noonday meetings became so popular that additional halls had to be opened in other parts of the city, including Park Street Church. Similar prayer meetings were led by Mrs. Finney in the church's basement vestry. Every available space was occupied by the crowds who came daily to pray. This

---

[1]Charles Grandison Finney, *Memoirs of Rev. Charles G. Finney* (New York: A. S. Barnes & Co., 1876), p. 385.
[2]*Ibid.*, p. 441.
[3]*Ibid.*

prayer plus Finney's forceful preaching extended the revival beyond Park Street Church to all of Boston and such neighboring cities as Charlestown, Chelsea and East Boston.

Signs of hostility against Finney's doctrine of sanctification first appeared in the spring of 1857 after the first phase of the campaign. Although it alienated a few from later participation, the volume of prayer which was associated with the second phase soon overcame it. Whereas this earlier opposition had been from the orthodox camp, a more virulent and unsympathetic attack was launched by Theodore Parker. In lectures delivered at the Music Hall in April, 1858, he criticized the churches, the emotionalism and the anti-intellectualism associated with the revival. Censuring Protestant ministers everywhere for working for the conversion of souls rather than against the more pressing evils of society, he accused them of making good church members and not good men. Speaking more particularly of Boston's various creeds, he made jest of the different gods delineated in them. Where certain creeds portrayed God as blessing saint and sinner alike, others pictured Him as variable, ill-natured and vengeful— "That is the God of the Park-street Church."[4]

Despite such bombast, many hundreds throughout the city were converted, with two hundred added to the membership of Park Street Church. Examining Committee records during 1854-58 contain numerous testimonies of candidates won to Christ as a direct result of the revival.

The year 1859 was a most auspicious time for Park Street Church to reminisce and recall its first half-century of service. Its life had been newly revived and its hopes restored. A recrudescent spirit was in process of revitalizing every department of the church. Its influence and prestige were second to none among America's Congregational churches. Its membership stood at eight hundred fifty-three persons.

Although there had been a thirty-sixth anniversary celebration on March 7, 1845, at the annual meeting, the proceedings were confined to one brief evening. Thirteen years afterward, at the yearly meeting of 1858, Deacon Edwin Lamson suggested that

[4]*Boston Courier,* April 5, 1858, p. 1.

a special fiftieth anniversary celebration be held the following year. The suggestion was adopted, and the committee on arrangements set Sunday, February 27, and Monday, February 28, for the semicentennnial observance. The first day of celebration was highlighted by addresses from Dr. Aiken, Dr. Linsley and Dr. Beecher, the church's surviving ministers. The semicentennial festival and banquet were held in the Music Hall the following afternoon. Introductory selections by the choir and the taking of photographs preceded the opening invocation by Dr. Aiken, "after which the edibles upon the tables were discussed in right good earnest by the 900 hungry guests." The program included speeches and the introduction of special guests, among whom was the daughter of Edward Dorr Griffin, Mrs. Ellen Crawford, the first baby to be baptized in the church. This was followed by greetings from churches mothered by Park Street Church. Rev. Henry M. Dexter of the Pine Street Church remarked somewhat jocularly that his church had been rightly named, in that "it had pined from its beginning, and had been in the woods ever since it was born."

The afternoon's activities ended with a review of missions at Park Street Church by William T. Eustis. Among his remarks were: (1) Eight members of Park Street Church had volunteered for foreign missionary service. (2) The total giving to foreign missions totaled approximately $100,000. (3) The membership of the Sandwich Islands Church was 22,535 souls, from whom $23,000 was being channeled annually to various Christian causes. (4) Two hundred missionaries had received their instructions in Park Street Church. Dr. Rufus Anderson, senior secretary of the American Board, was quoted as saying that "more missionaries have been dismissed from within its walls to their work in foreign lands than from any other."

The celebration ended with an evening service at which Pastor Stone, who was soon to leave on a six-month tour of Europe for reasons of health, was presented a draft for $2,000 and a $5,000 life insurance policy.

The first half-century of Christian activity at Park Street Church had been duly recognized. Its lay leaders and its godly ministers had been honored. Benevolent societies had praised the church's grand espousal to Christ and His global cause. Boston's orthodox clergy had duly commended its leadership in returning the doctrines of grace to Boston pulpits by creating new churches. The encomiums were richly deserved.

Since the construction of the cemetery in the Park Street meetinghouse cellar some forty years earlier, two hundred forty-two bodies had been interred in thirty-nine tombs. Early in 1861 a plan was initiated to remove the tombs. The Prudential Committee was authorized to negotiate with the tomb proprietors to secure consent for the removal of the dead and for the transfer of their tomb properties to the society. Initial efforts evolved into lengthy and arduous labor requiring much correspondence, numerous trips and interviews. Many times it was difficult to ascertain the owners, since the property had changed hands several times. However, by October 4 the committee had gotten the release of tomb rights from a majority of the proprietors, who had signed the following:

> Whereas, the tombs under the meetinghouse in Park Street have fallen into a dilapidated and offensive condition, therefore in consideration of one dollar paid by the Park Street Congregational Society, the receipt whereof is hereby acknowledged, we hereby agree to convey all the right we have to any tomb or tombs under said meetinghouse to said society whenever a majority of the owners of said tombs shall have signed this paper.

The dilapidation of the tombs was, on closer investigation, found to be deplorable beyond all anticipation:

> In some of them, portions of the brick walls had fallen in; the plastering overhead had broken away leaving only the lathing between the tomb and the floor of the vestry above. In some instances there was standing water on the floors of the tombs to the depth of several inches. Certain of the tombs were crowded with the caskets of the dead to the number even of twenty-five. These had been piled one upon another and had decayed until they were sunk and crushed together and their contents had become indiscriminately mingled. The examination convinced the committee that the work which they had in charge could not be too speedily entered upon

and had indeed been far too long delayed. The committee consulted with some of the most eminent physicians in regard to the deleterious effects of breathing such an atmosphere, and had their replies been made public the committee have no doubt the tendency would have been to have driven many of the worshippers from the house. The committee proceeded at once to select a suitable place for the interment of the remains to be removed from the dilapidated and almost dismantled tombs.

The society authorized the Prudential Committee to purchase a lot at Mount Auburn Cemetery in nearby Cambridge for reinterment. Having received the approval of nearly all the tomb proprietors, the society began cutting down the tombs. Of the two hundred forty-two bodies, ninety-one were transferred to Mount Auburn Cemetery, and one hundred fifty-one were taken to private lots throughout Massachusetts and other states. By 1863 the task had been completed except for four holdovers. The committee then applied to the city government to have the remaining tombs closed from further interments, and complained of their existence as a nuisance.

In the next few years the society managed to secure three of the four tombs, but at two to four times the standard rate. The final holdover did not come to terms with the society until 1893, when legal action was required to settle the matter.

The cost of this operation to 1863 was reported by the seven-man committee:

For purchase of tombs	$ 415.34
Boxing, removing bodies, and digging graves, etc.	806.32
Lot at Mount Auburn Cemetery	612.50
Curbstone around lot	280.00
Monument	470.00
Grading lot and digging graves at Mount Auburn Cemetery	215.00
	$2,799.16

The burial ground purchased by the Park Street Congregational Society on December 28, 1862, is Lot 3176 and contains 1,225 square feet. A simple granite monument sits on the lot. The olive leaf carved on its face is an enlarged copy of a sprig brought from Palestine by Pastor Stone in 1859. Since 1876, interments have averaged less than one per year. As of 1948 there had been one hundred twenty-four burials and two cremation interments.

From the first year of Stone's pastorate to the commencement of the Civil War, the American Peace Society convened its annual meetings in the auditorium of Park Street Church. The featured speaker at their 1849 convocation was Charles Summer, a prominent Boston lawyer and antislavery leader, and from 1851, United States senator from Massachusetts. In line with the society's purposes, his address unfolded the folly and evil of war for determining international controversies. Sumner proceeded to show how the war system could be overthrown by a massive project of educating men to the superior methods of peace. Pointing to a number of contemporary movements and legislative enactments, he forecast eventual peace among nations. The artless speech, though highly interesting and most fit for the occasion, foundered in unperturbed simplicity. The era of peace he hopefully foresaw was not to be realized. Within twelve short years, those of his own national household were to consign his hopes to a distant limbo.

Andrew Leete Stone's sermons before and during the war reveal him to be a typical New England clergyman on the subject of slavery and its issue. He said that even though the final alternative of war might be required to purge the land of the slave power, its use would be deemed justifiable. He felt that no more territory should be yielded, and no more legislation passed to feed the insatiable hunger of the slavery propagandists.

With the outbreak of hostilities in the spring of 1861, Stone viewed the rebellion not as a slavery issue but as a vicious attempt to overthrow the constituted national government. The war, he said, "is simply and solely a war for the maintenance of the Government and the Constitution." Since all lawful authorities had been ordained of God, he said participation in the war effort was a Christian duty as sacred as prayer and as solemn as the sacraments. It was every eligible youth's duty to enlist in the service of God and country to put down the rebel. "If need be [the government] must cut them down, it must mow them down—it must utterly exterminate them, if it come to that. Rebellion must be crushed out."[5]

As for those Northerners who joined and helped the South, Stone said such sacrilege could find its atonement only at the end of a rope:

> HANG TRAITORS. Above the terror of sword and bayonet, let there be the terror of the gibbet and the rope. Give not to treason, when it can be helped, the honor of a soldier's death. . . . Raze the nests of conspirators with axe and fire. This is the shortest and surest, time-saving and life-saving. Let the cautery burn this ulcer out. That is the message today of the law of love.[6]

Stone felt the fierceness of these declamations was justified on the grounds of saving the ripest fruits of world progress and mankind's most treasured hopes. He said the emancipation of four million slaves was worth the price of blood and wasted cities, of torn fields and grieving homes.

The early months of the war produced a number of galling defeats for the Union armies. In February of 1862, however, after the victory at Fort Donelson, the Northern spirit revived, and many, including Stone, believed the war would soon end. In a sermon that month he said he hoped the conflict would be ended by "the next national birthday."

With the coming of spring and summer, the Union campaign in the Northern sector faltered once more. An earlier call for 300,000 men to serve a hitch of three years or more was followed by a second call from President Abraham Lincoln for an equal number to serve a short term of nine months. This latter call resulted in the organization of the 45th Massachusetts Volunteer Regiment on August 8, 1862, and led to Stone's request for a nine-month leave to serve as regiment chaplain. Permission having been granted by the church, he was commissioned October 13, at the age of forty-six. In early November, Chaplain Stone and

[5]Andrew L. Stone, "God, the Governor," *Memorial Discourses* (Boston: Henry Hoyt, 1866), p. 8.
[6]Andrew L. Stone, *The War and the Patriot's Duty* (Boston: Henry Hoyt, 1861), p. 22.

fourteen other service personnel from Park Street left for their post in North Carolina. Eighty Park Street men served in the war while attached to twenty-nine different army groups; five were navy personnel.

The 45th (Cadet) Regiment reached its destination at Camp Amory, New Berne, North Carolina, on November 14, 1862. Two of its three major engagements with Confederate forces—at Kinston and Whitehall—occurred within two months after arriving in the South. Chaplain Stone performed his duties ably and courageously during this initial baptism of fire, walking among the troops in the heat of battle, encouraging, praying, comforting, and appealing to his men to keep the vows made to God in moments of peril.

After the battle at Whitehall, the cadets moved into New Berne Proper for provost duty. This temporary lull gave Mrs. Stone an opportunity to visit her husband during March. In her four weeks' stay, she opened up a day school for Negro children in a local church. The large enrollment of five hundred students provided some problems because there were no suitable textbooks and no steady faculty, the teachers being enlisted from soldiers who gave their free time from regular duty. The classes continued throughout the regiment's entire term of service. In addition, a Sunday school was begun in the Presbyterian church of New Berne largely for the benefit of Negro and poor white children.

Park Street's historical files contain a series of nineteen letters written to the church and its young people by Chaplain Stone from December, 1862, to June, 1863. Written in beautiful prose, they are a mine of information concerning his activities as chaplain. In his first letter, dated December 5, he related the nature of his ministry. On Sunday mornings he supplied vacant pulpits in the area. The two services for military personnel consisted of a 3 P.M. outdoor meeting and an evening prayer hour in the barracks. In addition to long hours spent in hospital visitation, many men consulted him in his tent, which was always open to visitors. Concerning the weekday prayer services, he wrote:

> Our prayer meetings are full of deep and tender interest. They are all well attended. Probably not less than 200 come

in on Sabbath and on Friday evenings, all indeed that the barracks will hold. The young men readily take part and a most happy influence is exerted by these exercises. Those who are not religious welcome the meeting to their barracks and often petition for it. We want only a copious libation of the Spirit. Beseech that for us even as we ask it always for you.

As chaplain, Stone needed a constant supply of various items for his soldiers: small items of clothing, food, books for the library, etc. Park Street's generous contributions during his term are noted in this letter of February 3, 1863:

I have been opening with glad and eager hands your precious and full freighted box. How exactly you have understood and supplied the wants of our suffering soldiers; and how eloquent each article is of the faithful hearts that will not suffer the soldier to be forgotten. . . . The opening box is as a fountain in this arid land. From beneath the rising lid wells up a stream of cherishing Northern love and care, into which the fulness of many hearts has emptied itself; and the stream is all the more refreshing because of this.

The letters continued through the spring—two to five each month—telling of his conversations with dying soldiers; of wandering, homeless slaves; of long marches through rain and mud; of drunkenness among the soldiers; of writing to the parents of the dead; and of many soldiers accepting the gospel. To the children of the church, he wrote touching pastoral letters on parental discipline, exhorting them to Christian obedience, and thanking them for their help in sending supplies.

After three months of police duty in New Berne, the regiment was moved outside the city to Camp Massachusetts, Fort Spinola, on the Neuse River. This site provided an excellent vantage point as an observation post. The bravery and the suffering experienced by the 45th is revealed in Chaplain Stone's final letter from the South:

This regiment has lost more in killed and wounded since we landed in North Carolina, not only than any other of the nine-months regiments in this department, but than all of them put

together. Not because we are braver than others, but because we have been in hotter fights and in hotter parts of the
field and more exposed.

The 45th Regiment returned to Boston on June 30 to receive
the praise and honor of the citizens and their civic leaders. Chaplain Stone was mustered out of the ranks one week later on July
7, 1863.

The participation of Park Street Church in the war effort extended beyond the loan of its minister for chaplain duty. The
Woman's Benevolent Society and a number of sewing circles
within the church contributed large amounts of homemade shirts,
socks, linens and delicacies. Such organizations as the Christian
Commission and the Boston branch of the Young Men's Christian
Association received considerable support by the church. The
United States Christian Commission was begun by evangelicals
at a YMCA convention in 1861 to meet the crises of the battlefield.
In its instructions to supporting churches such as Park Street,
numerous items needed by the military were listed. Concerning
books, the commission said, "Send no trash." With regard to
edibles: "Domestic wines are excellent in winter, but apt to spoil
in summer."

As the war neared its end, Stone spoke of the North's responsibility to restore and reconstruct the South—as brothers, not as
conquerors. He had introduced this theme to his people even
before his tour of duty. He felt that occupation forces should protect the freed slave and that there should be educational com-
missions, agents and directors of every sort to supervise the in-
tegration of all classes to a life of usefulness. Motivated by emancipation, the Negro would readily assume the necessary habits of
order, diligence and sobriety, and take his place in a new society,
according to Stone.

The news of General Lee's surrender at Appomattox Court-
house did not reach Boston until late Sunday evening, April 9,
1865. Since the churches had had no opportunity to celebrate the
event that day, special meetings of praise and thanksgiving were
convened throughout the week. Since Friday of that week was
the regularly scheduled fast and prayer day in the Congregational
churches, it was suggested that the occasion be used for continued

rejoicing. Before that fateful day ended, however, the buoyant spirits and the glad voices were abruptly stilled by the news that President Lincoln was dying.

The following Sunday, Pastor Stone mournfully spoke from Lamentations 5:15-16 to a hushed audience. He pictured the tragedy of a man being struck down in the midst of his greatness—not by age or illness—but by an evil assassin. The sympathy of the church to the stricken family was communicated by his prayer for divine consolation. He recalled Lincoln's words uttered only a few months before: "Yes, now I can say that I do from my heart love the Lord Jesus Christ."[7] Stone said, "His goodness was his greatness. His honest heart helped his straight-forward mind. He saw truth and duty more clearly by this inward illumination."

Recalling the suggestion to change the mood of the day of prayer, he lamented: "We cannot change thee, oh, weeping April! oh, month of tears! Pour down all thy warm showers: from our eyes the rain falls faster yet!"

The bitter news of President Lincoln's death had been preceded some months earlier by other tidings which had direct bearing upon Park Street's future. On September 18, 1864, Stone had addressed the church by letter: "I have received a unanimous and urgent call to become the Pastor of the First Congregational Church of San Francisco, California." He had then given the reasons for his planned acceptance. Boston and New England were established, he had said, and the position of Park Street Church was firm and secure. On the other hand, the California field was new; her period of formation and organization was upon her, calling for the wisest minds, the strongest hands and the purest spirits.

With reference to his physical weakness, he had added this practical note:

> The new field would allow me to use largely and freely all the capital of study and labor now locked up in manuscripts which are here so much idle Capital. The rest from the incessant production of fresh sermons . . . would greatly relieve me and recruit me.

[7]Andrew L. Stone, *A Discourse Occasioned by the Death of Abraham Lincoln* (Boston: J. K. Wiggins, 1865), p. 18.

Within the next two and a half weeks, the church and society had met in separate meetings to unanimously reject the pastor's proposal. Enumerating the needs of New England for every powerful and patriotic voice available, the congregation had strongly urged Stone to reconsider, and had promised to raise his salary to $5,500.

In his response Stone had agreed to reconsider but had alluded to certain doubts regarding his duty. To help resolve the matter, the church had convened an ecclesiastical council. The fifty-five-man assembly had met in the vestry at 3 P.M. October 20. Under the gavel of moderator Nehemiah Adams of the Union Church, the delegates deliberated the issue fully and carefully. A member of the San Francisco church was present to speak for his cause. After several hours, a resolution calling for the dissolution of the pastoral relationship had been announced and defeated: 22, no and 17, yes. This decision had then been forwarded to San Francisco.

At the turn of the year, the California congregation had communicated directly with Park Street Church. The letter had revealed something of the state of religion in their city of 150,000 inhabitants:

> Yet the number of Protestant Congregational Churches is but about one-third of your number. If we compare the Cities as to churches of all sorts you will outnumber us four to one. . . . The number of members in Congregational churches alone in Boston exceeds 5000; the total membership of all Evangelical Churches in this City cannot, we think, exceed 3000.
>
> We have four Congregational enterprises in this City, connected with which are 524 members, which is somewhat more than half of your single church membership and but one-tenth of your whole denominational force in Boston. Of these members four-fifths are in our own church. The Second Church is heavily in debt and needs immediate relief. The Third Church has about thirty members. The Fourth Society, a new undertaking, is dependent almost wholly on the First Church for the erection of its chapel and the purchase of its lot.

The importance of the First Church had been indicated further by its signal position as the chief supporter of all these churches as well as other benevolent, missionary and educational societies. The church had felt it could not afford to experiment with several candidates or untried novices. The demands of the times required a proven leader.

On January 6, Park Street Church had replied in strong terms:

> Our people had hoped that . . . you would have ceased from further efforts to draw our Pastor from us.
>
> It is time brethren that our church had rest from the disturbing influences that have been thrust upon us.

Park Street had then presented its own case for Stone's continuation as their pastor. A fact more far-reaching and of transcending importance beyond the wants of California was the national need for social and moral regeneration, they had said. The whole social fabric of the Confederacy required reconstruction after a New England model. Replying to the letter which implied the settled state of religion in Boston, the church's correspondent wrote:

> You are pleased to refer to a single Unitarian Church in your state. Boston alone has ten or more and another church edifice is contemplated ere long. The Millennium has not yet come in our own City. The "signs of the times" indicate that the Christian Church may yet be called to grapple with Catholicism and Infidelity in a struggle for mastery; and a crisis may soon be upon us, more trying to faith than the ordeal of civil war through which we are now passing.

Throughout the remainder of that year the church and society and their pastor received a series of letters and telegrams from the First Church and from individuals in California. This unremitting pressure was relaxed at the end of the year with Stone's renewed determination to heed their call. His letter of final resignation, dated December 30, 1865, called forth a dismissing council which, on the seventeenth anniversary of Stone's pastorate, concurred with the church's reluctant decision to capitulate.

At a special church meeting shortly thereafter, this resolution was adopted:

> Resolved, that the name of Rev. Andrew L. Stone is indis-
> solubly linked with that of Park Street Church, and that
> whatever may be our future record, the seventeen years of
> Christ-honored service performed by our departing brother
> will forever remain as a "green spot" in our history.

In his farewell sermon on February 4, 1866, Stone again clarified his reasons for leaving Boston. It was not because of any
bitterness, or rankling, or incompatibility of relationship, he said,
but wholly in order to harness the robust energies of the West for
Christ and the gospel, and to direct adventurous spirits in the
pursuit of Christian virtues and institutions. Turning to thoughts
of his ministry, he remarked how God had driven out early fears
to bless beyond expectation. "Scarce a communion Sabbath has
come and gone without adding some to our fellowship," he said.
The spirit of revival had been regular and constant, he continued,
"This church has believed in revivals, has prayed for revivals, has
labored for revivals, and refused to be comforted unless revivals
came." He concluded by praying for a fresh outpouring of the
comfort and power of the Holy Spirit.

Pastor Stone's departure from the city drew words of high
praise from sources other than Park Street Church. One historian
observed:

> When Dr. Stone came to Park Street it was a "half empty
> sanctuary" but after he began to preach, it became sprinkled,
> then darkened, then thronged with eager listeners, until the
> astonished and delighted parish were compelled to order a
> cord or two of camp stools for use on occasions of special
> service. . . . No man in this country except Henry Ward
> Beecher has preached to as many people in the last fifteen
> years as Andrew L. Stone.[8]

The record of more than a half-century of doctrinal fidelity,
Christian benevolence and revival, reached its peak during Stone's
ministry. Doctrinal uncertainties and grinding financial burdens
became memories. Church membership numbered nearly 900
persons with Sunday school enrollment at 600, a figure that would

[8]Abraham G. R. Hale, "Chaplain Stone and The Religious Life of The
45th Regiment," *History of the 45th Regiment Massachusetts Volunteer
Militia* (n. p., 1908), p. 225.

remain unsurpassed for one hundred years. With the nation once more at peace and the church in a state of vigorous health, a leader with exceptional ability was sought to lift the church to even greater heights of usefulness. Thirty-three months later a man of eminent and unusual gifts was chosen for Park Street's pulpit; but after six years of ministry, many were to ponder the wisdom of the choice.

12. *The Great Innovator*

William Henry Harrison Murray was unquestionably the most unique individual ever to pastor Park Street Church. This is not to say he was the most spiritual, nor was he the most successful. When he resigned from the church, he took a large part of the congregation with him, thus causing the only major schism in the church's history. He certainly was not the most effective pastor. His unbridled spirit left no room for patience with deacons who, to him, were terribly unprogressive and fusty.

But at the time of his departure from Park Street Church he knew what it was to taste the sweet fruit of success and achievement. His popularity was unexcelled, not because of his pastoral ministry however, but because of personal prowess in these most diversified areas of human endeavor: lecturing, preaching, sportsmanship, breeding horses, and authoring tales of the Adirondack wilderness. His nature was as free and as galloping as one of his Morgan thoroughbreds; consequently, the limitations imposed upon him by a rigidly Calvinistic New England pastorate were too galling for him to endure. He chose instead to leap the barriers.

One month after Pastor Stone's departure, Murray's name was introduced to the Pulpit Committee. Replies to inquiries regarding his qualifications, including one from a former pastor, Joel Linsley, indicated a consensus that he would not be best for Park Street Church. Thirty-two months later, however, the committee reconsidered his candidacy. During September, 1868, he was invited to supply the pulpit for two Sundays. Favorably impressed by the young minister and his record at the Congregational Church at Meriden, Connecticut, the pulpit committee ex-

164

tended a call. His reply of acceptance was dated October 16, and the installation service was a month later with Dr. Edward Norris Kirk delivering the sermon to a packed house.

The naturally creative mind and pungent tongue of the twenty-eight-year-old minister quickly won him the favor and adulation of the orthodox community and resulted in large crowds at Park Street Sunday after Sunday. In an effort to reach an even wider audience, the Prudential Committee voted in 1870 to advertise the preaching services in two of the daily newspapers. Also, an appropriation was made to print and distribute one hundred copies of Murray's sermons each week in public institutions.

Not many months had passed by before the congregation began to realize that their new pastor was not of common mold. As a realist and an innovator he began early to introduce ideas and methods which were novel to Park Street Church. These tended to create a hostile sentiment which was destined to grow to large proportions within six years.

One feature of the church's life which greatly disturbed the energetic pastor was its somewhat aristocratic nature which tended to prohibit the masses from its sanctuary and from the sound of the gospel. Speaking of this larger audience, he said:

> As I stand before you here, day after day, I catch the glimpse of another audience standing back of you, and enclosing you about as the many enclose the few. Many are wild and lawless and wicked, and some unfortunate, and they hear no preacher. . . . I see many churches going up, but none for these: voices by the score are preaching in this city today; but no voice preaches to them. The preachers of God are monopolized by the few, and religion has become a luxury. The table is spread with twice the amount of food that the sitters can eat,—spread for satiety, and not for necessity; and all the while gaunt faces look over your shoulders hungeringly. Shall they go unfed? I do not impeach your benevolence: I impeach the miserable fashion of church-building; and that inadequate system of religious administration in this city which makes provision for the spiritual needs of only two out of every five of your population.[1]

[1]William Henry Harrison Murray, *Park Street Pulpit: Sermons* (2d series; Boston: James R. Osgood & Co., 1872), p. 97.

Motivated by this intense desire to reach the rank and file, he inaugurated a wintertime series of lectures in the Boston Music Hall. Commencing on November 7, 1869, twelve Sunday evening lectures were delivered before large audiences. These meetings served not only to confront three thousand persons with the gospel each week, but also to encourage congregational singing. Murray believed that to remove the hymnal from the Christian was to revert back to pre-Reformation times. His attitude toward church music played an important role in influencing Park Street Church to accept the practice of congregational singing as a regular feature of public worship.

Of all his lectures, perhaps the most controversial was one entitled "The Moral Condition of Boston and How to Improve It." The four major moral and spiritual forces in Boston—church, mission school, public school, and City Missionary Society—were upbraided for failing to reach the poorer, downtrodden segment of society. Their labors, though diligent and well meaning, had not gone far enough or low enough on the social scale, Murray said. Individuals were being helped, but nothing was being done for the poor as a class. If the moral structure of Boston was to be improved, he said, the city had to be divided into districts and each church made responsible for the moral, spiritual and social needs of its district. He felt the churches and the police departments should work together, for the civil authorities well knew the problems of the poor and the vice-ridden. Virtue, under certain conditions of life, was impossible, he stressed, for the conditions had to change before it could exist. The dens of the city would stifle the worthiest saint. The causes of crime existed in the body as well as the mind. "The only way to reform the mind and soul is to reform the body first. Diet and cleanliness precede the Lord's Prayer in the alphabet of social ethics."

These Music Hall lectures served notice on Park Street Church and the evangelical community of Boston that Murray was determined to govern himself and his ministry according to his own ideas and not those of a former generation. A pioneer and trailblazer at heart, he had no fears or qualms about instituting untried programs and methods even in the sacrosanct headquarters of New England orthodoxy. Colonial ways and customs of church polity and practice easily became subordinate measures to the newer ideas of his pragmatic nature. He recognized that America was in a new stage of development, and that if the churches were to keep pace they had to relinquish some of their ancient patterns.

Regarding the administration of his church, whose membership approached one thousand in 1871, he said:

> Take this church and congregation, for instance: there is only one officer that really has charge of anything: I refer to the superintendent of the Sabbath School. That is in good hands, and gives the pastor no uneasiness. But, outside of this, the church is not connected officially with any branch of spiritual industry. We have no board for local charities, none for visitation of the sick and the transient, none for mission-enterprises, none for direction and leadership of the young, none for literary and social entertainment: All these branches of effort, so far as developed, are really running themselves. There is to them no really responsible head with whom the pastor can consult, from whom he can receive reports necessary to his own enlightenment and direction.[2]

A systematic, departmental type of organization was needed, Murray felt, to tap, direct and control the potential lay force of the church. He suggested that a twelve-man board of officers be elected, each member being the responsible head of one particular branch of spiritual activity. In addition, he said, a colleague pastor was required to assist in the program of leadership training and religious instruction on an adult level. Murray believed that the work of benevolent agencies could be done equally as well by the large city church. In a sermon on this subject during October, 1871, he said:

> I mean to do all I may to put the Church in such a position, that any other organization shall be seen to be superfluous; in such a position, that every gift of nature and grace in the membership shall be utilized, and so that there shall be an appointed and honored place in which every member may serve the Lord.[3]

[2]*Ibid.*, p. 17.
[3]*Ibid.*, p. 20.

Murray conceived the church's task to be twofold: to preach salvation, and to quicken public virtue. Therefore the church had to be in the vanguard of the city's humanities and culture; it had to become vitally connected with the city's moral necessities. He said that the church, with holy zeal and benevolent sympathy for all men, had to bind itself to the wise and diligent use of every appliance to reach, evangelize and elevate mankind. To Murray, few local churches measured up to this standard, including Park Street. Whether due to egotism or timidity, he felt the church had failed to adapt its program and ministry to the wants of the times, to enlarge the sphere of its outreach, and to capitalize on the opportunities for winning souls. As a result, he said, the more aggressive members of the orthodox community—the young men particularly—broke away from local church control to give vent to their Christian impulses by forming societies such as the Young Men's Christian Association, which stood as a living protest to the church's failure to reach the community.

These and many other statements of equal potency fell as bombshells upon the church and proprietors at Park Street. It appeared that in his attempt to adapt the church's program to the changing times, the youthful minister was berating the church for a misguided benevolence.

His religious beliefs as well as his social concerns were governed not so much by the established forms as by their relevancy to the hour. There was no basic departure from the essentials of the old faith, for Murray desired no change from or new interpretation of the basic facts of the gospel. He said, "My trowel shall never start the old cement."

As the pastor of a historic church, he often recalled the heroic stand of its founders who faced calumny and abuse without flinching or modifying their "offensive" doctrines, and to their banner he enlisted his own energies. He conceived his ministry to be that of preaching repentance and faith, and not the thought patterns of Calvin, Edwards or Woods. Thus his impatience with dogma and theological formulas was often interpreted as an indication of unorthodoxy. His strongly evangelistic spirit together with a sensitivity toward human need tended to blind him to the values of the academic or conventional, and to the need for Paul's teachings as well as those of Jesus.

When a new series of Music Hall lectures was inaugurated on November 3, 1872, it was in the face of growing opposition. Permission to continue the series was granted by only a small majority. In the intervening years since the first lecture series, Murray had made little headway with his ideas. Irritated by the seeming apathy of the people and their growing criticism of his manner and methods, his lectures became more critical than ever. *The Congregational Quarterly* objected to certain statements which accused the orthodox of bigotry and which denounced the presentation of the gospel in theological forms. With ecumenical spirit he uttered such words as these, which undoubtedly horrified his flock:

> How much those old preachers have learned of the love of God since when they fought each other, and moaned and grieved over each other's lapses, as they conceived, from the true faith! Taylor and Tyler no longer contend. Beecher and Nettleton are no longer separated. Woods has no longer need to labor to harmonize differences between brethren. Even Calvin and Channing have found a common platform at last, and stand, hand clasped in hand, happy in a common love, before the throne of an infinite and a like-experienced mercy.[4]

He felt theological opponents could be reconciled only by the gentleness of Christ, never by hammerblows and fighting. There was no reason, he continued, why men of divergent beliefs could not unite to improve the city's morals, or even to save from spiritual loss those overtaken by sin. He believed the failure of New England's religion rested with those who appointed Jesus to be the center of a mere theology instead of seeing Him as the Saviour and Helper of all mankind. In the study of Christian truth, Jesus was to be preferred above Paul; where the former was practical and compassionate, the latter was theological and rigid. Jesus was plain; Paul was mystery.

The public sensation caused by such preaching was matched by the reaction of the board of deacons. Murray's maverick spirit

[4]William Henry Harrison Murray, *Words Fitly Spoken* (Boston: Lee & Shepard, 1873), p. 142.

was certain to tangle with the more sedate ways of Park Street's diaconate. Midway in his pastorate he delivered an address to call attention to the abuse of this church office. He said deacons were, for the most part, no more than ornamental assistants at the sacramental service. Their election was due to their station, or social rank, or to some uncommon contribution to the church; thus their appointment was a reward, he said. Using satire with great effect, Murray summed up all deacons under three main types: Deacon Slowup, whose motto was "What has not been shall not be"; Deacon Sharpface, the grim and loveless heresy hunter who always became ecstatic at the smallest sign of apostasy, real or imagined; Deacon Goodheart, a simple, humble soul, who in his unselfish way served the pastor without pomp or pride.

He viewed them as self-appointed censors of pulpit doctrine who permitted no new thought or interpretation to brighten up a piece of stodgy theology. Criticizing the Examining Committee for investigating too deeply into the Christian experience of a candidate for church membership, he charged obscurantism and excessive rigidity. The church was inordinately "severe, strict," and bound by a stifling and "stiff" creed. The young pastor thought it rather remarkable that men such as Deacon Goodheart were to be found at all at Park Street.

Reference to Park Street's internal troubles appeared in a communication between two sportsmen who were friends of William Murray. The letter of Supreme Court Justice Alden Chester of Albany, New York, appeared in an editorial in *Shooting and Fishing*:

> Murray was the subject of quite severe criticism on the part of some of the more sedate members of his congregation, and he had differences with some of his deacons and other church officers. I have seen him attend church faultlessly dressed with a Prince Albert coat and wearing a Scotch cap. He was criticized for this as being undignified for a man in his position. He was also criticized because he liked horses and drove a fast horse through the streets, smoking a cigar. Some people also criticized his theology.
>
> There was a pastor of the Park Street Church before Murray by the name of Stone. A few years before, there had been

a popular New England circus known as Stone and Murray's
circus. Because of the differences between the critics and the
defenders of Murray in his own church and the excitement incident thereto, some of which found its way into public print,
the Park Street Church was oftentimes referred to as Stone
and Murray's Circus.[5]

The church officials undoubtedly tried to save the situation, but
neither their tastes nor dispositions were such as to be compatible
with his liberal ways. Although schism imperiled the church and
society, Murray continued to preach and propose programs in-
conducive to the restoration of harmony.

Ever since the Beecher years, the Park Street congregation had
become increasingly scattered throughout the expanding suburbs.
By the time of the annual meeting in February, 1874, the membership, including 275 absentee members, numbered 1,067 persons. This widely separated constituency demanded a ministerial
colleague to assist Murray.

On March 8 Murray announced to the church and society his
desire for such an associate. It was a simple, logical and practical
request, but there was more to it than met the eye. What exactly
lay behind this announcement? For five years Murray had attempted to win the church's approval for his various proposals:
reorganization of the boards and departments of the church,
evangelization of the masses, improvement of the city's moral condition, selling the meetinghouse and moving to a location more
central to its membership, and making the doctrines of Calvin
and Paul more humane. For five years he pleaded for what he
believed to be a more relevant church witness. A necessary in-
gredient in this program was an associate minister, who would
free Murray for preaching and lecturing. Since the Christian
ministry was an associated ministry, and since the early New England churches were established upon a colleague ministry, he
argued that there was ample biblical and historical precedent for
such an arrangement. To keep alive Park Street's tradition and its
ministry of preserving the preaching of the gospel, Murray urged
that careful deliberation be made concerning whether to utilize

[5]"Adirondack Murray in Boston," *Shooting and Fishing,* February 22,
1906, p. 409.

both ministers at Park Street, or to commission one to a branch
church to be erected elsewhere. He also suggested that the present site be vacated entirely if necessary. The crowded sanctuary
each Sunday called for expansion and consideration of a larger
meetinghouse, he said, and in any proposed new building, an adjustment in pew rents should make seating available to all classes.
To assist the church in calling an associate, Murray offered to surrender his annual stipend until the treasury could afford two
salaries. In the meantime, his personal estate and his literary
ventures would yield a moderate income.

The lengthy proposal concluded with the statement, which was
a harbinger of a not-too-distant resignation:

> To this city God called me; and here I propose to remain
> until death overtakes me, or age renders me unfit for service
> . . . but without assistance in the pastoral office, and a col-
> league in the pulpit, I cannot remain your pastor.

He did not know that by the end of that decade he would leave
not only Park Street Church and Boston but the entire ministry.

During the next weeks, committees from the church and the
society considered the proposals. On April 29, 1874, at a special
church meeting attended by 150 persons, two presentations were
made: a majority report favorable to the pastor, and an unfavorable minority report. The joint committee offering the majority
statement declared simply their acceptance of the pastor's request
for a colleague, but added one brief suggestion:

> Though we have not seen him out of the Pulpit and in the
> relations of Pastor, as we should have been glad to have done,
> we trust that in the future, he will so arrange his time and en-
> gagements, that he can give himself more fully to his work
> among us.

The minority report was in greater detail, with much unhappiness over Murray's pastoral labors. It said in part:

> There were many criticisms upon Mr. Murray's past course
> and much dissatisfaction was expressed as to the result and
> influence of his devoting so large a portion of his time to the
> delivery of lectures, and those too of such a character as he

has delivered for the past few years. A far more important matter, however, and one dwelt upon at length at that meeting was his neglect of his engagements. It has not been claimed that Mr. Murray has exhausted his strength in his labors with and for Park Street Church and yet it is asked that Park Street Church should furnish assistance in performing the duties which have not exhausted Mr. Murray's strength. Then Mr. Murray must have become overworked by the performance of labor which has been foreign to his Church. If Mr. Murray had "given himself to prayer and the ministry of the Word" as he indicated his duty to be, and had he found such labor to be too exhausting, then it would have been the duty of his Church to have provided assistance, or diminished the labor; but as he has given but a *small part* of his past labor and time, what will be the result of giving him assistance in the Church, but to enable him to lessen his labors with us, and thus enable him to devote more time to other matters so as to diminish the sum total of his work.[6]

The majority report won by a vote of sixty-six to thirty-four. It was adopted, and a committee was formed to find an associate pastor. Six months later, on October 11, Pastor Murray, still without an assistant, wrote his letter of resignation. He said he was unable to continue due to the size of the congregation and the extended boundaries of the parish. He deplored the attitude which hindered the society's reorganization on a larger scale and on a more advantageous site and, as a result, failed to minister to the city's less fortunate. Without their complete agreement on a colleague—the first step in his master plan—he said he had no alternative but to resign.

An ecclesiastical council with delegates from twelve churches convened in Park Street chapel on October 30, 1874, and recommended the pastoral relation be dissolved effective November 12. His final sermon was at the November 8 morning worship service. Speaking from John 12:32, he asserted the superiority of practical Christianity over theological theorizing.

While on a tour of Europe some years earlier, Deacon Ezra Farnsworth had written to his fellow parishioner, Charles C. Litchfield, concerning their minister:

[6]Park Street Church, Proceedings of Business Meetings, 1871-99, p. 28.

> I fear there will be danger that his popularity will make him vain and injure him, and I ventured to suggest that danger to him in a letter not long since; and to quote to him a remark his wife made to us when at Meriden, "that he would succeed in Boston if he kept near enough to Christ."[7]

It is questionable why Murray left Boston and quit the ministry when only forty years of age. His Park Street experiences certainly influenced him in this decision; however, he himself was more at fault than the church. The majority report and its acceptance by the church and the society indicated their willingness to cooperate. On the other hand, Murray remained intransigent. He lost the confidence of his deacons who suffered public caricature. He protested the unprogressive spirit of the church which forbade the modernization of its evangelistic outreach and its Christian witness to the community. But had not Park Street Church been a model of benevolent and missionary activity? Had not its constituents taught the poor and the ignorant in the city's mission schools? Had not its laymen participated as founders and leaders of a number of Christian societies and agencies? Apparently Murray's impatience and independency blinded him to the church's past achievements. His hopeful plans tended to eclipse the church's honored performance.

Murray was in many ways a good and a well-meaning man, yet he failed to avoid the pitfalls of a young, gifted and popular preacher. He failed to balance zeal with wisdom and prudence, and to discipline himself to perform the required duties of the pastoral office. However, his greatest failure apparently was in not keeping "near enough to Christ."

In a revealing and highly significant article written while yet at Park Street, Murray charged the churches with the city's moral failure. With more than 50 percent of the population unchurched, orthodox pews remained half filled. The churches, their pastors and their laymen stood condemned for not reaching the masses and for maintaining edifices too small to do the job. Repeating his favorite theme, he wrote:

[7]Letter of Ezra Farnsworth to Charles C. Litchfield, May 23, 1869, Park Street Church.

> The churches are rather religious club rooms, where four or five hundred favored disciples of Jesus can meet and be entertained and instructed with music and oratory of a sacred character, while the common people, who loved Him so when He was on earth and would love Him so now could they only have Him revealed to them, are rambling in the streets outside, or sunning themselves on the wharves and the Common.

With stinging rebuke he chided his own people with these words:

> What right, for instance, has the Park Street Church to lock up $600,000 worth of the Lord's property in such a way that it can give religious opportunities to only 1500 people in the morning and eight or ten hundred in the afternoon, when it might be so invested as to carry the strength and consolation of the gospel to ten or fifteen thousand people every Sabbath?[8]

Such minimal use of this vast property testified to a maladministration which was tantamount to "an actual betrayal of sacred trust," he claimed.

Murray had said the solution to Boston's moral condition would be the formation of a metropolitan church where thousands could hear the saving gospel. He felt a man large enough to hold an audience of three or four thousand each Sunday for ten years would make his opinions "the opinions of thousands, and his faith, the faith of the rising generation."

Murray decided to be that large man with or without Park Street Church. The first step toward the realization of his metropolitan church after leaving Park Street was the formation of the New England Church, an independent Congregational assembly. Organized in September, 1875, with nine charter members, it soon grew to a membership of three hundred. Services commenced in the Music Hall on the first Sunday in October with an overflow audience. Speaking from John 17:21, Murray announced the doctrinal basis upon which the new church was to stand. Its chief features indicated a "liberal evangelical theology and a wholly unsectarian policy." In May of that same year *The Congregation-*

[8]William Henry Harrison Murray, "A Metropolitan Church," *The Congregationalist,* December 11, 1873, p. 393.

alist reported the purchase of a lot on which a new church structure seating four thousand people was to be built and completed
by October, 1876. This metropolitan church was to feature a one-
thousand-voice choir, a quartet, three services each Sunday, and
annual sitting rentals of ten dollars. The benevolence of the
church was to be controlled by a thirty-member board, including
the highest state and city officials and members of the city's clergy.

Murray felt this church was the earnest of his grandiose hope.
Weekly services were held, with a Sunday school and a Monday
evening devotional meeting. The music included congregational
singing and a two-hundred-voice choir under the direction of
Professor Eben Tourjee. The main attraction, of course, was
Murray's ever popular preaching. The rapid increase in membership during the church's first year was largely due to many of
Murray's supporters from Park Street joining him in his new venture. During the closing months of 1875, one hundred forty-five
members of Park Street Church requested dismission to the New
England Church. In addition to the excellent musical and lecture
program, church interest was maintained with the use of Murray's
literary gifts. Special entertainments and sociables were frequently given, with Murray giving readings and recitations from his
Adirondack tales.

Midway in its third year, efforts were begun to raise funds to
build a permanent edifice. Murray was voted a year's vacation in
1878 to seek financial assistance. From this point, however, his
whereabouts and activities become obscure. The New England
Church, after three years of life, ceased its services. The metropolitan church and all the splendid plans associated with it were
never realized. Other "castles" fell during the next several years.
Leaving the ministry, Murray became involved in a number of
private business enterprises, all of which failed. Then, in 1886,
Mrs. Murray sued her husband for a divorce on grounds of desertion.

In reply to Murray's article on the metropolitan church, Professor L. Clark Seelye of Amherst College wrote a rejoinder in which
he rebuked Murray for his views and especially for publicly criticizing his church. Concerning the supposed waste and ill use of
the $600,000 investment in Park Street Church, Seelye told Mur-

ray he should be silent in light of the money lavishly expended on his personal farm and stud of fast horses.

Recounting the positive good done by the churches, Seelye said the best means for doing God's work was the Christian church, the minister and the people united in a common witness of Jesus Christ. The power of the lyceum was to make hearers only and not doers of the Word, for it did not provide the necessary power with which a man could strengthen and maintain his hold upon human hearts, according to Seelye. This could come only through a prudent, careful and patient nurture in a pastor's visits, counseling and prayers, he said. Seelye's ingredients of a successful ministry were the very things most neglected by Murray.

13. A Return to the Old Paths

Seventy years after the formation of Park Street Church, the evangelical forces in Greater Boston could boast of 121 churches with a total membership of approximately 58,000 communicants; 18,258 of these were associated with forty-three Congregational societies. The Suffolk West Conference of Congregational churches, of which Park Street was a member, was composed of nineteen churches with a resident membership of 4,842. Total missionary benevolences from these nineteen societies amounted to $123,733.76, the major share, $96,394.22, being designated for home missions.

This remarkable growth in the number and influence of these churches from humble beginnings soon after 1800 reflects the virility and power which characterized their combined witness. By 1880 three disturbing factors which had been visible on the horizon for several years had begun to make themselves felt. They were: a withdrawal from Congregational orthodoxy by a liberalizing element within the denomination; the moving of large numbers of native Protestant families from Boston to the suburbs; their replacement by European immigrants, most of whom were Roman Catholic. In the North End particularly, and in other areas as well, Protestant churches failed to keep pace with population growth and to adjust to the changing religious climate. With 35 percent of Boston's population foreign-born and largely unsympathetic to Protestantism, the Roman Catholic Church through its thirty churches and ninety priests began making more impressive strides than ever toward its present powerful position. The difficulties which were to confront William Murray's successor were twofold: the internal problem of mollifying the wounds of a battered congregation, and the external one represented by these changing social, religious and theological conditions.

Dr. Charles S. Robinson of New York City did not accept a call extended him by the church and society in June, 1875. A year later, the name of Dr. John Lindsay Withrow of the Second Presbyterian Church, Indianapolis, Indiana, was recommended. The Pulpit Committee visited him to personally convey the congregation's desire to have him as their pastor at an annual salary of $7,000. In his acceptance dated June 13, 1876, he wrote:

> Now let me dare to enjoin every believer of your venerable and honorable body to beseige the throne for a double portion of piety upon your new pastor. If Park Street pulpit has God's Spirit in it the radiation of power will be irresistible.

The installation service was held September 14, 1876, nearly two years after the resignation of William Murray, who then was beginning his second year at the New England Church across the street in Music Hall.

During the centennial celebration of 1909, Dr. Conrad recalled the state of the church when Dr. Withrow became pastor: "For the first time in nearly three quarters of a century there was grave unpleasantness in the church."

The first task confronting the new minister was to win the confidence of his officers. The attitude of those remaining had become so overly firm as a result of their controversy with Murray that it appeared no minister would be free from their understandable but undue interference. By prudent and patient leadership, Dr. Withrow proved himself; within a few months he had won their full support. Aiding him was his contention, rejected by Murray, that it was the duty of the Examining Committee to not only hear the profession of a prospective candidate for membership, but also to be satisfied that a conversion had actually occurred.

The decline in membership during and after the Murray ordeal ceased soon after Dr. Withrow's arrival. Five months after his installation, twenty-five persons joined the church. Thirty-five others were enrolled in classes preparatory to membership. The

Monday evening young people's prayer service, which had been held in a small room, was forced by enlarged attendance to move to the more commodious chapel.

On Sundays the congregation heard once more the doctrines which had characterized its pulpit before the Civil War. With the relaxation of tension and the restoration of harmony, the pews began to fill once more. In the latter years of Dr. Withrow's ministry, the evening service was often extended with a prayer session in the lower chapel. As many as four hundred persons attended these after-services, which resulted in the deepening of spiritual life, the reclamation of impenitents and many conversions. This return to normalcy was reflected by regular additions in membership. Of the three hundred persons who joined the church in the next three years, half were added in the first ten months of the new pastorate.

Shortly after Dr. Withrow's ministry began in Boston the church appointed a committee to revise the constitution and Articles of Faith. Due to the growth of the church over the years, its rules had undergone natural periodic changes. However, the Articles and Confession of Faith had remained unchanged for sixty-eight years. The proposal to modernize them was strongly opposed by certain church members. This opposition was illustrated in a letter of protest written by Peter Hobart, an active member of the society, in which he warned against any move that would jeopardize its character and witness. His undated letter of 1877 listed the doctrinal points designated for elimination:

> That the Father, Son and Holy Ghost are *one* God, equal in power and glory.[1]
>
> That God from all eternity according to the counsel of his own will and for his own glory foreordained whatsoever comes to pass.
>
> That God in his most holy, wise, and powerful providence preserves and governs all his creatures and all their actions.
>
> That by the fall, all mankind lost communion with God, are under his wrath and curse, and liable to all the miseries of this life, to death itself and to the pains of hell forever.
>
> That God out of his own good pleasure from all eternity elected some to everlasting life, entered into a covenant of

grace to deliver them from a state of sin and misery and introduce them into a state of salvation by a Redeemer.

The protest continued:

> In the Covenant also, some words and some important sentences it is proposed to omit. Is it possible that we are seeking to conform to the views and perhaps the suggestions of some who would join us but for these words and sentences to which they take exception, because they do not relish them or may not comprehend their meaning?
>
> To bring our church down to the understanding of ignorant and uninstructed persons for the sake of enlarging our membership, is, it seems to me, lowering our dignity as a church and is a conformity to the world, which might be an offence to the Great Head of the Church. It would involve repeated change and great danger.

The protest concluded with a warning that the proposed amendments would introduce confusion and disharmony into the church.

During the first seventy years of the church's existence all candidates for membership had to subscribe to the original Articles of Faith. The altered symbol, adopted February 27, 1877, required subscription by the pastor and deacons only, the sole obligation resting upon the people now being their acceptance of the Confession of Faith as found in Article IV, Section 7 of the amended bylaws.

One reason for this revision was to restate their beliefs more simply; there was no doctrinal departure. The 1809 Articles had emphasized certain doctrines then under attack, while other areas of belief were bypassed. With the adoption of the Articles of 1877, the only real change was one of emphasis and form rather than one of faith. This position was clarified by Withrow at the church's seventy-fifth anniversary on March 2, 1884, when he declared the church's intention to hold fast to the doctrines of the founders.

However, Hobart's letter indicated that there was another and more practical reason behind the change: to facilitate the admission of new members at a time when the city's population was

[1]This statement was left in the Articles.

being reconstituted as to national origins and religious affiliation. Although the amended statement was not as detailed or as forthright as its predecessor, it is doubtful that this factor had any measurable effect on the increased enrollment during the Withrow years. Actually, truths omitted from the 1809 Articles were incorporated into those of 1877, and they were precisely the doctrines then being dishonored: resurrection and final judgment. The amended Articles also included references to specific Bible passages.

The fears of men like Hobart were understandable in that hour when the centers of orthodoxy were once more being convulsed, this time by a "Christocentric," but liberal, theology—a theology which robbed God of His sovereignty, which rejected the concept of imputed sin, and which emasculated the doctrine of vicarious atonement.

Within the Congregational denomination, the doctrine of final retribution became the keystone of theological debate and controversy. The liberal belief in the fatherhood of God rendered impossible any thought of future, everlasting punishment. Related to this belief was the concept of probation after death.

The controversy arose out of the contention of a missionary that heathen who had never been afforded the sound of the gospel would be awarded an opportunity to hear and believe. Although this fitted in agreeably with the thought of the newly arrived liberal theologians at Andover Seminary, it caused considerable concern among the more conservative members of the American Board. The new theology, these men argued, was culpable in its substitution of the individual consciousness for the authority of biblical revelation and, in the area of polity, in its abolition of certain established requirements for ministerial ordination, which would, in time, fill the churches with unorthodox men.

Among the voices frequently raised against the new theology was that of Dr. Withrow, who blasted those who called the opponents of the new movement "a helpless minority," anchored to the past. Including himself in this minority, he showed that the churches which had the largest membership, the largest Sunday schools, the most extensive mission work, the highest level of benevolence contributions, and the largest regular prayer meetings, were served by pastors in this "helpless minority." He admitted their anchored position by saying they were anchored to the idea that it is forever wrong for pastors and professors to subscribe to creeds and covenants with mental reservations in order to teach contrary to the intention of the founders. He said the minority was not synonymous with falsity, and that some day, the minority would become the majority as sound and pious men rose up to denounce these errors. To illustrate this last point, he reminded his readers of the helpless condition of Old South Church in 1808 and its remarkable revival shortly thereafter.

Dr. Withrow's resounding declamations continued to be heard from the national platform of the American Board in its seventy-fifth annual convention of 1886 in Des Moines, Iowa. In its opening meeting the Park Street pastor, speaking on the subject of a post-mortem gospel, raised some pertinent questions: Why send missionaries? Why the urgency? If the priest and the Levite knew the Samaritan was coming to help the innocent victim, was not their disinterest justified to some extent? He further observed that Gordon Hall must have been mistaken when he raised his anguished voice to cry: "Oh, fly for the salvation of the heathen! Persuade a thousand to come. Oh, brethren, hasten to the field!"

The vigorous oratory of Dr. Withrow and his colleagues played a significant role in the convention's vote to approve the board's actions in guarding the faith from the encroachment of error and to encourage them to continue to do so.

In an address prepared for the seventy-fifth anniversary of Park Street Church, Dr. Edmund K. Alden, secretary of the American Board, said that the relation of a church to the spread of the gospel throughout the world was the test-question both of the quality and the breadth of its Christianity. The zealous support Dr. Withrow gave the American Board in its controversy over the new theology was only the latest example of Park Street's laudable commitment to the Christian witness, he said. His reference to Dr. Withrow's commitment indicated the distinguished manner in which Park Street Church had met the "test-question." Here are some of the highlights of its missionary record over three-quarters of a century:

1.The church supported Dr. Edward Dorr Griffin in the founding of the American Board of Commissioners for Foreign Missions.

2. The Foreign Missionary Society of Boston and Vicinity was formed in Park Street Church soon after Dr. Griffin's installation.

3. Dr. Griffin participated in the ordination of the first five missionaries from the western hemisphere to bear the gospel to pagan lands.

4. The monthly missionary concert was inaugurated in 1816.

5. The Sandwich Islands Church was formed in 1819.

6. Ellen Stetson, a member of Park Street Church in 1819, and the first female missionary under the American Board, was assigned to the Cherokee Indians at the Arkansaw [sic] Mission, where she served for twenty-seven years.

7. In 1822, Park Street Church sent its first male missionary, Levi Chamberlain, to assist the initial contingent to the Sandwich Islands.

8. Park Street Church, through its pastors and laymen, was represented on the Prudential Committee of the American Board for a total of eighty-five years from 1812-84.

9. The total foreign missions contributions during these seventy-five years exceeded $150,000.

The interest in worldwide missions by the society as a whole was fully matched by the women of Park Street Church who, through various local organizations, established an unparalleled record of charitable and missionary activity.

The Woman's Benevolent Society, the first organization of its kind, though actively supporting several evangelical agencies which appeared in the early 1800's, enlarged its program after 1850. That year the Park Street Benevolent Sewing Circle was formed to relieve the wants of the poor, especially their lack of clothing. Mrs. Andrew L. Stone served as its first president for fifteen years. When a mission school was organized five years later in the Haymarket section of the city by Misses Sylvia Dana and Lizzie Gilbert, the circle provided clothing for the children. It also prepared garments for needy students at Oberlin Seminary. With the start of the Civil War hostilities in 1861, the Woman's Benevolent Society and its associates—the Soldier's Circle and the Park Street Benevolent Sewing Circle—began making large numbers of shirts, socks, linens and edibles. After the war this ministry continued in behalf of frontier missionaries in western America. The women worked closely with the Young Men's Christian Association, often putting on bazaars to raise money for the association's projects.

Before 1866 these women's activities were largely of a charitable and benevolent nature. Then their initial labors for foreign missionaries began, with interest centered in Crete. In November, 1878, the Sewing Circle women formed an auxiliary to the National Women's Board of Foreign Missions. Although the women had supported the Board of Foreign Missions, the auxiliary's purpose was to stimulate individual interest and enlarge their usefulness through more personalized commitment. The $648 raised in their initial year was given to their first missionary, Miss Anna Young Davis, who sailed for Japan in September, 1879. Four months later this local auxiliary joined fifty-two other auxiliaries in the Suffolk West Association to form the Suffolk Branch of the Woman's Board of Foreign Missions in Boston. This branch organization, which originated in Park Street Church on March 26, 1879, supported fourteen missionaries with contributions of $8,500 in its first year. With the retirement of Anna Young Davis in 1893, the Park Street Auxiliary undertook the support of Miss Belle Nugent of India, for whom $522 was appropriated in 1893.

In the autumn of 1879, under the leadership of Dr. and Mrs. Withrow and others, preliminary steps were taken to create a women's society for home missions. After a series of delays, the Woman's Home Missionary Association was organized on February 26, 1880, with its inaugural meeting in Park Street Church three weeks later. The purpose of this association was to do for women and children in America—among Mormons, Indians, Southern freedwomen, Chinese, etc.—what the Woman's Board of Foreign Missions had been doing in other lands.

In 1917 the women's department of the church was completely reorganized. The existing societies and circles were merged into one organization with a new constitution: The Woman's Benevolent Society of Park Street Church. It was this society which, for nearly a quarter of a century thereafter, carried on the only real missionary interest in Park Street Church.

The spiritual refreshing which came to the city's churches in 1877 as a result of the Moody campaign had its origin in a meeting held in the Park Street Church vestry on April 15, 1876, when fifteen men gathered to consider a proposed invitation to the evangelist. On the following May 8, a conference of representatives from seventy-eight evangelical churches voted to invite Moody to Boston. The meetings, which began on January 28, 1877, were held in a six-thousand-seat tabernacle in the south end of the city. That evening, Park Street Church suspended its regular service to join the revival effort. The campaign continued through April, attracting a full house each evening with large numbers of Christians attending the numerous daily prayer meetings conducted throughout the city. The first of the noon prayer services was held the next day at Park Street Church. Fifteen minutes before the noon hour, the doors were closed due to the overflow crowd. The increasing numbers forced a relocation of the meeting to Tremont Temple and then to the tabernacle itself. Other halls used during the campaign included Meionaon Hall, Clarendon Street Baptist Church and the Berkeley Street Church. In addition to these noon meetings, special services were provided for youth, women, businessmen, furniture dealers, the press, and the wholesale distributors of the Faneuil Hall marketplace.

The enduring importance of this Boston campaign lay not so much with the spiritual harvest as with matters of social concern, such as temperance. Of the many who became Christians during this three-month campaign, a large number had been drunkards—so many, in fact, that temporary homes were established in close proximity to the tabernacle, to care for their physical needs. One reporter observed that the "work assumed a prominence and netted such wonderful results, as the history of no previous effort of the evangelists in other cities exhibits." Assisting Moody in this temperance effort were such notable evangelical leaders as Frances E. Willard, Theodore L. Cuyler, Stephen H. Tyng and John Wanamaker.

The $15,000 cost of remodeling the first floor of the meeting-house in 1868 after the removal of the tombs remained an outstanding debt for nearly a decade. Soon after Dr. Withrow's arrival at Park Street, an appeal to discharge this mortgage debt resulted in a subscription which freed the society from debt for the first time in its seventy-one-year history. By this date the society's current expenses were being met almost entirely from these three major sources of revenue listed in the treasurer's report of 1879:

Pew taxes	$ 7,091.96
Pew rents	2,851.31
Basement room rents	600.00
	$10,543.27

Total receipts for that year amounted to $11,098.13.

Encouraged by the financial health of its treasury, the society, on the recommendation of its Prudential Committee, voted on April 13, 1880, to proceed with plans to alter the sanctuary. Having recently subscribed $15,000 for the payment of the old debt, the church and society pledged an additional $12,323.38 for this reconstruction. With the meetinghouse closed after June 1, new black walnut pews were installed; the pulpit steps were removed from the front to the sides, necessitating the removal of the wing pews; the organ was repaired; and the floor was recarpeted. In addition to general interior painting, frescoing and upholstering, the downstairs vestry partitions were changed to provide for better use of available space and to increase the vestry capacity. These modernizations proved fortunate in the light of the declining years which were soon to follow; for had they not been made then, the edifice would have been in a far worse state of disrepair at the next opportunity for renovation nearly a generation later.

This decade of advance under the wise leadership of John Lindsay Withrow came to an end at the close of the year 1886. With their pastor in Des Moines for the annual meeting of the American Board, the church and society were notified of his impending departure at the morning worship service of November 21. Having accepted a call from the Third Presbyterian Church of Chicago, Illinois, Dr. Withrow wrote in his letter of resignation dated December 24, 1886: "Called now to yet larger responsibilities and heavier burdens, I gratefully praise God's name for the years and labors we have had together here." The Third Presbyterian Church at this time had a membership of 2,300, with a Sunday school enrollment of 3,000.

After hearing this letter read at a special church meeting on December 24, the following statement testifying to Withrow's conscientious devotion to his ministry was moved and adopted:

> When he came he found us comparatively weak and scattered. He leaves us strong and all united. He found us in debt. He leaves us without debt or liabilities, and a surplus in the treasury, as has been the case from year to year of his pastorate. Under no other pastorate since the organization of the church has this been the fact. He found our house of worship needing repairs. He leaves it in as fair condition as when it was built at first. Repairs have been made at an expense of about $20,000, including a new organ placed in the church, so that within and without it is very pleasing to the eye as well as comfortable for use.[2]

The resolution listed these spiritual advances: continual conversions, a harmonious church, regular additions, and large attendance at the stated services.

Dr. Withrow's final Sunday, January 2, 1887, found Park Street Church full to overflowing. With every seat taken, extra chairs were required for the large audience. Speaking powerfully on I Samuel 2:30, "Then that honour me I will honour," Dr. Withrow recalled the happy years of his Boston ministry, and then concluded with a final exhortation:

> Keep the faith, brethren, as you have kept it here for so long; the old faith, which our fathers toiled and sacrificed so much to transmit. Give this pulpit to no minister that is liable to be "turned about with every wind of doctrine." And when you shall have committed it to the care of one whom you are led to trust, may it never occur that he, or any of his successors in office, will turn a theological somersault out of the creed which the pastor and deacons must sign, into some fanciful fetch-up of his own fabrication, or fashionable speculation of a passing hour.[3]

[2]Park Street Church, Proceedings of Business Meetings, 1871-99, p. 281.
[3]"Dr. Withrow's Farewell," *The Congregationalist*, January 6, 1887, p. 5.

The following day an ecclesiastical council, presided over by Dr. Edwards Amasa Park of Andover Theological Seminary, declared the pastoral relation dissolved.

The brief testimony of *The Congregationalist* to Dr. Withrow reflected the feelings of the hundreds who left the meetinghouse on January 2: "His success has been solid as well as brilliant, and his departure seriously weakens the Evangelical force of this community."

14. Years of Decline

During Dr. Withrow's absence in November, 1886, the church not only heard of his intended resignation but also entertained as guest preacher the man who, within one month, was to become its next minister. Rev. David Gregg, scholarly pastor of the Third Reformed Presbyterian Church, New York City, supplied the Park Street pulpit on Christmas Sunday. The church's satisfaction with Gregg plus Dr. Withrow's recommendation led to his call on January 12, 1887. With his acceptance, Park Street was assured a pastor in the shortest possible time—a new and welcome experience. The installation sermon on February 16 was delivered by Dr. William M. Taylor of the Broadway Tabernacle Church, New York City, with the invocation and Scripture reading by Rev. George A. Gordon of Old South Church.

On the morning of February 20, the meetinghouse was filled for the new pastor's opening sermon. Speaking from Romans 16:3, he declared:

> One thing this pulpit never intends to do—that is, to waste time in trying to prove a text of Scripture. It will always be accepted as true and infallible without proof, and it will always be used as a sledge hammer to drive home the bolt of truth.[1]

Gregg's attitude toward the theological controversy then raging in the denomination was soon made known to his congregation. In a sermon delivered in the summer of 1887, he cautioned against undue fear and anxiety which could dictate unwise and impatient action. Though a denomination might fall away from its biblical

---

[1] *The Congregationalist*, February 24, 1887, p. 63.

moorings, the true church of Jesus Christ was in no danger, he said; it could never be overthrown. He predicted that the Congregational denomination would become "worm-eaten" if it permitted the "warm doctrine" of a probation after death to rob the churches of their faith and power. He further warned of surrender to the enemy in order to preserve the church: "Compromises, even for the sake of what looks like the present preservation of the truth, are deadly and full of destruction. Cleave to the direct and written law of God, and let come what will."[2]

In the church's letter of call to the candidate, reference was made to "an unusually large proportion of young people" who were anxious to cooperate with him in an aggresive witness to the community. Gregg's appreciation of this youthful spirit together with his love for young people directed a goodly portion of his pastoral care toward them. His sermons on the ideal young man and woman, published in 1897, are masterpieces of biblical instruction and wisdom. Special meetings were provided from time to time for the spiritual strengthening of the young. The following notice which occasionally appeared in the pages of *The Congregationalist* attests to the church's concern for youth:

Fathers and Mothers of New England—An Open Letter from Park Street Church, Boston; David Gregg, D. D. Pastor: Have you a son who has left your fireside and has come to this great city? Removed from the sympathy and restraint of his home and home church, is he among us homeless and churchless? If he is, and if you wish him brought under the *care* of the church and into the *friendships* of the church, send us his name and address, and we will invite him to become one of our church family, or introduce him to the friendship of some sister church. Have you a daughter among us desiring a church home? Then tell us this, and we will take *her* into our church family and surround her with the sympathy of our noble young women.[3]

Dr. Gregg's faithful ministry to young and old alike proved to be a source of great encouragement to Park Street Church during these critical years. It appeared for a time that his pleasant man-

[2]David Gregg, "Is the Church of Christ in Danger?" *The Congregationalist*, October 20, 1887, p. 363.
[3]*The Congregationalist*, February 21, 1889, p. 61.

ner and his allegiance to orthodoxy might stem the tide against
the contemplated departures to the suburbs of many of the members. Dr. Gregg's acceptance of a call from the Lafayette Avenue
Presbyterian Church, Brooklyn, New York, quickly caused such
hopes to fade. Though Park Street sought to keep its pastor, there
were too many factors favorable to his leaving. His closest associations were in the New York City area—both family and professional—and his heart was more with the Presbyterians than
with the Congregationalists. In addition, the Brooklyn congregation offered him a salary of $10,000, which figure exceeded his
income in Boston by $3,000.

On Sunday, November 16, 1890, the Park Street congregation
heard two powerful sermons from guest preacher, Dr. Samuel H.
Virgin of the Church of The Pilgrims, Brooklyn, New York. At
the close of his morning discourse, with Dr. Gregg present, he
read the pastor's letter of resignation, which said in part:

> In giving back into your hands the pulpit which I have
> held in trust for you, I humbly ask you to forgive all weak-
> ness and failures. No one is more conscious of these than I
> am. I can only say I have tried to the full extent of my ability
> to be true to God, and to you and to the gospel of Jesus
> Christ. You have been most kind and forbearing, and my
> pastorate in your midst has been all any man could ask. I
> shall always carry you in my heart, and I shall be disap-
> pointed through all eternity if I do not meet everyone of you
> in the Father's house above.[4]

Dr. Gregg's farewell message on November 23 dwelt on Park
Street's physical and spiritual glory. Referring to its prominent
site in downtown Boston, he said, "Its influence as a public monitor
and an individual educator is unsurpassed." The height and grace
of the spire in comparison with the dome of the State House a
block distant inspired this comment:

> This steeple runs ten feet higher than the State House,
> and illustrates a beautiful truth. It is the Aaron of the Com-
> monwealth standing beside the Moses of the State, and illus-

[4]Letter of David Gregg to Park Street Church and Society, November 15,
1890, Park Street Church.

trates this significant truth: The gospel should ever soar above the law.

He conceived the church's sublime mission to be threefold: to maintain a loyal defense of the full truth as it is in Jesus, to demand of men the reincarnation of Christ in a holy life, and to stand as an exponent of a worldwide philanthropy. The church was to be related to the world in the sense that the roots of humanitarianism are imbedded in the soil of Christian truth, he said.

Gregg's brief pastorate permitted him to do no more than was done. The exodus of members from Park Street was merely postponed; however, this in itself was an accomplishment of a sort. On the other hand, his early departure might have saved the congregation problems similar to those being encountered by so many other churches at that time; that is, problems relative to a more liberal view of Jesus and Christian doctrine. Dr. Gregg's later writings reveal theological interpretations more in keeping with the new theology than with the orthodoxy jealously guarded by Park Street Church. A volume published in 1921 contained brief sayings on a variety of subjects which might well have been written by a theological liberal. In 1909, due to his inability to attend Park Street's centennial, he sent a congratulatory message listing what were to him the cardinal points of the church's creed: the fatherhood of God, the brotherhood of man, the presence of inner light in the soul, the Bible, God's revelation through human experience, Jesus Christ, the value of God, the reign of the Holy Spirit, and the Golden Rule as the law of life. His reference to the soul's inner light is a reflection of his admiration of Quaker beliefs. His high regard for the Religious Society of Friends was revealed in a sermon dealing with their role in the making of America, in which he not only lauded their message and their methods but, with equal vigor, censured the Puritans and their reforming ancestors as being in need themselves of reform. In grand language, he praised the society for their substitution of a gospel of hope for a gospel of despair. These views were not in harmony with the faith subscribed to by Park Street Church.

Faced once more with the difficult assignment of securing another pastor, the pulpit committee was immediately attracted to Dr. Samuel H. Virgin because of sentimental attachment and his

gifts of leadership. Having received a unanimous call from Park
Street, Dr. Virgin said a separation from his church would be
detrimental to many families weak in the faith, and to impending
plans for local advance.

Not until January, 1893, was the committee successful in locating a minister. Rev. Isaac J. Lansing of the Salem Street Congregational Church, Worcester, Massachusetts, accepted a call on
January 30. Both the letters of call and acceptance reflected the
rising influence of scientism upon theological belief. The church's
communication stated:

> Generations swiftly pass away; God's Word is eternal.
> While welcoming the best thought of the age, Park Street
> Church has little reverence for so-called progress which tends
> toward the destruction of all creed.

To this, Lansing replied:

> So long as all sciences have their working formulas, in-
> dividual men and bodies of Christians will need formulated
> statements of belief and conduct. I am not so much afraid
> of creeds as of no creeds, and I have usually found earnest
> Christian believers the most tolerant, and assumed liberals
> the most intolerant, concerning freedom of opinion in re-
> ligious thinking.

His answers before the installing council of March 8, 1893,
revealed the following opinions: Salvation is received on redemp-
tive rather than on social grounds; the theory of inspiration is in-
cidental to the fact; the primary work of the church is to help the
myriads who have not heard of Christ; concerning critical views
of the Bible, in regard to higher criticism: "I believe in the largest
liberty of the human mind. If the critics uphold injurious principles I contest them. It makes no difference to my religious life
whether Moses or Aaron wrote the Pentateuch. I don't care if
there were four Isaiahs."

After the examination, Isaac J. Lansing was formally installed
that evening with Dr. Withrow preaching the installation sermon.
Dr. Gordon of Old South Church delivered the pastoral charge,
urging his colleague to courageous service in the context of love
and tolerance and not in that of combat and controversy.

The rising expectations which accompanied this new beginning were short-lived. In addition to an increasing loss in membership, Park Street Church and all of Boston Protestantism was now confronted by the powerful ecclesio-political force of the Roman Catholic Church. Although former pastors had orated against the hierarchy, Lansing was the first pastor of Park Street Church to make a diligent and serious study of the Roman Catholic Church and to present lectures on the basis of his findings.

While in his Worcester pastorate, he inaugurated a lecture series which gave him a reputation as an ardent foe of the Roman Church. A special series of twelve "patriotic" addresses were delivered under the general title "National Danger in Romanism" before large and enthusiastic audiences. Quoting voluminously from Roman Catholic sources, the scholarly presentations were widely acclaimed and soon published for even wider circulation. These quotations show the militant manner in which his lectures were presented:

1. "Romanism is not a religion, but a system of government bearing all the marks of despotism: absolute authority and total control."[5]

2. "Romanism is so prolific of crime, that where the papacy rules, conscience is debauched, morality degraded, and criminality encouraged."[6]

3. Concerning the church's relation to police departments in large cities, Lansing said: "When I know that a very large proportion of the police of great cities are of the same nationality, in the same ecclesiastical tradition, and all dominated by the priests, I see in it all a fixed plan to precipitate a catastrophe for American liberty."[7]

4. Boston's population in 1848 was 128,000, with 65 policemen; in 1888, with a fourfold increase in population, the police force

[5]Isaac J. Lansing, "Despotism in Church and State The Principle of Romanism," *National Danger in Romanism* (Boston: Arnold Pub. Assn., n. d.), p. 89.
[6]Isaac J. Lansing, *Rome's Avowed Purpose to Control the State and Her Success in Great Cities* ("Envelope Series, enlarged," Vol. II, No. 3B; Boston: Arnold Pub. Assn., 1892), p. 306.
[7]*Ibid.*, p. 308.
[8]*Ibid.*, p. 314.

had grown thirteenfold. "Boston today is almost a Roman Catholic city."[8]

5. The extent of Catholic control is indicated by the degree of Protestant fears to dissent:

> Why do timid Protestants tremble before the possible boycott of Romanism? Why is one's name thought to be almost synonymous with fanatic if he tells the historic and eternal truth concerning this hoary despotism? It is because the heel of Rome is on us, even here in Massachusetts. . . . It is because the community is careless, and Rome is gaining the ascendancy. I say to you in the name of history which never falsifies, in the name of truth as clear as the sun in heaven, that the despotic power claimed by Rome is forever incompatible with free intelligence and with its free expression.[9]

Although these lectures were well received and widely heralded throughout New England, they did appreciably little to withstand the accelerated progress of the Roman Catholic Church. Related to this progress was the declining membership of Park Street Church. In the final five years of the nineteenth century, church membership dropped from a high of 918 to 376, and in the Sunday school, from 445 to 250.

In the interim between the Gregg and Lansing pastorates, society members began relinquishing their pews before moving to the suburbs. The treasurer's report of 1892 shows the surrender of seventeen pews valued at $3,970; four pews in 1893 valued at $1,520; and eight pews in 1894 valued at $2,900. Meanwhile the treasurer's list of those who had not paid taxes and rentals grew longer. In 1887 there were twenty persons in arrears, ranging from one to nine quarters; in 1888, twenty-four persons; in 1890, thirty-one persons; in 1893, fifty-nine persons; and in 1895, seventy-eight persons holding back $1,478.12. The treasurer's report of 1896 indicates that the society anticipated tax income from only thirty-two pews and rental fees from one hundred forty-seven pews. Gallery pewholders were permitted to exchange their pews

[9]Lansing, "Rome's Despotic Intolerance of Free Opinion," *National Danger* . . . , p. 126.

for those on the main floor at a rate of 50 percent of the valuation difference.

The increasing drop in membership with the resultant monetary loss caused special action. The Prudential Committee was told to investigate the "feasibility of altering the basement and front of the church . . . for business purposes" and to report on the desirability of such a plan for producing additional income. On the basis of architect's plans, the committee reported the need for: (1) wider and straighter flights of front stairs, permitting an easier exit to Tremont Street in place of the narrow, winding staircases; (2) a narrow stairway to the vestry from each of the rear or west corners of the auditorium; (3) high stores with handsome plate glass fronts, with the meetinghouse to be raised six feet, making the store floors level with the street and providing three feet of air or storage space beneath; (4) removal of the old iron fences and side steps from the front of the building.

These plans—initially formulated during the final days of Dr. Gregg's pastorate—were rejected by the church as being too radical. Due to the ensuing pulpit vacancy, the matter lay dormant until 1894. In the meantime the society had to ask its members for special pledges to meet current operating expenses.

At a special society meeting on May 28, 1894, alteration proposals appeared again on the agenda. The Prudential Committee recommended that the entire first floor be reconstructed, with new iron girders replacing old timbers; brick piers in the basement be replaced with iron columns; the basement floor be lowered fourteen inches for better commercial use; an indirect steam heating system be installed; and three basement stores with plate glass fronts be constructed.

The recommendations were adopted, and a building committee was appointed to hire architects and receive contractors' bids. In succeeding weeks the committee reported the general soundness of the timbers supporting the auditorium and presented the low bid of $31,000. Early in 1895 the church was officially notified, and upon its agreement the treasurer was authorized to borrow $35,000 and draw up a mortgage on the society's real estate. The shops, which were completed in 1895, produced an income of $3,256.67 the following year, and $5,440 in 1897. The first tenants were florists John Gormley and Son and fruit vendor V. Giana-kopolos.

As the decrease in membership continued to play havoc with the treasury, another difficulty arose over the society's inability to continue paying Lansing's $7,000 salary. The problem was so acute by January, 1896, that the society had to cut his annual salary to $4,500 and revise the terms regarding his vacation. This action generated a chain of events which ultimately led to his resignation.

Upon notification of this vote, Lansing responded by letter:

> I am aware, as you undoubtedly are, that the proceedings of the Society as had, and as reported to me, have no force and effect, without my approval, to change the terms of the contract existing between the Society and myself prior to this meeting of the Society. I cannot and do not accept the proposed changes.

Several meetings during the fall and winter of 1896 between the society and its pastor failed to achieve a satisfactory solution. They only hastened Lansing's decision to resign. On the basis of an unofficial suggestion conceived in the minds of Rev. A. H. Quint, Rev. George A. Gordon and Rev. Elijah Horr, Lansing proposed that he be assured of his regular salary should he resign at the end of March, 1897. Both the church and society agreed to this proposal. The 1898 financial statement shows $8,291.67 as the final outlay for the pastor's salary. In addition to the $35,000 loan for the basement alterations, the society borrowed $2,000 to meet the final salary payment and $7,000 for current expenses. So at the time of Lansing's departure, liabilities totaled approximately $45,000. In the annual meeting of 1897 the society voted to liquidate this mortgage debt with a new loan of $55,000. In all these important business meetings, attendance usually averaged less than twenty.

Lansing resigned on March 10, 1897. The dissolving council convened three weeks later on April 1. Although the members described the outgoing pastor as an able preacher—sound in the faith, and of unquestionable rectitude—the council did not officially recommend him to other Congregational churches. A stormy debate took place in the council's lengthy executive session concerning the advisability of such a statement.

Apparently the roots of disharmony did not lie with any one particular party. Both church and pastor, faced with seemingly insurmountable obstacles, were forced to acknowledge their inadequacy. Although the basement stores did provide some financial relief, they appeared too late to salvage Lansing's ministry, nor did they halt the continuing membership decline. The vigor of the church and society was markedly hampered in its Christian witness as a result of this depressed state of affairs, which would not show an upturn for another decade.

15. The Low-Water Mark

Three distinct movements characterized the life of Boston in the late nineteenth century: (1) increasing industrialization, (2) expansion of immigration, (3) intensive urbanization.[1] The first two movements provided the fuel for the economic growth of the city, whose port served as a gateway to America for thousands of aliens. Whereas prior to 1840 the bulk of immigrants had come from Great Britain and Germany, after this date the Irish formed a large segment of the incoming population who, for the most part, were unskilled and virtually penniless. By 1875 a total of 60,000 foreign-born Irish were residing in Boston. By the close of the century, this national class composed 40 percent of the city's population. Jews and Italians also began making their entrances at this time.

This huge labor pool was immediately put to work in the many industrial mills of metropolitan Boston. The resultant burgeoning economy brought great wealth to the community and to a number of fledgling entrepreneurs; however, one-third of the citizens suffered economic tensions and social ostracism. At the same time, the native population resented this competition for jobs and the fact that a few enterprising aliens were experiencing greater success. Native hostility, the instability of the immigrant, physical deterioration of certain neighborhoods, and oppressive factory conditions combined to drive the large middle class from the city into the largely rural suburbs. The recently established streetcar system aided immeasurably in this displacement. Whereas in 1850 the metropolitan region of Boston encompassed a radius of

[1] Sam B. Warner, Jr., *Streetcar Suburbs* (Cambridge: Harvard University Press & MIT Press, 1962), p. 5.

three miles with a population of 200,000, in 1900 the region extended to a radius of ten miles with a population of over one million. Whereas in 1850 Boston was a closely knit city located about its harbor, within fifty years it had become two cities: the industrial and commercial center about the port was located within the outer suburban complex of residences and manufacturing subcenters.

The fluctuating state of Boston's Congregational churches amid these significant social and economic conditions is revealed by approximate representative statistics for 1886-95 provided by the Maverick Church in East Boston, Phillips Church in South Boston, the Winthrop Congregational Church in Charlestown, Park Street Church, and the Shawmut Church in the South End. The total membership of these five churches in 1886 was 3,408; in 1895 it was 2,892, indicating a *net* loss of 516 communicants. However, the actual number of persons leaving these churches was 3,473—a 100 percent statistical change in membership personnel. Losses amounted to 20 percent of the membership for each church each year. Benevolence contributions decreased 45 percent—$38,428 to $21,116. These figures emphasize population shifts more than actual net losses in membership. Such losses, especially in Park Street Church, would be characteristic of the succeeding ten-year period.

In the interim months while the Park Street pulpit was vacant, the church experienced its usual difficulty in securing a replacement. Under the circumstances, it appeared that the church's best hope lay with one of its former ministers. An attempt to recall David Gregg proved unsuccessful. However, Dr. Withrow, who was supplying the pulpit during the first week in January, 1898, promised Deacon Orlando E. Lewis to give the matter earnest consideration. Despite the fact that more than 1,600 persons had united with the Third Presbyterian Church of Chicago since Dr. Withrow's arrival, and that the vote of Park Street Church favoring a call was ninety-six to twenty-four, the invitation was accepted. The church and society heard the news from Dr. C. I. Scofield, guest preacher from Northfield, Massachusetts, who, during a Sunday morning service late in June, 1898, read the acceptance telegram from Dr. Withrow. The jubilant congregation roundly applauded the announcement and sang the "Doxology." At the conclusion of the service the tower bell was rung so furiously that passersby wondered as to its meaning. His return was viewed as an omen of a bright future, for his sole motive in returning to Park Street was to preserve its life and testimony on its historic site. Neither a $4,000 cutback in salary nor the intercessions of such prominent Chicagoans as Marshall Field and the McCormick family could persuade him from the Boston call.

The first indication of a possible sale of the church building appeared in the fall of 1897 in connection with the basement stores. In September the Prudential Committee voted to insert a clause in the stores' leases to safeguard the society "in case of the sale of the Church." The next February a subcommittee of the Prudential Committee, having been appointed "to consider the future of Park Street Church, [and] to advise such a course as may be necessary to perpetuate the same," reported: "The general feeling was the church should be kept in its present edifice, and that it was already in a good field for usefulness. . . . To sell and remove to another location would not be advisable."

Dr. Withrow felt Park Street should preserve its conspicuous location and remain a downtown church. Despite his high hopes and sincere intentions, the diminishing church rolls and the continued low treasury, together with the social and cultural changes, forced him and the congregation to qualify their future hopes. After four years Dr. Withrow conceded the unlikelihood of continuing at the Park Street location. The hour of decision came in December, 1902. On Sunday, December 7, this notice was read from the pulpit:

> A special meeting of the Park Street Church will be held in the church chapel on Saturday, December 13, 1902, at 7 o'clock P.M. to hear and act upon a communication from the Society relative to the sale of its realty on the corner of Park and Tremont Streets in Boston;
> If it seems advisable, to concur with the Society in the said matter, or to determine upon what conditions it will concur;
> To discuss its policy in view of, or in event of, a sale in

order that it may provide for the perpetuity of the church and safeguard its interests;

To take such action as may seem wise in the premises and to appoint such committees, with or without power, as the occasion may warrant;

To transact any other business which may legally come before the meeting.[2]

At the December 13 meeting Deacon D. Chauncey Brewer acted as moderator. This communication from the society, relating its decision to sell Park Street Church to the Park Associates Trust, was read:

At a special meeting of the Park Street Congregational Society, December 11, 1902, legally called, the following votes were cast:

Voted that the Park Street Congregational Society accept the written offer dated December 11, 1902, of One Million Two Hundred and Fifty Thousand Dollars ($1,250,000) made by the trustees of the Park Associates Trust for its realty on the corner of Park and Tremont Streets in Boston, and that the Treasurer and Clerk of the Society, and the Chairman or Chairman *pro tempore* of its Prudential Committee, be and are hereby authorized in behalf of the Society to execute the purchase contract for record and to execute and finally deliver a deed conveying the property subject to the following conditions:

1. Provided the conveyance may be legally made.

2. Provided that the Church concur with the Society, and authorize representatives of its Board of Deacons to countersign the instruments in behalf of the Church, if they be requested to do so.

3. Provided that the money received from the purchasers may be legally received and controlled by the Society and the Church affiliated therewith as fully and absolutely as is the realty which it herein has arranged to convey, but for the purposes originally designed by the founders of the Park Street Church and the parties joining in the Indenture to the Society dated August 18, 1835, and more especially provided that the rights of individual pew proprietors, the Park Street

[2]Park Street Church, Proceedings of Business Meetings, 1899-1922, p. 43.

Congregational Society and the Park Street Church can be fully safeguarded by such a conveyance, the purchase money becoming available for the erection of such a church edifice as the church shall require in which the pew proprietors may be assigned pews in lieu of their holdings in the present building, and for the creation of an endowment, the principal and interest of which shall be under the control of the Society or trustees acting therefor, and the net income of which shall be appropriated for such purposes as the body ecclesiastic shall lawfully indicate with the concurrence of the body corporate, or for such ends and objects as the Church and Society may by agreement between themselves determine.

That the Clerk be instructed to certify to the Church the vote of the Society accepting an offer for its realty, and that the Church be hereby asked to concur therewith and authorize representatives of its Board of Deacons to countersign the instruments in behalf of the Church, if they be requested to do so.[3]

The church voted thirty-seven to two to concur to the society's action.

At 10 P.M. committees of the church and society met in a joint session to determine whether two-thirds of the male members present would authorize the sale of the realty "and its consequent use for other than religious purposes," as required by a previous indenture. This motion was adopted:

That since the Indenture of August 18, 1835, limits the use of the meetinghouse for religious purposes only, unless changed by two-thirds of the male members of church and society,

That we, the male members of the Park Street Church and the Park Street Congregational Society . . . hereby expressly authorize the Park Street Congregational Society upon the delivery of a deed of their realty, July 10, 1904, to grant the use of their meetinghouse on the premises conveyed in the said Indenture of August 18, 1835, to any and all persons for other than religious purposes.

The society's committee reported the results of the joint session at a meeting on February 24, 1903. The society then voted to

[3]*Ibid.*, p. 44.

erect a new meetinghouse with similar facilities and to assume the title to the new site according to covenants in the 1835 indenture, thereby guaranteeing the church the integrity of those covenants. The purchase money was to be held in a separate bank account and invested in first mortgages on Massachusetts real estate and in stocks and bonds. The clerk and treasurer were authorized to seal and deliver the conveyance deed and other documents necessary for completing the sale.

One reason for this decisive determination after the earlier contrary decision is revealed in a statement by Dr. Withrow in which he asked, "Are we right in allowing so vast a sum to lie hid in a napkin, when the income of it would do so much?" The purchase amount not only would make possible a new meetinghouse at a more convenient location for the widely distributed membership, but also would provide a church endowment of half a million dollars, plus smaller endowments for mission agencies. Dr. Withrow said, "The spirits of angels had a hand [in the offer to buy Park Street Church]. Brethren, it is the Lord's doing."

One month after the sale, a group of prominent citizens, having no religious connection whatsoever with Park Street Church, began a drive to save the meetinghouse and its spire from commercial takeover. Recognizing the historic value and architectural grandeur of the edifice, they organized The Committee for The Preservation of Park Street Church. They hoped to raise sufficient contributions from the general public to purchase the building from its new owners and to persuade the state legislature to allow the building to be used for whatever purpose it deemed best, but without any exterior alteration.

At about the same time, the Park Associates Trust suddenly found it inadvisable to continue with the sale due to the tightness of the money market and the unadvantageous publicity about the transaction. As a result of its failure to proceed with the contract terms, which required a payment of $312,500 by April 1, 1903, the trust forfeited its initial deposit of $25,000 to the society.

Meanwhile, the church had waived its rights of indenture, giving the society unconditional authority to dispose of the property. But, by May, 1904, it still remained unsold. During that spring the society's Prudential Committee, in consultation with architects, devised an alternate plan, entailing a smaller auditorium and the utilization of the entire vestry floor for stores. Rent from these stores could be used to erect a new chapel elsewhere in the city, to provide $12,000 annually for operating expenses, and to pay at least the interest on the loan necessary for the remodeling. While discussing these plans, the society received a new proposal from the Boston Herald Company. If the church and society would raze the meetinghouse and erect a five-story building suitable for newspaper publishing, the Boston Herald Company would lease it beginning January 1, 1906, for at least twenty years at an annual rent of $52,000.

On June 6, 1904, the Prudential Committee voted to submit these two plans to the society and to recommend acceptance of the Herald proposal. To forestall any decisive action by the society, opposition leaders immediately set in motion plans to preserve the meetinghouse. This reminder appeared in a general letter sent to the entire constituency:

> It surely was never contemplated by those who made great sacrifices to establish Park Street Meetinghouse that at some later time the property acquired through their efforts and self-denial should be used for any other purpose than the perpetual worship of God and for religious and charitable work in connection with the Church. To take the proposed action may not only be illegal, but would seem to disregard the intentions, wishes, and purposes of the founders.[4]

They presented an estimate of receipts under the Herald lease plan as compared to rental income if the present edifice were remodeled. They said competent realtors had advised them that the proposed Herald building, being adapted to printing, would be worthless in twenty years. Since this plan would net the church less than 3 percent of that income which would be derived from the less radical remodeling proposal, they urged the church to reject the lease as a bad business proposition.

They further reminded the church of the sentiments of their previous pastor, Isaac J. Lansing, and of Dwight Lyman Moody who declared that Park Street Church was the grandest place for

[4]Letter to Members of Park Street Church Protesting the Proposed Demolition of The Church Edifice, June, 1904, Park Street Church.

gospel work in New England. To raze a historic and sanctified edifice in order to construct a building for commercial purposes, they said, seemed extremely foolish:

> An establishment to publish a daily and Sunday paper should never replace or support this church. And that paper, confident of success, announces in its editorial that to a large extent it can do the work of the pulpit and "will feel that the mantle of the old divines of Park Street has fairly descended upon its shoulders." Shall the church assent to this humiliation?[5]

Although this effort failed to deter the church from voting sixty-eight to fifty-nine for the lease plan, it did make a considerable impact upon the society. Thanks to the work of The Committee for The Preservation of Park Street Church, public pressure against the plan was by then influencing more and more people. Many society members especially had become aware of the plan's unfavorable implications. As a result, the Prudential Committee's attempts to win their official support utterly failed. In the society's crucial meeting of June 21, 1904, the proponents of the lease plan capitulated without an official vote.

The sale of the church, which seemed a certainty in December, 1902, became an abandoned hope within two years. As a result of this difficult testing period when the church and the society repeatedly experienced alternating hopes and disappointments, Dr. Withrow felt a revived witness was still possible for Park Street Church. At its annual meeting on January 3, 1905, Dr. Withrow made a bold request, the fulfillment of which was to augur a brighter future for the church. He asked the church to secure an associate pastor who, by means of his physical, mental and spiritual gifts, could revive its waning life. He offered to pay every expense of the search and to relinquish two-thirds of his salary so his colleague might receive the largest possible income. After the church's approval and the society's concurrence, a joint committee began a diligent search which culminated the following November with the acceptance of Dr. Arcturus Z. Conrad.

Dr. Conrad had ministered to the Boston congregation on

[5] A Statement of The Results of The June 20, 1904, Meeting Relative to The Future of The Edifice, Park Street Church.

earlier occasions during the 1890's. As the months of searching passed, the pulpit committee focused its attention almost entirely upon this prominent clergyman who was engaged in a preaching mission in England. Preliminary efforts to interest him were capped by a personal telegram from Dr. Withrow. As a result, Dr. Conrad returned to America in October and ministered again to the church. On October 25, 1905, at a special meeting called to hear the joint committee's recommendation for an associate pastor, the church voted unanimously to extend an invitation to Dr. Conrad. His salary was set at $6,000. Dr. Withrow's income was fixed, at his own request, at $2,000. The letter of call of November 1 was accepted five days later.

The new associate pastor had most recently been the minister of the 1,100-member Old South Church (Congregational), Worcester, Massachusetts. After a highly successful ministry of eleven and a half years, he was forced, on physician's orders, to resign due to nervous prostration. Although his church had been willing to give him a prolonged two-year leave of absence, his health demanded freedom from every pastoral and pulpit responsibility. After his physical and mental restoration in 1905, he accepted the Boston invitation to initiate a program that would soon restore Park Street Church to its former place.

One year after Dr. Conrad's installation, the senior minister, now sixty-nine and recently a widower, decided to terminate his ministerial career. After resigning on January 8, 1907, he was elevated to an emeritus position, and awarded an annual honorarium of $1,000 for life. Dr. Withrow steadily failed in health during the next thirty-three months. He died September 24, 1909. Interment was at Mount Auburn Cemetery in nearby Cambridge.

Dr. Withrow's passing not only came at the close of a pastorate, of a severe trial by Park Street Church, and of a century of fidelity to the faith and vision of its founding fathers, but it also marked the entrance into new and larger fields of service hitherto unknown and untried. During this transitional period, the *Boston Journal* offered this advice to Park Street Church:

> About now it may well be asked by the rank outsider, who
> is longer on business than he is on church government, if

Park Street Church cannot make a success on "Brimstone Corner," which has been advertised all over the country, where in the city can it make a success? We suspect churches are not unlike folks. If they have the goods, it doesn't make much difference where they are,—people will find them. If they haven't the goods, it doesn't matter where they are, either. Our advice to Park Street Church is, Quit fussing, and get the goods.[6]

The history of Park Street Church for the next generation shows that in securing Arcturus Z. Conrad as pastor, they got "the goods."

---

[6]This quotation, found in *The Preservation of Park Street Church Boston*, p. 74, and attributed to the *Boston Journal*, July 1, 1903, does not appear in this issue of the *Journal*. Research has failed to locate the original quotation.

16. A Notable Renascence

After nearly one hundred years of Christian service in New England, Park Street Church found itself in a situation not unlike that of a century past. Fearful of the future, beset by huge pecuniary problems, and pressed by a resurgent liberalism, the times required another Griffinlike stalwart to preserve and strengthen the church's witness to the doctrines of grace. The ministry of Arcturus Z. Conrad met this need.

Recognizing as providential the failure of the church and society to sell their realty, the fifty-year-old associate pastor set out to test a plan of his own which comprehended a future for the church on its original historic corner. Having been given a free hand by his co-workers in the church, Dr. Conrad conceived a plan to raise $10,000 for the refurbishing of the edifice by capitalizing upon the general interest of the city as represented by The Committee for The Preservation of Park Street Church. Within three months after his installation, the plan was announced in a Sunday bulletin:

> We hereby notify the interested public of Boston that we want $10,000 for purposes of improvement, painting and general renovation, necessary for the successful maintenance of church work at the corner of Park and Tremont Streets. The treasurer or either of the pastors will be pleased to receive your subscription and duly credit the same to the Improvement Fund. This is a most serious and earnest request.

A month later a letter of appeal was sent to The Committee for The Preservation of Park Street Church, in which Dr. Conrad cited obstacles thwarting continued growth: the death of prominent members, changes of residences, and a trolley-car congregation largely precluding family attendance in church and in Sunday school. He said this solicitation for $10,000 was wholly his own idea and was being made unofficially, on an individual basis only; however, he was confident that the society and its Prudential Committee would render their wholehearted approval and cooperation. He then outlined the conditions under which the money would be expended: the realization of a constituency and an income sufficient to warrant continuation at the present location; total contributions to be spent entirely for the improvement of the meetinghouse; failure to keep Park Street Church at its location was not to be construed as a breach of faith or violation of trust with any contributor; gifts of money must in no wise compromise or interfere with the church's autonomy of action; should the edifice be sold due to the church's inability to continue, the $10,000 was to be returned to the committee.

The appeal soon received support from civic-minded citizens unrelated to Park Street Church. Aided by such generosity, the required goal was reached within a few weeks. Dr. Conrad relayed the information to the Prudential Committee by a letter which further indicated the method of expenditure:

> I beg to state that this amount is held to my personal credit for the purposes stated.
>
> I therefore request the Prudential Committee to authorize me to proceed to make such repairs and changes as shall seem expedient.
>
> I further request that a committee of two be appointed by the chairman of the Prudential Committee to cooperate with me in this work.

Upon the appointment of James F. Rollins and Alfred H. Colby as committee assistants to Dr. Conrad, the work of restoration was begun, the major share of the $10,000 being expended for carpeting, interior decoration and exterior painting.

With the completion of these first improvements, additional remodeling programs were initiated throughout the remainder of Dr. Conrad's pastorate. During the summer of 1910 major alterations were made to the entire pulpit platform. The high pulpit was lowered and the platform widened. Small choir boxes were constructed on either side. In addition, a new $10,000 organ was purchased and placed, for the first time, at the front of the auditorium. Stairs on either side of the platform, connecting with the first floor, replaced long, narrow closets used to store choir gowns. Four years later the building's exterior was enhanced by the removal of the paint from the brickwork. For several decades all exterior painting had included the bricks as well as the wood-work. The first fire escapes which were attached to the edifice in 1909, per order of the city authorities, were removed in 1914 and replaced with a more modern system.

At the conclusion of his first full year at Park Street in 1907, Dr. Conrad offered his people a realistic hope for a brighter future. In his annual message:

> I feel prepared to speak with a confidence that would have been impossible a year ago. It is my belief that our church will be self-supporting . . . two years hence. . . . Nothing is surer than that the tide has turned and is steadily increasing in volume and force. We may expect a healthy growth with a somewhat increasing ratio during the coming year.

After three years of ministry, the Sunday morning crowds had more than doubled; the number in the evening services had quad-rupled. Prayer meetings were regularly attended by two hundred to three hundred persons. Social attitudes among members and the general morale of the church markedly improved with the aid of monthly suppers attended by hundreds. The revived spirit of hospitality was immediately noted by visiting worshipers. Dr. Conrad's labors were extended beyond his church soon after his arrival in the city. By 1909 he had become president of the Florence Crittenton League of Compassion; the Home for Deaf Mutes, Aged or Blind; and the Evangelical Alliance of Boston. He was also chosen a director of the New England Sabbath Protective League, and vice-president of the Bible Club of Boston.

At a meeting held in Park Street Church during February, 1900, more two hundred ministers met to discuss the failing spiritual condition of the churches, and the need for revival. A report lamented the small number of converts, the apathy of Christians toward soul-winning, and parental carelessness in rear-

ing children. It condemned the laity for their reticence and
failure to assist their ministers in encouraging revival. The report
also suggested to the pastors that their congregations would be
bolder in their witness for Christ if they were more bravely and
enthusiastically led.

Eight years later Dr. Conrad, as president of the Evangelical
Alliance of Boston, summoned these same church leaders to formulate plans for a Greater Boston Simultaneous Campaign under
the leadership of evangelists J. Wilbur Chapman and Charles
Alexander. This series of meetings, under the general chairmanship of the Park Street pastor, opened in more than twenty cities
in and about Boston on January 26, 1909, and continued for nearly
a month. The central services were held twice daily in the huge
auditorium of Tremont Temple. Noonday meetings also were
conducted daily at the temple, with overflow crowds meeting in
Park Street Church or Faneuil Hall.

Many thousands attended the preaching of the several evangelists required by the campaign. Special services were provided
for professional, industrial, business and student groups. The
meetings, especially on Sundays, packed not only the two-thou-
sand-seat auditorium of Tremont Temple but also such nearby
churches as Park Street Church, Tremont Street Methodist Episcopal Church and the Bromfield Street Methodist Church.

During the forenoons of the final week, a Christian workers'
conference on soul-winning was conducted in Park Street Church
by Dr. Chapman. The campaign closed with four days of meetings in the city's largest auditorium, Mechanics Hall. Six thousand
persons gathered at each service to climax a month of intensive
effort toward the conversion of sinners and the revitalization of
the churches. Many hundreds became Christians and nearly every
one of the one hundred sixty participating churches reported large
additions to their memberships. The campaign's success was indicated by evangelist Chapman who referred to it as the greatest
experience of his life. Dr. Conrad's outstanding and energetic
leadership before and during the campaign was noted by Methodist Bishop Willard F. Mallalieu at Park Street's centennial celebrated just a few days after the conclusion of the campaign:

> In my judgment, evangelical Christianity in Boston and
> New England owes a greater debt of gratitude to your pastor
> than to any other living man for the work he has done in the
> recent evangelistic campaign.[1]

Although the pastor's annual report of 1908 suggested the practicability of uniting the church and society by an official act of
incorporation, no definite action was taken until the winter of
1915. On December 30 at a special meeting held after the weekly
prayer service, Alfred H. Colby, representing the board of deacons, read the draft of a petition to the state legislature calling
for the enactment of a bill to merge Park Street Church and Park
Street Congregational Society into one corporate body under the
name of Park Street Church. The petition recommended three
amendments to Chapter 81 of the Acts and Resolves of 1835 plus
four additions necessary to the adjustment of old laws by which
the congregation had been governed. This presentation was
readily adopted and then sent to the society for concurrent action.
Upon its approval, the church deacons and the society's Prudential Committee formed a joint committee to submit the petition
to the General Court of Massachusetts. On April 13, 1916, the
consolidating act was passed: "The corporation hereby established
shall be deemed to constitute the same ecclesiastical and legal
entity which was founded [in 1809]."[2]

In accordance with the terms of the joint petition, the church
and society notified the commissioner of corporations of their approval on April 28 and May 5, respectively. The joint committee
then proceeded to draw up Articles of Faith and bylaws for the
new corporation, which were presented and adopted on June 26.
Its first annual meeting was held on January 9, 1917, with Alfred
H. Colby as moderator.

When Dr. Conrad came to Park Street Church, the Sunday
school was at a very low ebb due to the flight of families into the

[1] Arcturus Z. Conrad, *Commemorative Exercises at The One Hundredth
Anniversary of The Organization of Park Street Church* (Boston: Park Street
Centennial Committee, 1909), p. 250.
    [2] Commonwealth of Massachusetts, *Special Acts and Resolves Passed by
The General Court of Massachusetts in The Year 1916* (Boston: Wright &
Potter Printing Co., 1916), p. 215.

suburban areas. Enrollment figures had dropped sharply from a
high of seven hundred in 1890 to one hundred sixty in 1905. But
the new spirit which pervaded the church soon afterward, plus
the new pastor's zealous interest in the school's development, provided the needed spark. By 1908 the Sunday school had adopted
a fixed year-round program with no summertime break. An important factor in the school's revival was the teachers' meeting
prior to the prayer service on the second Friday evening of each
month. This time was utilized for discussion, instruction and
prayer that "increasing numbers of Park Street Church may become interested in our Bible School."

Church records indicate the school was not properly organized
until early in the twentieth century. Although there were approximately fifteen classes in 1905, it was not until Dr. Conrad's
day that the school was established on more functional and departmental lines. A kindergarten was begun in 1901, a home department in 1907, and a cradle roll with twelve members, in 1915.
With the passing years, new classes were opened for college-age
youth, for young married women, and for national groups such as
Greeks. In 1914 a class for men was organized by Gleason L.
Archer, dean of Suffolk Law School. Despite the initially low attendance in all departments, continued hard work and progressive
innovations steadily raised total enrollments to 250 in 1910 and
to 428 a decade later. By the close of Dr. Conrad's thirty-one-
year pastorate, the membership figure had levelled off at 350 with
weekly attendance having declined to approximately 125 students
and teachers.

Youth Organizations

The first organization specifically designed for Park Street's
youth was the Christian Endeavor Society formed about 1885,
four years after the founding of the parent organization by Rev.
Francis E. Clark. The new society's interests were immediately
reflected in its support of Rev. James Smith of India and, on the
home front, of the North End Mission, where opportunities were
afforded for personal evangelism.

On January 7, 1906, a dozen youths formed the Young People's
Society of Christian Endeavor, which in two years grew to a

membership of fifty-seven boys and girls. The older group then changed its name to the Senior Christian Endeavor Society. Its enrollment in 1908 was thirty-four.

In December, 1914, a club for boys aged twelve to seventeen was founded through the efforts of Bertrand W. Taylor, its first president. The club, which met every other Saturday, was to aid in the physical, mental and moral development of its members by means of athletics, debates and discussions. A similar organization for girls was begun by Irene C. Scott in November of the same year. Named the Altruria Club, its object, as indicated by its motto—the Golden Rule—was to assist the needy wherever possible. In 1917 the fourteen members were organized into a Philathea Class.

Adult Clubs

During Pastor Gregg's years at Park Street Church, the young men's Sunday school class met in the apartment of Charles E. Richards on the first and third Saturdays of each month, October through May, for debate, mutual improvement and fellowship. On January 18, 1890, as an outgrowth of these gatherings, twenty-four men organized the Park Street Club. Its first officers were: A. A. Maxwell, president; Alfred H. Colby, vice-president; J. E. Worthen, vice-president; Charles E. Richards, vice-president; C. Julian Tuthill, secretary; and George F. F. Roberts, treasurer. Annual dues of two dollars were assessed against the membership, which soon numbered sixty-two men. Debate and parliamentary practice provided useful instruction for ambitious young men interested in self-culture and, in time, scores of men were attracted to the club. A highlight of each year's program was the governor's night when the state governor or another notable figure addressed a large audience. The club has always drawn influential and famous personalities to its rostrum—presidents of universities, high officials in state and city government, prominent clerics, and business executives. Calvin Coolidge was an honorary member for a number of years.

On October 22, 1915, a similar organization was founded and named the Men's Club of Park Street Church. According to the constitution, its purpose was the advancement of God's kingdom, the promotion of the interests of Park Street Church, civic betterment, and personal improvement. In 1948 these two organizations merged to form the Park Street Club with purposes more in harmony with the latter society. The club's present monthly dinner meetings feature outstanding speakers of local and national repute. The 1964-65 diamond anniversary season featured two professors from Harvard University, an evangelical youth leader, and three prominent businessmen. The Park Street Club is the oldest men's club in continuous activity in the Congregational denomination in America.

In December of 1899 women church members organized the Park Street Woman's Club as an outlet for intellectual and social development and for the promotion of Park Street Church. For more than sixty years it has provided numerous charitable and benevolent services to the community and to the church's missionaries.

Missionary Outreach

During the years of Dr. Conrad's pastorate, especially in the 1920's when many denominations became alarmed over the theological liberalism of their missions personnel, the missionary program of Park Street Church underwent a significant change. It had been the church's custom for many decades to receive a special collection the third Sunday of each month for the several agencies of the Congregational denomination. In face of the rising apostasy, Park Street became more and more loath to support these agencies; as a result, its benevolence contributions during this time remained static. Missionary gifts particularly were channeled by designation to evangelical societies in order to avoid total giving to the denomination. The Prudential Committee, apart from denominational wishes, formed its own decisions regarding the amount and designation of its benevolence funds. The only American Board missionaries receiving support after September, 1929, were Mr. and Mrs. Richard Webb, under appointment to Angola, and Miss Eleanor Wilson of the Marshall Islands. Thus Park Street's missionary outreach during the Conrad years was very limited, but it evolved into a nationally acclaimed enterprise after 1940.

Park Street's emergence from the doldrums, with its renewed attractive powers energized by Dr. Conrad's indefatigable labors and consequently drawing hundreds of new members, markedly strengthened the treasury and paved the way for progressive fiscal advance. The three prime sources of income—store rentals, Sunday collections, and pew taxes and rents—showed steady gains.

With the church's incorporation in 1916 and the passing of the parish system, the Prudential Committee recommended that pew-holders relinquish their pews by transferring them to the church. The acceptance of this suggestion terminated the pew tax levy; however, rents for sittings continued to be charged:

> The desire of large numbers of people to enjoy a definite location in the church leads us to continue the pew-rental system for the present. So far as we have been able to see, the advantages very decidedly outrank the disadvantages.

The rental system was finally discontinued in 1949, although long before then most of the seats had been freed and made available to the general public.

The basement stores continued as the most productive source of income for many years, yielding over $21,000 in 1915. Tenants included the Houghton-Gorney (florist) Company, the E. F. Kemp (nut) Company, the Mary Elizabeth Tea Room, and a mill-end shop. Before the 1929 economic depression, yearly rentals ranged as high as $16,000. In addition to these receipts, the church's treasury was strengthened through investments, legacies and special funds. In order to conduct these fiscal matters in a more efficient and businesslike manner, a program was initiated to standardize the church's bookkeeping system and to eliminate reduplication and waste.

With growth and new life visible on every side, Dr. Conrad began giving serious consideration in 1913 to raising an endowment fund to secure Park Street's financial future. Because of the poor business climate, preliminary action was postponed until

January, 1921, when a five-man committee was appointed to prepare a plan for creating such a fund. Reasons for this trust were: (1) to guarantee in perpetuity the continuance of Park Street Church, (2) to guarantee an evangelical ministry in a downtown location, (3) to eliminate the use of the basement for commercial purposes. Three months later, after the weekly prayer service on April 1, articles establishing The Park Street Church Endowment were unanimously adopted.

The immediate goal before raising endowment money was to remove an outstanding mortgage debt of $50,000, which had been on the books for twenty-five years. In a general letter to the entire church membership, the Endowment and Debt Committee said that application of the $5,000 yearly surplus for the next four years, plus a $30,000 subscription, would again free the church from debt. The committee hoped to burn the canceled mortgage in 1925 on Dr. Conrad's twentieth anniversary at Park Street. Thereafter, the $5,000 to $10,000 expected annual surplus would be applied to the endowment fund, with the goal of $200,000 hopefully reached in approximately twenty-five years.

The "$50,000 Mortgage Crusade" officially got under way on January 3, 1922, at a supper meeting of the church—"one of the greatest evenings in the 113 years of history of Park Street Church." Within one hour, $22,000 was pledged amid great enthusiasm. The support of nonmembers sympathetic to the cause was enlisted through the pages of *The Congregationalist* and the *Christian Endeavor World*. All assets belonging to special and invested funds were transferred to the endowment trust. In that first year 613 persons and nine organizations within the church made subscriptions toward the payment of the outstanding debt, which was finally canceled on October 29, 1925. The mortgage was burned on November 3 during the celebration of Dr. Conrad's twentieth anniversary. The Park Street Church Endowment reached its goal in 1953.

Dr. Conrad's gifts of leadership, which were necessary for restoring the edifice and reviving the church's pulse, were equally matched by his skill in the pulpit. The didactic, expository sermons presented each Sunday morning and the evangelistic mes-

sages of the evening drew large audiences year after year. A full
sanctuary was the rule more than the exception. His sermon titles
alone were sufficient to attract many, especially students, and
members of other churches, who formed a large percentage of the
Sunday evening audiences. For example: "Proven But Not Persuaded: The Word that Defies Dungeons, Demons and Death";
"When the World Slams the Door in Your Face and Goes Back to
Bed"; "The Tragedy of Undramatically Settling Down to Nothing-
ness"; "Handicapped, Hobbled, Harried and Hindered, Yet Arriving." A popular feature of the Sunday evening service was
the question-and-answer period in which the pastor answered
questions from the public. The weekly church bulletins carried
the questions for each Sunday, thus helping to ensure a large
audience. The wide range of topics covered is indicated by these
representative queries:

1. Are not the lipstick inebriates a serious menace today?
2. What proportion of leisure should be spent for pleasure?
3. If law controls, how can liberty be a fact?
4. Why would it be an egregious blunder for the United
States to recognize Russian Sovietism?
5. Should not bank deposits be guaranteed?
6. On what basis are delegates to the Republican Convention selected?
7. Is not the present cost of coal unreasonable?

It was a time in America's religious history when the major
Protestant denominations were in convulsion over the modernist-
fundamentalist struggle, with the evangelical churches on the
short end of ecclesiastical control and power. Park Street Church,
in line with its past history during similar doctrinal controversies,
remained faithful to the Word of truth. The catastrophic acceptance of a humanistic gospel by a large segment of Protestantism
during the 1920's and 1930's though a final denouément for
many, was bitterly protested by others. Among the latter group
was Dr. Conrad, who recognized the Christian faith as a fighting
faith and Christianity as struggle. In the midst of this denominational upheaval and apostasy he declared:

We are too much afraid of open collision. We spend our
time parleying about consequences. The apostles told the
truth and told it straight without such adjustment as emascu-
lates the truth declared.

.   .   .   .

The atmosphere of true spirituality is not rose scented. It
smells of battle. The men who have shaped the destiny of
nations have been men who have breathed the flame that was
designed to consume them and who have grown vigorous in
such an atmosphere.[3]

Dr. Conrad's sympathy and support of the fundamentalist cause
did not extend to an acceptance of their label:

How far would I go with the modernist? Not a step. Yet
let me make it plain, please. I am not a Fundamentalist. I
refuse to be thus labeled, because I cannot accept their ex-
treme positions. Many of my brother ministers class me with
the Fundamentalists, and to be sure I am a thousand times
nearer them than the modernists.
Let me tell you what I am; I am an evangelical Christian.[4]

That there was no question about his opinion of modernism, the
following typical quotation reveals: "The adulterated, eviscerated,
emasculated gospel of modernism blasts everything it touches.
Avoid it as you would avoid a pestilence."

Dr. Conrad's outspoken declamations not only touched religious matters but social and political issues of the day as well.
His sermons reflected a live interest in politics, civics and social reform. Concerning German participation in World War I, he
declared:

We must crush the Hohenzollern hyena that is throttling
humanity, the beast who thinks only might is right, and desire the only law to be followed. . . . We must blast our way
to Berlin, bring Germany to our feet, and dictate our peace
terms to the beast at a table in the heart of Germany. We

[3]Arcturus Z. Conrad, *Invisible Collisions: Two Goblets of Wine* (Boston:
Hamilton Bros., 1928), pp. 12-16.
[4]"What Dr. Conrad Thinks of Modernism," *The Boston Post*, July 18,
1926, p. B-7.

must make it impossible for Germany to drink the blood of
humanity again.[5]

An avid supporter of Herbert Hoover's reelection in 1932, Dr.
Conrad saw Franklin Delano Roosevelt one who espoused much
that he vigorously fought against and hated; for example, recognition of Soviet Russia and repeal of the Volstead Act. An uncompromising advocate of prohibition, he deplored every effort
then being made to repeal the eighteenth amendment of the
United States Constitution. In 1930 Dr. Conrad became the
founder and president of the Prohibition Loyalty League, which
hoped to enlist public opinion in favor of retaining the controversial amendment. His vigorous support of the dry position through
this league consumed so much of his time that the church finally
requested him to resign as president.

The election and administration of Roosevelt as president added
more fuel to the fires of protest. The highly touted "brain trust"
became a favorite target of the Park Street minister. Branding the
New Deal as socialistic and dictatorial, he denounced it as a wild
and worthless program. He suggested to the President that he
confess the poverty of his godless schemes and call the nation to
repentance and prayer.

An implacable foe of graft and political corruption in local
affairs, he upbraided city and state officials who perverted their
mandates to serve their own bellies. In like manner, he thundered against professional sportsmen who played games on the
Lord's Day, and against the promoters of horse and dog racing
in the state. There was much to protest. From pulpit, from platform, and with pen, Dr. Conrad rained down holy fire upon the
altars of crime and godlessness. Boston's saints loved it. The
moral community respected and applauded him.

These prophetic sermons of Pastor Conrad, characterized by a
high degree of sensitivity to spiritual and social evil, began to
reach a wider audience through the means of radio in January,
1923. Park Street's entrance into using this new medium was
encouraged by the vision of Dr. Conrad and the Matheson family,
members of the church and owners of station WHDH. This radio

[5]"Crush the Hohenzollern Hyena, Says Dr. Conrad," *The Boston Post,*
July 1, 1918, p. 6.

station, built in part with money raised by Dr. Conrad, carried
the Sunday morning and evening services, though not continuously, for the remaining fourteen years of his pastorate. In 1926
a two-year contract was signed with the WNAC (CBS) network
to air the entire Sunday evening service, and three years later,
the morning service every second Sunday. On May 3, 1929, over
the same network, Dr. Conrad began a weekly fifteen-minute
broadcast at noon, called "Dr. Conrad's Friday Inspirational."

During the 1930's two issues, one local and one national, caused
minor tremors of excitement in Park Street Church. The first was
Dr. Conrad's marriage to his second wife. The other was the
national economic depression.

Not long after being introduced to Harriet Adams of Limerick,
Maine, during a student preaching mission in 1885, Conrad had
made her his bride. For forty-six years the couple was practically
inseparable—until May 8, 1931, when Mrs. Conrad died. Eighteen
months later, on November 9, 1932, the seventy-six-year-old minister remarried. The second Mrs. Conrad was a likable, attractive
woman in the church, and, like his first wife, was musically gifted.
During the summer services, Jean Livingston often substituted
as church organist. But the union created an uproar in the church,
because the bride was only twenty-seven years old. Several members requested letters of dismission, and a few officers, particularly
the more elderly, resigned.

Upon the announcement of the engagement in the press and the
ensuing feeling of shock by a segment of the religious community,
a letter of protest was immediately sent to Dr. Conrad by Deacons
William Carrick, Frank H. Bosson, John Clugston, John C. Fer-
guson, Martin K. Shamlian, David W. Moffatt, Harry R. Finley
and William Buchanan:

> Dear Pastor: Regarding the press announcement of your
> engagement to marry a woman fifty years your junior, we be-
> lieve it is an unwise action on your part. We believe that it
> has entailed a great loss of respect for the church as well as
> for yourself.
>
> While we appreciate the work done in the twenty-seven
> years of your pastorate, we believe that by this action on your

part, you have undone a great deal of what has been accomplished.

We therefore hereby express our regret that a man and
minister of your attainments should place himself and the
church in a position of public ridicule, and with our regrets
express our disapproval of this action.[6]

For several weeks the meetinghouse halls hummed with conversation pro and con, heated and restrained. Many wondered
about the possible extent of the repercussions and their effect upon
the church's witness and reputation. Dr. Conrad appeared to be
genuinely surprised by this consequence of his marriage. A short
time afterward he was quoted as saying: "This is the first ripple
of disapproval that I have ever had in my forty-seven years in the
ministry."

The attitude of the great majority of the church, however, was
revealed in an unusually well-attended meeting—three hundred
forty-six present—on January 10, 1933, when a vote of confidence
in Dr. Conrad was expressed through a resolution:

> Park Street Church hereby declares its complete confidence
> in her pastor and leader, Dr. A. Z. Conrad. We record our
> profound appreciation of the truly wonderful work accom-
> plished under his leadership during the past twenty-seven
> years. We assure Dr. Conrad of our sympathetic cooperation
> as he leads on to even greater work, under Jesus Christ. We
> pledge to him our loyalty and pray that health and strength
> may be given him to "CARRY ON" with the same untiring
> devotion that has been so evident in the past.

By this date, the initial uproar had considerably quieted. Some
who had contemplated transferring their letters refrained from
doing so, while others who had already changed to different
churches returned—and in a short time, so did normalcy.

Of lesser significance to Park Street Church, yet a cause of
some concern during the years 1930-35, was the national economic depression. The membership declined by nearly three hundred
members during this five-year period, some moving to the Maritime Provinces, others to rural areas in New England to live with

[6]Letter of deacons to Arcturus Z. Conrad, November (?) 15, 1932, Park
Street Church.

families or friends. Sunday school enrollment also suffered losses
for the additional reason that car fare was now a luxury for many.

Certain of the church's deposited monies suddenly became un-
available due to bank closings. Annual budgets were trimmed to
the absolute minimum. Newspaper advertising was canceled.
The incomes of the church's salaried workers were reduced. Pastor Conrad requested a $3,000 cutback in his $10,000 salary.

Viewing the depression from another standpoint, many in the
church expected the economic conditions to drive the nation back
to God. Revival was prophesied, but none was forthcoming. Dr.
Conrad's hopeful prophecy of a spiritual refreshing was not to
come for nearly two more decades.

Despite these two jolts to the social and financial health of the
church, the Park Street constituency in 1935 was riding the crest
of a highly successful pastorate of thirty years. A generation of
faithful, energetic ministry under Dr. Conrad had revolutionized
the character of the church and its meetinghouse. The time had
arrived, however, for a change in leadership. Recognizing that
not many years remained for him, Pastor Conrad began to prepare
his people for this change in his annual report of 1933:

> In the very nature of the case, a comparatively short time
> will necessitate the transfer of the heavy burden of leadership
> to someone whom none of us know but whom God will raise
> up to carry on this great historic church.

A little over a year later, upon the independent advice and recommendations of Dr. Clarence Cacartney, Dr. J. Gresham Machen
and Dr. Harold Paul Sloan, Dr. Conrad approached Rev. Harold
John Ockenga, the twenty-nine-year-old minister of the Point
Breeze Presbyterian Church, Pittsburgh, Pennsylvania, concerning
a move to Park Street Church as his associate. During the next
two years, the offer was twice urged upon the young minister and
twice declined.

Because of the harmonious relationship which had existed between him and Dr. Withrow during their copastorate, Dr. Conrad
advised a repetition of that initial experiment in order to facilitate
and maintain pastoral continuity. Furthermore, he was convinced
that Ockenga was the man to eventually assume the reins of
leadership.

During the summer of 1936 Ockenga supplied Park Street's pulpit twice. Not long afterward, Dr. Conrad convened an informal meeting of his officers to request Ockenga as his associate at a salary of $6,000, volunteering to surrender an additional $4,000 of his income to assist the church. During the latter half of August, the candidate committee consulted with many individuals regarding Ockenga's ministerial qualifications. A subcommittee met with him on September 2 and was highly impressed.

The general candidate committee called for a special meeting on September 15, 1936, to make known its findings and recommendations. The church was reminded of the many great preachers it had heard in recent months and years: Harry Rimmer, Donald Grey Barnhouse, Stewart M. Robinson, F. P. McConkey, John H. McComb, Harold Laird and others. The committee also recalled that Ockenga had preached in Park Street Church on three separate occasions from 1934-36, and that a majority of the membership highly favored him. Recognizing him to be a man of spiritual and intellectual depth, the committee recommended his election with the following benefits: a salary of $6,000, raised to $7,000 should he become sole pastor, a vacation of two months with pay, a full-time secretary, and payment of moving expenses.

Upon the conclusion of the balloting, Ockenga received 228 votes. Of the other names presented, none received more than three votes each. A subsequent motion for unanimity received prompt passage. It was voted that Dr. Conrad's salary be fixed at $3,500 for the duration of the copastoral association.

The church's official call to Ockenga received this response:

> Since your gracious action of September 15th you have been constantly in my mind and prayers.
>
> For many years your steadfastness in faith in the Lord Jesus Christ, and your love unto the Christian brethren have been known by me, as they are also known throughout a wide section of the Bible-believing world. Many of us have rejoiced and thanked God for this testimony of the Park Street Church. Now the full meaning of this witness comes directly home to me, as I contemplate sharing the great responsibility and privilege with you.[7]

[7]Letter of Harold John Ockenga to Park Street Congregational Church, n. d., Park Street Church.

Although the Point Breeze Church tried to dissuade their pastor, his decision had been made. He began his duties on November 15, 1936.

While these historic events were taking place, the eighty-year-old senior minister continued to decline in health. An operation in May, 1936, was followed by another on January 11, 1937, from which he never recovered. Death came in his hospital room on January 22.

The funeral service was held in the church on the afternoon of January 25 before a packed auditorium. That morning a continuous line of men and women passed by the bier as the body lay in repose at the front of the sanctuary. Addresses were by Nathan R. Wood, president of Gordon College, and by a relative, Rev. J. Lee Mitchell of the First Congregational Church, Attleboro, Massachusetts. Pastor Ockenga preached on the resurrection theme, "I am the resurrection and the life." Burial was in Mount Auburn Cemetery.

Among the many tributes to Dr. Conrad, perhaps the finest was offered by the Board of Deacons. It said in part:

> We believe our church lost in his passing one of the greatest pastors of its history and one of the outstanding preachers of this generation.
> Coming to the church in 1905 at a time when the membership was dwindling and there was real concern as to whether this church would survive, with indomitable courage and tireless energy, he, through the grace of God, brought our church to the greatest height in its history.

By his astute leadership, Dr. Conrad had enabled the church to hurdle every obstacle and to rise to higher levels of evangelical influence in a city no longer friendly to the biblical gospel. The meetinghouse had been preserved and beautified, the membership enlarged, and the treasury once again placed in a strong financial position. Every department of church life had been revitalized. With a loving pastor guiding its people, a wise administrator directing its fortunes, and a fighting pulpiteer proclaiming its faith, Park Street Church had become once again a powerful evangelical force in New England.

17. *Beginnings Revisited*

On September 23, 1936, Harold John Ockenga addressed the Point Breeze Presbyterian Church requesting action toward terminating his pastorate:

> After much meditation and careful thinking I have come to the conclusion that it is the divine will for me to accept a unanimous call to become pastor of Park Street Church, Boston. . . . It is with deep regret that I petition the Session to call a congregational meeting to join with me in requesting from the Presbytery of Pittsburgh a dissolution of this present pastoral relationship. This involves separation from places and people I love dearly, and the breaking of relations which have been most precious, but it appears necessary. It is desirable to consummate this action November 14th . . . .

This announced decision heralded the commencement of an association with Park Street Church which, to all practical purposes, would end only by retirement or incapacitation. Dr. Ockenga's Boston ministry began on Sunday, November 15, 1936. In the morning worship service that day, Dr. Conrad, who was confined to his room by failing health, introduced the thirty-one-year-old copastor by telephone:

> I commend my brother, Dr. Ockenga, as a man of God as one upon whom God has already signally laid His hand of approval; also, as one who is committed to proclamation of the truth indicated particularly in God's Word as "Christ and Him crucified."[1]

[1]*The Park Street Spire,* December, 1961, p. 4.

228

Three days later Ockenga was formally installed by the Suffolk West Association of Congregational Churches. The installation sermon was delivered by Dr. Clarence Edward Macartney, pastor of the First Presbyterian Church, Pittsburgh, Pennsylvania.

The four guiding principles which have undergirded and directed the ministry of Dr. Ockenga at Park Street Church from its inception in 1936 have been these: a worldwide missionary vision, a passion for evangelism, the Christian education of the whole man, and the power and control of the Holy Spirit. Drawn from the post-resurrection orders of Christ to His disciples, this four-pronged guideline has been the key to the successes achieved during the past thirty-one years. Furthermore, this philosophy reflects the motivations behind three historic institutional beginnings in the first decade of the nineteenth century: Andover Theological Seminary, founded in 1808, Park Street Church, in 1809; and the American Board of Commissioners for Foreign Missions, in 1810. Wisely led by Edward Dorr Griffin, noted for his missionary passion and zeal for Christian education, Park Street Church became a leading supporter of these evangelical institutions. Although the church's entire history has been characterized by a fidelity to this threefold commission, the present ministry has greatly enlarged its scope, producing motivations and incentives conducive to more vigorous and more personalized involvement by the members.

William Henry Harrison Murray, speaking concerning the administration of city churches, set forth these qualities of leadership:

> The administration of a prominent city church demands that the pastor possess the rare powers of tact, judgment, general ability; the qualities that make a preacher, plus those that make a statesman—the ability to both anticipate and provide for future contingencies.[2]

Harold John Ockenga has been well suited to his position. Among the goals which he set for the church and for himself in 1937 was the securing of a part-time ministerial assistant. His request to the Prudential Committee led to the employment of a student on a temporary basis. Since that time there has followed

[2]William Henry Harrison Murray, *Park Street Pulpit: Sermons* (2d series; Boston: James R. Osgood & Co., 1872), p. 16.

a steady succession of high-caliber young men who, in addition
to assisting the senior minister in the achievement of his goals,
have contributed to various church departments. Among their
responsibilities have been church visitation, direction of the junior
church, Christian education director, youth adviser, dean and
lecturer in the Boston Evening School of the Bible, campus evangelism, supply preaching, Sunday school teacher, the Mayflower
Pulpit ministry, counseling, church correspondence relative to
visitors and new communicants. Their names: John A. Huffman,
Jr., Clarence Kerr, Reginald A. Berry, Gleason L. Archer, Jr.,
Louis F. Hutchins, Calvin S. Malefyt, Dale E. L. Fisher, Daniel P.
Fuller, Alvin F. Desterhaft, George G. Squires, J. Murray Mar-
shall, Sherwood M. Strodel, Thomas A. Erickson, Harold O. J.
Brown, Paul E. Toms and Robert Ives.

Dr. Ockenga's missionary passion developed during his student
years through a series of religious experiences—conversion, dedication, a deeper-life encounter, and a definitive commitment to
the missionary challenge. Recognizing his individual Christian
responsibility, he determined in 1929 to become a missionary to
Kansu, China, under the auspices of the China Inland Mission.
In the light of the shakeup in Presbyterian circles in the late
1920's and the general modernist-fundamentalist struggle, he was
influenced by Dr. Frank Stevenson and Dr. Clarence Macartney
to remain in the homeland to assist in strengthening the orthodox
Presbyterian position so that future missionaries might enjoy evangelical rather than liberal auspices. Heeding their counsel, the
newly graduated seminarian vowed to enter the pastorate only
on condition that his churches would support orthodox missionaries.

Due to the absence of a missions emphasis during the Conrad
years, Dr. Ockenga came to the church at a time when participation in and support of missionary causes was at a low ebb. The
Woman's Benevolent Society continued active, but the church as
a whole remained largely uncommitted. In 1935 the membership
of 1,566 persons only partially supported one missionary couple,
Mr. and Mrs. Richard S. Webb (now retired), and contributed

a total of $2,235 to missions. Repeated stress by Ockenga on the values of a stronger missions program resulted in a gradual yearly increase in contributions, reaching a figure of $9,043 in 1939, the year prior to the inauguration of the annual missionary conference. In the twenty-seven years that followed, Park Street Church contributed five million dollars to the support of home and foreign missionary effort.

It all started in a church meeting on January 9, 1937, seven weeks after Dr. Ockenga's ministry began. On that occasion, this motion was presented and adopted:

> That it be recommended to the Benevolence Committee that it appoint annually a subcommittee on Missions, consisting of three members, . . . to increase the interest of the members of Park Street Church in local, national, and foreign missions, and to increase their contributions thereto. . . .

Under the careful instruction of the new pastor and the direct impetus afforded by the Benevolence Committee, the members awakened to the need for greater involvement. This involvement was made possible by means of an experiment new to Park Street Church—a week-long missionary conference. (The idea, originally Dr. A. B. Simpson's at Old Orchard Beach, Maine, was popularized by Dr. Oswald J. Smith of Toronto, Canada.)

After three years of missions emphasis by Dr. Ockenga, coupled with much prayer and planning, the first missionary conference was held April 28 to May 5, 1940. With Oswald J. Smith as conference chairman and major speaker, and with representatives and missionaries from ten mission agencies, meetings were convened four times on Sunday and twice daily. Signs of awakened concern by members became immediately apparent. Within one year the church announced the partial support of twenty-three missionaries, four national workers, twelve students, and eleven missionary children on sixteen fields throughout the world.

Dr. Smith continued as the presiding conference chairman through 1946, when Pastor Ockenga assumed the leadership. For seven years, under the instruction and guidance of the Canadian missionary statesman, Park Street Church learned the procedures for such an intensive campaign. Over the years since that beginning there have been some modifications of the Smith plan with adaptations suited to the local situation, but the scheme in use today is basically that originally conceived by Dr. Simpson. After ten years of conferences, ninety-five missionaries from thirty-eight mission agencies were receiving personal support from Park Street.

In 1951 an 11 A.M. meeting was added to the enlarged daily schedule of seven services. Two years later the conference was extended to ten consecutive days: Friday through the second Sunday with the first Saturday set aside as a day of prayer. In 1955 thirty-seven boards were represented on the conference program. The number of supported missionaries advanced to one hundred twenty-nine.

At each annual conference there are from ten to twenty missionary candidates who have been examined and approved by their boards and by Park Street Church. They appear before the audiences each day to introduce themselves and give a brief account of their conversion and call. In this way, the church's interested members and friends become reasonably acquainted with the candidates seeking financial assistance.

Park Street Church has in recent years encouraged a personal response to the missionary challenge by asking individuals to designate the specific use for their contributions. This plan not only enlarges the interest of the individual member, it also creates incentive for continued giving and praying. Thus, many of the church's constituents aid in supporting particular missionaries and particular projects.[3] Some choose to employ their gifts wholly for needed equipment and tools.

As of November, 1966, Park Street supported ninety-three evangelical missionaries, all from missionary agencies committed to the biblical gospel of Jesus Christ. Eligibility as a candidate for Park Street support requires: (1) accreditation and recommendation by an acceptable missionary society; (2) completion of society requirements in areas of testing and indoctrination; (3) submission of notice of recommendation by the agency and a statement on the rate of support to the treasurer; (4) presenta-

---

[3]Park Street treasurer's reports for 1956-58 show a total of $263,627.33 specially designated for the periodical *Christianity Today*.

tion by the candidate to the church board of a statement relative to his life, training, Christian experience, marital status, Christian service, etc.

This information is then submitted to the Committtee on Qualifications of Candidates for review and appraisal. Approved candidates are invited, through the missionary agency, to attend the annual conference.

The high level of organization, preparation and implementation is carried on and maintained by the Board of Missions and Benevolences (called the Benevolence Committee prior to 1959), whose fifty-eight-man membership includes the Board of Deacons, the pastor, twenty-four members of the church, the missions treasurer (ex officio), and representatives from the Board of Trustees and the Woman's Benevolent Society. This board, through its several subcommittees, determines the missionaries, mission societies, and other evangelical groups which are to receive support. Chairmaned by the pastor, the board is at all times accountable to the congregation. The financial administration is the responsibility of the missions treasurer who performs his duties, without salary, under the guidance of the pastor and a small executive subcommittee of the board.

The support of a missionary by Park Street Church, after his initial reception, is contingent upon continued acceptable service. This support does not remove a missionary from the jurisdiction and control of his board which continues to bear responsibility for supervision and discipline. The church begins its financial assistance of the missionary the day he departs for the field. The amount varies but is usually at the current full-support rate. Parents receive half support for each child. Assistance may be terminated after a six-month notification.

In 1940 the church established a missionaries' reserve fund for the retirement needs of its home and foreign missionaries and for their children's education. A trust separate from all other accounts, it is supported by payments from the missions treasury. These are invested, with the income being deposited proportionately into the missionaries' accounts.

This emphasis on missions, begun by Dr. Ockenga in 1937 and resulting in contributions exceeding five million dollars since

1940, has helped rather than hindered commensurate growth in other major areas of church life. Figures show that the church's giving in 1941, one year after the first conference, was two and a half times greater than in 1936; missionary contributions in 1949 alone exceeded the amount given in the first fifty years of the church's history; in 1935 total income was $20,000, but by 1952 it was approximately $300,000—a budget increase of 1,500 percent; giving for local church expenses increased 700 percent from 1935 to 1963, while missionary totals climbed from $2,235 to $308,534.

Dr. Ockenga is convinced that the local church is the key to world missions and that the missionary conference is the most effective means of conveying the missionary challenge. Dr. Ockenga, in recalling the lessons learned from twenty-five years of conference experience, has written:

> Over against the common denominational practice of central board control of apportionments, of block giving, and of secretarial mediation, I have learned that the important thing is the participation of the local church.[4]

The importance of this lesson has been amply illustrated by Park Street's outstanding contribution to world evangelization and by the fact that more than sixty of its members now serve as missionaries, with scores in other areas of Christian service.

A careful look at Ockenga and his ministry will reveal signs of Arminian (Methodist) and Holiness influences which have helped to balance an intellectual capacity with simple piety and spiritual fullness. His subscription to the Apostles' Creed and the Westminster standards is maintained alongside a belief in an experience subsequent to conversion when the Christian fully surrenders his life to Christ, an experience sometimes erroneously called "a second work of grace." His faith in a sovereign, electing God does not rule out man's ability to receive or reject salvation.

Dr. Ockenga is closely akin to the fundamentalist and has admitted to being one, although, in the contemporary scene, he feels the term to be unfortunate and sees in the fundamentalist

[4]"What 25 Years of Missionary Conferences Have Taught Me," *World Vision Magazine,* March, 1964, p. 23.

movement elements of weakness from which he has dissociated himself. A theological conservative, he is opposed to every hierarchical tendency and modern ecumenical merger.

From this variegated theological background and doctrinal position, Dr. Ockenga preaches a thoroughly biblical, well-outlined message, usually of an expository nature, geared more to the intellect than to the emotions. His comparatively highly sophisticated audiences regularly include many men and women from the academic, professional and industrial communities. A balanced diet of biblical truth is presented, not only theologically but historically, biographically and practically.

As pastor of Park Street Church for thirty-one years, he is well acquainted with Boston, its dominant religious and political power, the Roman Catholic archdiocese, and the liberal segment of Protestantism. Over the years of his pastorate, each of these has been the subject of sermons. In the Marian year of 1950, upon the dogmatic annunciation of the assumption of Mary, Dr. Ockenga presented the orthodox Protestant view that the mother of Jesus, though highly esteemed, was, as all other humans, in need of saving grace and hence could not be regarded as a mediatrix between man and the Saviour. In a city whose citizens are approximately 80 percent Catholic and where the papal church is the strongest single religious force, Park Street Church, led by its courageous pastor, has maintained a faithful and admired witness to the historic doctrines of grace, encouraging the Christian community to a resistance of Roman Catholic power throughout the state.

Dr. Ockenga's posture toward the liberal Protestant establishment is revealed more by active example than by his sermons, though he does not fear to speak against his opponents. Park Street's decision to remain outside the recently formed United Church of Christ, about which more will be said later, illustrates this posture.

The radio ministry of Park Street Church, begun in 1923, has been greatly enlarged in the past twenty years. The decade of greatest expansion occurred during the 1950's when both Sunday services were broadcast the year round over WBZ and WHDH, 50,000-watt stations, the latter on sustaining time. In 1957 Dr.

Ockenga initiated his Sunday morning expositions of the National Sunday School Association lessons. In addition, the morning sermon was taped for rebroadcast on WCOP.

Also in 1957, Park Street Church entered the field of television with Dr. and Mrs. Ockenga appearing weekly on a public service program over WHDH-TV called "I Want An Answer." At the present time Dr. Ockenga appears on a fifteen-minute weekly program called "We Believe" which is offered to Park Street Church on sustaining time by WHDH-TV and which reaches an estimated 50,000 viewers.

The current radio ministry of Park Street Church includes these Sunday broadcasts:

7:35- 8:00 A.M.	WHDH	AM-FM	Sunday School Lesson
8:00- 8:30 A.M.	WCOP	AM-FM	Rebroadcast
10:45-11:45 A.M.	WEZE		Worship Service
7:30- 8:30 P.M.	WEZE		Worship Service

A more recent outlet for the witness of Park Street Church and its pastor came into being in April, 1955, with the appearance of a publication named *The Park Street Spire*. Designed to extend the outreach of the church's ministry and to provide information about its doctrines and programs, the magazine, in its first ten years of existence, has achieved national recognition by the Evangelical Press Association as a first-rate magazine. Under the guidance of the Radio-Publication Department, *The Park Street Spire* has grown in sufficient popularity to attract more than 1,700 subscribers in forty countries, nine Canadian provinces and forty-one states. Approximately half of the church's membership receives the publication through subscription.

The contiguity of Boston Common to Park Street Church has been a factor in initiating a somewhat unique method of evangelism for a downtown church in Boston. On Sunday evening, May 30, 1943, the outdoor ministry of Park Street Church began on the Common. Servicemen and civilians who normally crowded the downtown park in that war year were easily attracted to Dr. Ockenga's pulpit. City permission, though at first denied, was later granted since the Park Street pastor had already inaugurated the meetings before large and attentive crowds. The church bulletin for June 6, 1943, reported:

> Last Sunday night at 9:00 P.M. over 3,500 people gathered on the Lafayette Mall for our Singspiration and to hear Dr. Ockenga preach. The mighty bell rang for fifteen minutes and a capacity congregation poured out from the church to mingle with hundreds who had been on the mall listening to the broadcast of the sermon preached in the church. Thousands of others immediately joined the crowd to see what was happening.

The preaching site was soon changed from the Mall to the adjacent and more adequate Parkman Bandstand, but only after repeated requests for permission to the Park Department and the mayor's office. From this ideal outdoor location, the services continued throughout the summer with the church's supply ministers carrying on during the pastor's vacation. At each meeting several responded to the gospel invitation. On one occasion fifty persons professed Christ. The success of this evangelistic effort dictated its continuance the following summer. The meetings continued to draw thousands each Sunday and grew in popularity with the general public, but not with the Roman Catholic authorities who, in 1945, pressured the city to cancel the church's permit.[5] This action forced Dr. Ockenga's withdrawal from the Common, but it failed to silence his voice. That year the meetings were conducted from the church's front steps on one of the busiest corners of the city; however, the crowds were necessarily reduced in size and the stopgap measure did not prove altogether suitable.

Dr. Ockenga sorely needed a more satisfactory preaching point than the meetinghouse steps. Through the conversion of a Roman Catholic businessman, Park Street Church was presented with a most unique pulpit. Charles Dooley, owner of the Mayflower Hotels on Cape Cod, had been converted to Christ through Dr. Ockenga's preaching during Holy Week, 1945. He offered to erect a small balcony pulpit on the exterior wall of the church facing the corner of Park and Tremont streets. The Mayflower Pulpit was used for the first time on May 29, 1946, with formal dedication

[5]Harold Lindsell, *Park Street Prophet* (Wheaton: Van Kampen Press, 1951), p. 76.

on June 2. Since that date, during the summer months of each year, the gospel has been proclaimed to thousands who might never have heard, and hundreds have experienced redemption in Christ. The pulpit is also used during Holy Week and the annual missionary conference.

From its earliest years Park Street Church, being an evangelical church grounded on the fundamental doctrines of Christianity, has been continuously active in witnessing to a lost world. This feature of its long life has been especially prominent during the years of the present pastorate. Since his arrival in Boston in 1936, Dr. Ockenga has prayed for and encouraged his congregation toward a spiritual revival. His hopes for a city-wide awakening in 1940, at the bicentenary celebration of the Whitefield revival, failed realization. Each year, well-known evangelists were brought to the church in an effort to arouse the city to the claims of the gospel and to a more aggressive evangelical witness. Such outstanding clergymen as Paul S. Rees, Robert Munger, Howard Ferrin, Robert McQuilkin, Alan Redpath, Harry Hager and Bob Jones, Sr., were invited during the 1940's. Many were converted and Christians were reclaimed, but there was no awakening on a scale desired by the Park Street pastor.

Not until 1949 did Dr. Ockenga see the kind of revival for which he had been praying for over a decade. Out of the Youth for Christ organization emerged a young evangelist, Billy Graham. Dr. Ockenga's initial efforts in 1948 to interest other clergymen in the then unknown evangelist were unsuccessful. He then proposed to his ministerial colleagues to bring Graham to Park Street Church for a ten-day campaign. If they approved of the evangelist's ministry, a later invitation could then be made under city-wide auspices. After a general acceptance of this proposal, Graham made his first visit to Boston at the call of Park Street Church. By the date of his first meeting on December 31, 1949, the great Los Angeles campaign had served to catapult him into national prominence, which aided considerably in creating interest in his Boston appearance.

After a preparatory service in Park Street Church on Friday evening, December 30, the Boston campaign opened the following evening—New Year's Eve—in Mechanics Hall, an auditorium seating six thousand persons. The hall was completely filled, and hundreds were unable to enter the building. At the close of the lengthy meeting, approximately one hundred fifty persons made decisions to confess Christ as Saviour.

The remainder of the campaign had been scheduled for Park Street Church. But believing that the hour for revival had arrived, Dr. Ockenga, after consultation with key church officials, engaged Mechanics Hall for Sunday, January 1, 1950. Although this change was executed within a very few hours, the afternoon meeting that day was filled once more. Because of the heightened interest in the Graham services in the days that followed, and the prior engagement of the city's several halls by other interests, it was necessary to shift the meetings during the next two weeks from Park Street Church to Mechanics Hall, to the Opera House, and finally to the huge Boston Garden. On January 16, the last day of the campaign, hundreds gathered in Tremont Temple at various hours of the day to pray for that evening's meeting. By 7:30 P.M., more than 25,000 people had filled the huge sports arena and the streets outside. The response was tremendous as masses of people from all over New England came to the garden to hear the simple gospel message from Graham. Over a thousand made spiritual decisions in favor of the Saviour. After this first phase of the revival effort, Dr. Ockenga wrote a personal letter to each convert, signing his name and encouraging each one in his newly experienced Christian life.

The second phase of the campaign began March 27 with a converts' meeting at Park Street Church and continued for approximately a month with concluding services at Boston Garden and on the Common. During this four-week period Dr. Ockenga traveled with the Graham team to a number of their meetings throughout New England, speaking on topics related to revival. The final meeting on Boston Common was convened on a cold, wet Sunday afternoon; nevertheless, 50,000 persons came to hear the dynamic evangelist. Dr. Ockenga also called upon the assembled thousands to repent and accept God's righteousness in Jesus Christ. He then led the crowd in a prayer for peace, the words being repeated by the audience, phrase by phrase.

In the first four months of 1950, a total of 186 additions were made to the Park Street membership. Total admissions for the year numbered 254, with 74 of these by profession of faith. The revival also had a salutary effect upon contributions to the church's missionary program. The 1950 figure exceeded that of the previous year by $27,000, one of the highest increases for any one year in the twenty-seven-year history of the missions program under the present leadership. Prayer meeting attendance numbered between 400 and 500 during the revival year. The accelerated interest in spiritual matters produced by intercessory prayer and powerful preaching sparked new life and energy into the church. Three years after the campaign, the auditorium, seating 1,000 people, was still being packed to the doors every Sunday morning, with 800 to 900 in the evening service. The songtime hour after each Sunday evening service attracted 200, and the weekly prayer meetings, though down somewhat from the high of 1950, were still drawing up to 300 persons.

In the pastor's report for 1957, however, it was observed that revival was again desperately needed in Park Street Church and among Christians throughout New England, and that the general spiritual condition of the Christian community was at a low ebb. Dr. Ockenga began to pray for a repetition of the 1950 experience. In the intervening years Billy Graham had grown in power and stature as a commanding international figure on the religious scene. Successful campaigns at home and abroad since 1950 had lifted him to the pinnacle of achievement as an evangelist and religious leader. Believing that Graham's ministry was well suited to the refreshment and salvation of the city, Dr. Ockenga once again requested his Board of Deacons to invite the famous evangelist for another crusade. Graham accepted upon condition that the campaign be adequately supported, whereupon the matter was placed in the hands of the Evangelistic Association of New England, which produced a pledge of support from more than three hundred churches in the metropolitan Boston area.

After a series of preparatory visits to Park Street Church by members of the Graham party in January and April, this second major city-wide crusade commenced in mid-September, 1964, and continued into October with nightly meetings in the huge Boston Garden. Throngs of people from every state in New England filled all the seats each night. Thousands were converted and many were brought into the churches. Approximately two hundred persons were referred to Park Street Church as a result of the crusade. An ecumenical flavor was added to the campaign with an endorsement of the meetings by Richard Cardinal Cushing, head of the Roman Catholic archdiocese of Boston, and his highly publicized "brotherly" visit with Graham. Much time, money and prayer was expended for the crusade by Park Street Church, as once again it showed itself a leader of Christian causes in New England and its key city.

Thus the evangelical witness of the Park Street pulpit is being carried on today by preaching, by radio, by pen, by evangelism. In the city, in the region, and throughout New England its voice is being heard by multiplied thousands every week as it persuades men to accept the old-fashioned gospel of grace.

Park Street's Christian education program is carried on in these five major departments, which are subject to the central Board of Christian Education: Sunday school, youth work, support of Christian schools and colleges, the Boston Evening School of the Bible, and the Christian Education Conference. A sixth department, until recently, was the Vacation Bible School. Immediate responsibility for the proper functioning and planning of these departmental programs rests with the minister of education and an associate.

During the past twenty years, efforts to coordinate and integrate these various ministries into a unified whole met with only minor success. The Christian education report for 1957 commented on the difficulty encountered by the Christian Education Committee to educate the church on the value and importance of a full-orbed program. It pointed out the unpopularity of its task and the relative indifference of the members.

An Education Minister and the Sunday School

This somewhat lethargic condition began to show marked signs of improvement with two significant actions. In the spring of 1954 the Christian Education Committee, which had been functioning as a part of the Benevolence Committee, became a separate body. It assumed its own budget and the responsibility to raise and control the necessary funds. The committee was composed of the pastor (chairman), the treasurer of Christian education, the Sunday school superintendent, the dean of the Evening School of the Bible, the presidents of the youth societies, plus fifteen members of the congregation.

The second change was the employment of a trained and qualified minister of education. Although the church had appointed several assistants to direct the youth and Sunday school activities over the years, the program as a whole did not become satisfactorily established and integrated until the early 1960's. The present minister of education, Sherwood Strodel, has been largely responsible for advances made in recent years. An important factor has been the recruitment of parental interest and assistance in the educational program.

Whereas during the first hundred years of the church's history the Sunday school kept pace with the church constituency statistically—a ratio of one-half to two-thirds—the present century has witnessed a wider ratio. In 1935, Sunday school enrollment numbered three hundred fifty, approximately one-fifth of the total church membership. During the present century, Park Street Church has gained a reputation primarily as a preaching church, a pulpit where orthodox believers could find strength for their faith. Although Park Street has never deviated from its original orthodox beginnings, Boston and its churches have radically changed, and this has placed the church in its present unique position. The emphasis, therefore, at least in the minds of the church's members and friends, has been on the preaching rather than the educational ministry.

A second reason for the comparatively small enrollment is the distance traveled by the church's constituents. Although the church is located in the heart of the city, most of its members live in approximately eighty suburbs surrounding Boston, which makes it a suburban church in an urban meetinghouse. The entire educational program must continually confront problems relative to time, travel and scheduling.

Furthermore, until recently the Sunday school has not provided classes for every age group and taste. Unmarried adults, though not always willing to do so, have had to meet with married adults. From time to time similar difficulties with other age groups have tended to place a damper on increased participation.

In addition to these somewhat peculiar reasons, Park Street has had problems common to all church schools: a general disinterest, and the odd concept that only juveniles require instruction.

Within the past three years, however, this wide ratio between church and school enrollments has narrowed. Present Sunday school figures are approximately 750, with an average attendance of 400. The Sunday school is divided into these departments and classes:

Departments	Classes
Nursery	
Beginners	3
Primary, grades 1-3	5
Junior, grades 4-6	6
Junior High, grades 7-9	5
Senior High, grades 10-12	1
College	1
Adult	5

In addition, a well-organized and effective youth church is conducted during the Sunday morning service. Approximately 175 children of nursery to high school age attend this separate worship hour.

The Boston School of the Bible

An educational ministry of Park Street Church which extends to persons outside its own constituency is the Boston School of The Bible. Conceived by Dr. Ockenga and formulated in conjunction with Dr. Howard Ferrin, president of Providence Bible Institute, the school was designed to teach new converts the basic doctrines of Christianity, to train laymen engaged in religious instruction, and to provide advanced courses in such areas as New Testament, Old Testament, theology, church history and missions. After preliminary planning during the fall and winter of 1942-43, first classes were convened in October, 1943. A total of 474 students from more than 100 churches enrolled in the credit courses.

In the succeeding years, attendance continued to climb with 586 enrolled in 1950, representing some 200 metropolitan churches and more than a dozen denominations. In recent years the enrollment has hovered around the 200 mark.

The school's faculty is drawn largely from Gordon College and Divinity School, Barrington College (formerly Providence Bible Institute), and the church's ministerial staff. An advisory committee composed of pastors, educators and interdenominational leaders in the area has aided greatly in the formation of the curriculum and teaching staff. The continued progress and growth of this lay institute was given major impetus in the spring of 1966 with the arrival of Dr. J. C. Macaulay of London, Ontario, Canada, to assume the deanship. With wide experience as a pastor, educator and writer, the new dean not only is responsible for carrying on the school's ministry at Park Street but also for offering extension classes in numerous other Massachusetts cities.

The registration fee of $15 entitles the student to enroll for one to four courses for the entire twenty weeks, and enables the school to be self-supporting. Since its inception the school has ministered to more than 6,000 students.

The Christian Education Conference

An annual feature of the church calendar for eighteen years has been the Christian Education Conference. Begun in 1949, its purpose has been to acquaint the public with the offerings of Christian education; to afford Christian schools an opportunity to inform laymen of their services, curriculums, problems and challenges; to give students and parents an opportunity to interview personally representatives of various Christian schools; and to inspire wider support for the cause of Christian education through prayer, recommendations and financial aid.

The three-day meeting, usually held during October or November, is highlighted by guest lecturers and workshop sessions in which the challenge and work of the Sunday school and other educational facilities are considered and discussed.

An important conference feature is the reception of pledges for local Christian education. The entire educational outreach is supported from funds pledged at the annual conference and from weekly Sunday school offerings. In 1965, pledges of $24,000 were required for the local program alone. Sunday school collections are now totaling just over $3,000.

Park Street Church also supports several Christian schools and colleges through its Christian Education Conference. In 1964 the board received $7,500 for this purpose in designated funds from individuals. The total budget for Christian education presently stands at $37,900. Included in this figure are expenditures for summer camping, evangelism conferences for youth, scholarships and office overhead. Of the $30,400 budget for the local program (exclusive of gifts to colleges), half is for salaries.

Summer Vacation Bible School

Park Street's first Vacation Bible School convened in 1957 as a result of a laywoman's concern for the children living in the immediate locale. But after six years, the school ceased its activities due to problems peculiar to a student body composed largely of children from low-income families. The few teachers who volunteered their services, being unfamiliar with the backgrounds and manners of their students, felt inadequate in relating teaching to life. Recruitment of children produced only limited results. Teaching staffs were seldom sufficient to properly manage the school. This project, designed to make Park Street Church sensitive to the spiritual needs of its immediate environment, closed operations in 1962.

On the whole, however, employing an aggressive and able minister of education has enabled the church to develop along educational lines more rapidly in the past five years than at any time in its history. There has been a marked growth in interest and participation by the youth. Capable leadership has produced better-trained layworkers and assistants. Financial contributions have increased as the members have awakened to the values of a well-integrated Christian education program.

The Collegiate Ministry

Upon Dr. Ockenga's recommendation, a committee was appointed in 1948 to make suggestions for beginning a ministry to the 100,000 college students in and about Boston. On October 5 it advised that a Sunday morning Bible class for collegians be formed, with advertisements placed on several campuses. After approval by the Board of Deacons, the sponsorship and support of the class was placed in the hands of the Benevolence (Missions) Committee. The church employed a minister to students, Rev. Calvin Malefyt, pastor of the Clarkstown Reformed Church, Nyack, New York.

With the help of a nucleus of Christian students, thousands of students were contacted by letter, in person and by notices in campus periodicals. Within three years the ministry was expanded to include a popular collegiate club, meeting Sunday evenings, and a singspiration. Average attendance at the club meetings rose to 140 with an active membership of 350 students. Attendance at the morning Bible class averaged less than 100.

Malefyt's responsibilities, apart from these Sunday meetings, involved student visitation, counseling, and lecturing to youth of theologically diverse backgrounds. Many hours were spent unraveling knotted personal relationships among students, both American and foreign. Consultations with college deans were occasionally required to find satisfactory solutions to social, spiritual and emotional problems.

The harvest from this campus evangelism has been rewarding. The roster of Christian students rose measurably as young men and women were confronted with the validity and trustworthiness of the Christian gospel. Many testimonies have certified the sanctifying influence of this ministry.

The healthy growth of the college program has been due to five factors: (1) the uncompromising presentation of the gospel; (2) a contact with every Congregational freshman in the college community; (3) the dedication of Christian students; (4) personal interviews, whenever possible, with the several hundred who attend the collegiate activities at the church; (5) a strong church pulpit.

When Malefyt left in 1961 to resume a pastoral ministry, Harold O. J. Brown, a Fulbright scholar and graduate of Harvard University, assumed the post until the summer of 1965, when he was succeeded by Dr. Robert Ives. Despite ever present opposition from campus authorities and evidences of hostility from the liberal clergy, the work continues as a significant service to the academic world.

Dr. Ockenga has always been very much aware of the need and importance of Park Street being an evangelical beacon in a city hostile to the evangelical faith. If the church's founding was dictated by a sorely pressed, declining orthodox community, its present continuance is necessary for the same reason. In addition to the spiritual concerns already recorded, however, Dr. Ockenga has devoted a major share of his time over the past twenty-two years to the restoration, refurbishing and expansion of the physical properties. His administrative gifts and visionary zeal are well illustrated by this aspect of his pastorate. With unlimited and expanding horizons ever before him, he has pressed hard and successfully for the utmost utilization of the building's five floors.

In 1939 a suggestion was included in the pastor's annual report relative to closing the basement stores. Many were fearful from a financial standpoint, as rent from these businesses often totaled more than $20,000. In a business meeting on October 15, 1943, the church, having been convinced of the proposal's validity and necessity, voted to: (1) dispense with the stores at the end of the lease period, January 1, 1945; (2) to restore the basement—one-third of the building's floor space—to religious uses; (3) to appoint a committee to ascertain methods for its utilization and adaptation. To help pay for this remodeling, a drive was begun the next year to raise $50,000 in war bonds. The bonds were then taken over by the Endowment Fund, which released the cash for remodeling. The remainder of the funds was provided by various legacies and loans.

The tenants had moved by the end of 1944. After nearly fifty years of commercial usage, the stores were dismantled and the entire basement and subbasement reconstructed. In their place was built a chapel, a row of staff offices, a kitchen, and the Hawey Assembly Room seating three hundred persons.

In November of 1953 the church purchased the adjoining property at 1 Park Street. The acquisition of this two-story commercial building, thirty by eighty feet, which had been used as a florist shop, was to play a significant role in future expansion plans. The site, which nearly became the property of the Paulist Fathers, was purchased for $175,000. At present the first floor is devoted to educational uses, and the second floor has been made into offices for the missions department and the pastor.

The first phase of the restoration program having been completed by 1946, the church entered the second phase with the installation of a modern self-service elevator and stairwell at the northeast corner of the building, and a new sidewalk-level entrance. This entrance and elevator had been greatly needed by the elderly and infirm who found it difficult to ascend the thirty steps from the street to the auditorium and the forty-eight steps to the balcony. The new elevator, completed in 1959, was named the Calder Memorial in memory of Malcom T. Calder, who was church treasurer when he died in 1952.

Among the items necessary for an enlarged ministry in the newly refurbished meetinghouse was Park Street Church's fourth organ. In 1957 the church's demands for a more versatile instrument led to the purchase of a new three-manual organ from the Aeolian-Skinner Company. This new instrument, which required nearly three years to manufacture and eight months to install, was built to meet tonal and control requirements in four areas: the church service, concert work, radio broadcasting, and recording. The organ was given in memory of Albert O. Wilson, a recent trustee and treasurer of the congregation, and was dedicated at a special service on January 1, 1961.

On a Sunday evening late in the summer of 1962, after the congregation had left the meetinghouse, a section of plaster fell from the sanctuary ceiling. An immediate engineering survey revealed the need of an entirely new ceiling. A substitute ceiling was erected at once, and for seven months the extensive work continued. Despite the lofty staging down the auditorium aisles and across the ceiling, the weekly ministry continued, though with considerable impediment. Thirty-two tons of steel were used to reinforce the trusses and beams supporting the roof and spire.

Four years earlier, similar evidences of decay in the tower

caused pieces of trim to fall to the street, revealing extensive rust and rot which required nearly $80,000 for repairs.

Thus, under the careful leadership and wise guidance of Dr. Ockenga, with the aid of loans and legacies, through the generous subscriptions of the members to the Restoration Fund, the Emergency Fund, the Loyalty Fund, and the Recovery Fund, the present-day edifice is at a peak of beauty, strength and utility.

That expenditures for repairs totaled more than $820,000 during the period 1944-64 is more remarkable when considered alongside increased annual missionary contributions of from $45,000 to $321,000, a widely broadened Christian education program, an enlarged staff, and a general-expense budget which has climbed from $46,000 to $105,000.

With the historic building in excellent condition, and the church free of all debts incurred by its restoration, new plans have been recently formulated toward a radical revision of the existing facilities. Hemmed in on two sides by busy thoroughfares and on a third side by an historic cemetery, the only direction for physical development is along Park Street. The meeting-house is no longer adequate either for the present or for the proposed programs of the future. The church's educational, college and pulpit ministries have been curtailed due to insufficient space to accommodate those participating in its life and testimony.

In 1962, members of the church's joint boards subscribed $12,000 to finance a professional study of the problems associated with expansion. After two years of investigation, the Hutchinson Report was presented to the boards for analysis and deliberation. Out of their yearlong discussions came an integrated plan for additional changes in the present church structure and the erection of an eight-story building at 1 Park Street. The plan provides for a doubling of the present floor space, additional sanctuary seating, a new prayer-meeting chapel, a sixty-four-seat choir and organ loft, increased Sunday school capacity, an enlarged banquet and assembly room, new kitchen facilities, modern rest rooms and a more adequate nursery. Other provisions include an adjacent pastor's manse, centralized business offices, a more commodious church parlor, and modernized heating and air-conditioning units.

The plan's total cost is presently estimated at $1,050,000, of which $830,000 is scheduled for 1 Park Street. In addition, the church cabinet has strongly recommended that the upper four floors of the new building be extended over the roof level of the meetinghouse by means of cantilever construction, thereby doubling Sunday school space. The estimated cost for this added proposal is $200,000.

With the inner city involved in a huge reconstruction program of its own, with the redevelopment of slum and commercial areas into centers of high-rise residences and governmental offices, Park Street Church is preparing to meet the challenge of the new Boston.

The leadership, vision and faith of Dr. Ockenga, which have enabled Park Street Church to develop markedly in the various areas of its life, have also captured the attention of the evangelical community across America. As a result, Park Street has experienced a problem peculiar to churches having successful pastors. Running parallel with the church's achievements over the years has been the continual effort by numerous churches, institutions and organizations to woo Dr. Ockenga from his Boston charge in order to engage him in other causes. Recognized as a choice servant of God, generously endowed with spiritual and administrative gifts, Dr. Ockenga has been asked to assume positions, which occasionally have been resented by the church. Calls to become executive secretary of the National Association of Evangelicals in 1944, and president of Fuller Theological Seminary a decade later, threatened the continuance of the pastoral relationship. The seminary invitation was the more serious.

With the spirit of ecumenism and denominational cooperation having captured the imagination of the liberal Protestant church with renewed and concerted vigor over the past generation, a number of evangelical churches launched the National Association of Evangelicals in 1942. This was to give itself a national voice with which to speak out in behalf of its own interests as well as to counteract moves thought to be unwarranted and

against the best interests of religious freedom by such organizations as the National Council of Churches of Christ in America.
Since the National Association of Evangelicals was conceived
largely through the vision of Dr. J. Elwin Wright, director of
the New England Fellowship and a close friend of Dr. Ockenga,
the Park Street pastor was quickly enlisted as a founding father
of the organization. At the constitutional meeting held in Chicago
in May, 1943, he was elected its first president.

After the association's initial formation, Dr. Wright, its promo-
tional director, asked Park Street's deacons to release their pastor
for specific tasks necessitating prolonged absences from the city.
Having received their permission, Dr. Ockenga devoted considerable time in the ensuing months for the new society. Two years
later, when the association asked him to become its first full-time
executive secretary, he declined, choosing to continue his pastoral
ministry.

The National Association of Evangelicals was founded to create
a national platform from which evangelicals could publicize their
views and beliefs on the current theological, ecclesiastical, social
and political issues of the day, and from which concerted action
could be initiated. The earlier organization of the American
Council of Christian Churches, an ecumenical movement among
the fundamentalist Protestants, failed to allay the need for a
united action group as contemplated and conceived by such leaders as Dr. Ockenga. In this rejection of the fundamentalist American Council of Christian Churches may be found the seeds of
the "new evangelical" movement, which has caused considerable
anxiety in certain tents of the orthodox camp.

In the spring of 1942, having in mind the recently formed
American Council of Christian Churches and historic fundamentalism in general, Dr. Ockenga indicted his fundamentalist
brethren for their denominational divisiveness and controversial
spirit which he believed to be unjustifiable. Indicating disgust
for this strife, he declared the sole ground for division to be the
cross of Calvary and not such matters as baptism or church polity.
Decrying the exclusive spirit of separatism as practiced by some,
he stressed the need of fundamentalists to cease their excessive

intolerance and to enter the main stream of the evangelical movement.[6]

The phrase, "the new evangelicalism," was coined in an address delivered by Dr. Ockenga at the first convocation of Fuller Theological Seminary in 1947. Its outlines, sketched in the founding National Association of Evangelicals' convention address of 1944, were enlarged in the autumn of 1957 before a Park Street audience. Criticizing the fundamentalist's gospel as asocial in content and ethic, he proceeded to point out three major deficiencies of fundamentalism: (1) a wrong attitude toward those not holding identical views of doctrine; (2) a wrong strategy producing unnecessary fragmentization; (3) a wrong accrual in the loss of every strategic battle with modernism and the resultant loss of influence within the denominations.[7] As an answer to both a truncated personal (fundamentalist) gospel and a truncated social (modernist) gospel, Dr. Ockenga offered the new evangelical gospel, defining it in these terms:

> The New Evangelicalism then is orthodox Christianity established upon an authoritative and dependable Bible, proclaiming the Gospel truths in a positive, constructive, and dynamic manner, avoiding the fragmentization that comes by personal controversies, and applying the Christian teaching to the societal problems of our day so that Christ and Christian truth may be expressed both in personal and social life with power and fruitfulness.[8]

Dr. Ockenga's declination of the request of the National Association of Evangelicals to become its national secretary in 1944 was due to the fact that he had been at Park Street Church only seven years and therefore had not had sufficient time for the realization of his hopes for his congregation, and because the new era of missions at the church had been introduced only four years before and vitally needed his leadership.

[6]See Harold John Ockenga, "The Unvoiced Multitudes," *Evangelical Action,* compiled and ed. by Executive Committee of National Association of Evangelicals for United Action (Boston: United Action Press, 1942), pp. 32-33.

[7]Harold John Ockenga, "The New Evangelicalism," *The Park Street Spire,* February, 1958, p. 2.

[8]Harold John Ockenga, "The Pastor's Study," *The Park Street Spire,* January, 1958, p. 7.

A second and more formidable threat to the longevity of his Boston ministry appeared in 1954, which he considers "the year of my great decision in reference to Park Street." Actually, there were two great decisions that year. The first one was revealed to the congregation following the communion service on Sunday morning, June 27, 1954. Dr. Ockenga read a letter in which he said he planned to resign in order to become associated with Dr. Charles E. Fuller of Pasadena, California. He was to become Dr. Fuller's successor on the Old-Fashioned Revival Hour beginning January 23, 1955; the president of Fuller Theological Seminary; and executive vice-president of the Fuller Foundation with a lifetime contract.

The background of his decision was conversations with Dr. Fuller during 1946-47, when the famous radio preacher approached him concerning the possibility of founding a college-level school of evangelism and missions. Disinterested with any such plan on the collegiate level, Dr. Ockenga offered a counter proposal for a graduate seminary, indicating his willingness to serve as a trustee should such a school be founded.

With Dr. Fuller's acceptance of this latter proposal, plans were hastily formulated toward founding the new seminary in the fall of 1947. Dr. Ockenga agreed to become president-in-absentia and to be responsible for selecting a competent faculty and curriculum.

Upon assuming the presidency, he assured Park Street Church that the new relationship was to be maintained at long distance and that no further commitments had been made by either party. The letter of resignation, therefore, was received with great unhappiness. Between 1947 and 1954, although the church had been most generous in making its pastor's services available, the seminary had not been satisfied with the existing arrangement. Pressures from the Pasadena campus continued to mount unremittingly for Dr. Ockenga's full-time services.

Immediately after the resignation announcement, the pastor's cabinet met to prepare recommendations for submission to the congregation. At a special meeting on July 16, the cabinet reported discussions with Dr. Ockenga regarding his decision. They stated that upon examining the means he used to arrive at his resolution, "we have not found a clear revelation of the Lord's direction in his decision." They observed that, under the strenuous circumstances generated by the double burden of church and seminary, the clear discernment of God's will was most difficult.

Their report being concluded, the assembled 389 members (an unusually large gathering for business) proceeded to vote on a motion calling for a reconsideration of the resignation. The result was 367 yea, 18 no, with 4 not voting; a motion for unanimity was then quickly passed. A committee of eight informed the pastor of this action in mid-July.

Faced with this overwhelming expression of love and loyalty, Dr. and Mrs. Ockenga reviewed and reevaluated their decision during the remainder of that summer, spending much time in "prayer, fasting, and meditation upon God's Word and search for divine principles."

On September 10, 1954, the resignation was reversed, and the cloud of joy which had settled over Pasadena in June moved to rest over Brimstone Corner. The significance of this reversal for the future of both pastor and church is revealed by Dr. Ockenga in his 1954 annual report:

> As you know, I have burned all my bridges behind me by putting other men in positions of leadership which otherwise I could have taken. Now you will have to bury me at Mount Auburn or put me out in due season from decrepitation.

Park Street Church has always been a self-governing, self-sustaining, wholly autonomous local church according to the best traditions of Congregationalism. In 1931, as a result of the union of the Congregational churches with the Christian churches, Park Street entered a new organization known as The Congregational and Christian Churches (1,200,000 members).

In 1940, preliminary discussions toward further union were begun by the Congregational Christian Commission on Interchurch Relations and Church Unity as the result of the catalytic action of a number of Congregational Christian and Evangelical and Reformed ministers in St. Louis, Missouri. These discussions soon included the Evangelical and Reformed Commission on Closer Relations with Other Churches. After four years of preliminary meetings, the national bodies of these two groups voted to proceed further with these conversations with a view toward possible union.

A careful examination of the official Basis of Union by Park Street's officers revealed several items fraught with peril: (1) the proposed new denomination, though presbyterial, was to be non-creedal; (2) constitution-making was scheduled after the consummation of the union and the creation of a new general synod; (3) the individual Congregational Christian churches would be in possible jeopardy of losing their physical properties; (4) new standards for the education, ordination and placement of ministers were planned for adoption; (5) the glory of the Congregational way was endangered by a hierarchical system complete with centralization of authority and ascending levels of denominational judicatories.

After a denominational request in 1945, the churches of the Massachusetts Conference of The Congregational Christian Churches registered a straw vote on the proposed merger. In its annual meeting on January 22, 1946, Park Street gave a clear indication of its intention: "Park Street Church goes on record as being opposed to any union of it or of the Congregational Christian Church with the Evangelical and Reformed Church."

After two years, during which time the Basis of Union was revised, the individual congregations were asked to vote for or against the union no later than April 1, 1948. During January of that year, the Park Street cabinet, having carefully restudied the pertinent literature, unanimously adopted three resolutions:

> 1. That the Park Street Church . . . declares its opposition to the proposed union of the Congregational Christian Churches and the Evangelical and Reformed Church, as set forth in the Basis of Union. . . .
>
> 2. That the Park Street Church respectfully declares that should such union be consummated, it will not in any manner whatsoever enter into or become a part of such union or the United Church of Christ, or adhere thereto, or become responsible to or for the same.

3. That in taking this action the said representatives of
Park Street Church are convinced that they are acting within
the will of God and under the guidance of the Holy Spirit.

Three weeks later, the voting congregation met in annual session
and formally adopted these resolutions as their official position.

This historic action was dictated by: (1) the tendency of modern union movements toward centralization of authority and dilu-
tion of theology; (2) the invalidation of the autonomous principle;
(3) the delay in drawing up a constitution until after the formation of the new denomination; (4) the noncreedal feature of the
United Church of Christ; (5) the acceptance of a Presbyterian-
type of polity.

Although the plan of adoption required the affirmative vote of
75 percent of the Congregational Christian churches for passage,
less than 70 percent voted in favor of the plan. The proponents
of union, undaunted by this temporary setback, continued their
pursuit of the goal. In the meantime, Park Street Church printed
a sermon of Dr. Ockenga's relative to this issue and the church's
position and mailed a copy to every Congregational church in
America. At the annual meeting of the Suffolk West Association
of Congregational Christian Churches on April 27, 1948, Park
Street Church, through its delegates, indicated its continued opposition to the merger by registering a further negative vote.

Although the pressure of lawsuits and the opposition of the
conservative elements within the Congregational Christian
churches tended to slow down the drive for union, the new
United Church of Christ came into existence in June, 1957, and
a constitution was approved by the General Synod on July 7, 1961.
That same year, upon the joint recommendation of the official
boards, Park Street unanimously passed (139-0) resolutions dis-
approving the new constitution and calling for a separation from
the United Church of Christ. The results of the two votes were
officially communicated to the United Church of Christ that same
day.

From that hour, Park Street Church has continued its independent existence as a self-governing local body. At the present
time the church is affiliated with the National Association of
Congregational Churches (formed in 1959 by some two hundred

nonuniting assemblies, liberal and orthodox), and with the Conservative Congregational Christian Conference.

From the foregoing record, it may be legitimately concluded that Dr. Ockenga's ministry has been, without question, the most extensive, the most well rounded, and the most successful of all those which preceded his over a period of one hundred twenty-seven years. The fortitude, the progressive vision, the administrative leadership, the righteous hatred of humanistic religion by whatever name, and the gift of preaching, so evident in his pastoral predecessors, have all been demonstrated by the present minister of Park Street Church for nearly a generation. It can never be said that the mantle of leadership passed on to Harold John Ockenga in November, 1936, has not been worn with dignity and with concern for the faith of Him who is the Head over all.

Conclusion

Park Street Church is indeed the citadel of orthodoxy in New England—and remarkably, an enduring one. During the length of one hundred fifty-nine years, Boston grew from a town to a city and from a budding commercial center to a highly industralized metropolis. Political power changed hands to become the sole possession of men under papal influence; the influential centers of orthodoxy dried up and were incorporated into the network of liberal Protestantism; and the lay Protestant church as a whole yielded to the ascendant lay Roman Catholic church its dominant power in city government, its hold on a large portion of the landed wealth, and its influence over the minds of a major segment of the citizens.

In the face of these radical changes, situated in the midst of the inner city, and surrounded by ecclesiastical, political and academic communities (in recent decades) fundamentally hostile to its evangelical posture and witness, Park Street Church has kept a steady course from its beginning to the present without essential deviation or any semblance of apostasy.

Park Street Church today numbers 2,300 members who reside in seventy or more towns encompassing Boston. Their religious backgrounds recall former affiliations with some fifteen to twenty denominations. The intellectual level of the congregation is such that at least 40 percent have a college education or its equivalent. At the Sunday evening services, a large percentage of the audiences are composed of students. To these who attend the services of the church, Dr. Ockenga faithfully presents the truths of the

Word, applying its testimony and its principles to the spiritual and moral needs of man.

The contemporary influence of Park Street Church is varied: to the United Church of Christ, it is a source of admiration, though a thorn in the side; to the evangelical churches of New England, it serves to encourage and guide in matters of mutual concern. Beyond New England, and aside from the missionary outreach which encompasses the globe, the influence of the church is largely mediated through its pastor by virtue of his numerous official and unofficial responsibilities and associations.

In this northeast region of the United States, where past years have witnessed the closing of thousands of churches and the take-over of hundreds of others by religious bodies unfriendly to the old-fashioned gospel, Park Street Church continues in its original meetinghouse on its original site, a staunch champion of the cause and kingdom of Jesus Christ.

Bibliography

BOOKS

ALLEN, WILLIAM. *Memoir of John Codman with Reminiscences by Joshua Bates.* Boston: T. R. Marvin & S. K. Whipple & Co., 1853.

"American Heritage" Editors. *The American Heritage Book of The Pioneer Spirit.* New York: American Heritage Pub. Co., Inc., 1959.

ANDERSON, RUFUS. *History of The Mission to The Sandwich Islands.* Boston: Congregational Pub. Board, 1874.

The Articles of Faith and Covenant of The Bowdoin Street Church. Boston: T. R. Marvin, 1843.

The Articles of Faith and The Covenant of Park Street Church. Boston: T. R. Marvin, 1825.

BEECHER, CHARLES (ed.). *Autobiography and Correspondence of Lyman Beecher, D.D.* New York: Harper & Bros., 1864, Vol. I.

———. *Autobiography and Correspondence of Lyman Beecher, D.D.* New York: Harper & Bros., 1865, Vol. II.

BEECHER, EDWARD. *Baptism with Reference to Its Import and Modes.* New York: John Wiley, 1849.

———. *The Conflict of Ages.* Boston: Phillips, Sampson & Co., 1853.

———. *History of Opinions on The Scriptural Doctrine of Retribution.* New York: D. Appleton & Co., 1878.

Bowen's Picture of Boston. Boston: Abel Bowen, 1829.

BUCK, EDWARD. *Massachusetts Ecclesiastical Law.* Boston: Gould & Lincoln, 1866.

CLARK, JOSEPH S. *A Historical Sketch of The Congregational Churches in Massachusetts.* Boston: Congregational Board of Publication, 1858.

The Confession of Faith and Covenant of The Central Congregational Church, Boston. Boston: T. R. Marvin, 1842.

260

The Confession of Faith and Covenant of The Mount Vernon Congregational Church in Boston, Massachusetts. Boston: T. R. Marvin, 1846.

Confession of Faith and Covenant of Union Church, Essex Street, Boston. Boston: Crocker & Brewster, 1839.

CONRAD, ARCTURUS Z. *Boston's Awakening.* Boston: The King's Business Pub. Co., 1909.

———. *Commemorative Exercises at The One Hundredth Anniversary of The Organization of Park Street Church.* Boston: Park Street Centennial Committee, 1909.

COOKE, PARSONS. *Recollections of Rev. E. D. Griffin.* Boston: Massachusetts Sabbath School Soc., 1855.

DUNN, JAMES B. (comp. and ed.). *Moody's Talks on Temperance.* New York: National Temperance Soc. & Pubn. House, 1877.

DWIGHT, WILLIAM T. *Select Discourses of Sereno Edwards Dwight, D.D. with a Memoir of His Life.* Boston: Crocker & Brewster, 1851.

EARLE, ALICE MORSE. *The Sabbath in Puritan New England.* New York: Charles Scribner's Sons, 1893.

ELLINWOOD, LEONARD. *The History of American Church Music.* New York: Morehouse-Gorham Co., 1953.

FINNEY, CHARLES GRANDISON. *Memoirs of Rev. Charles G. Finney.* New York: A. S. Barnes & Co., 1876.

First Annual Report of The American Society for The Promotion of Temperance. Andover: Flagg & Gould, 1828.

Garrison Children. *William Lloyd Garrison, 1805-1879, The Story of His Life.* New York: Century Co., 1855, Vol. I.

GOULD, NATHANIEL D. *Church Music in America.* Boston: A. N. Johnson, 1853.

GREGG, DAVID. *A Book of Remembrance.* New York: Fleming H. Revell Co., 1921.

HAYWARD, JOHN. *The New England Gazetteer.* (14th ed.), Boston: John Hayward, 1841.

HILL, HAMILTON ANDREWS. *History of The Old South Church.* Boston: Houghton, Mifflin & Co., 1890, Vol. II.

HOLMES, PAULINE. *One Hundred Years of Mount Vernon Church, 1842-1942.* Boston: Mount Vernon Church, 1942.

JENKS, WILLIAM. *A Memoir of The Rev. Louis Dwight.* Boston: T. R. Marvin, 1856.

JOHNSON, ALLEN (ed.). *Dictionary of American Biography.* New York: Charles Scribner's Sons, 1927, Vol. I.

JOHNSON, OLIVER. *William Lloyd Garrison and His Times.* London: Sampson, Low, Marston, Searle and Rivington, 1882.

KILHAM, WALTER H. *Boston After Bulfinch*. Cambridge: Harvard University Press, 1946.

LINDSELL, HAROLD. *Park Street Prophet*. Wheaton: Van Kampen Press, 1951.

MANN, ALBERT W. (comp.). *History of The 45th Regiment Massachusetts Volunteer Militia*. N. p., 1908.

Mayors of Boston. Boston: State Street Trust Co., 1914.

Memorial of Samuel Hall Walley. Boston: T. R. Marvin & Son, 1866.

Memorial Volume of Salem Church. Boston: Salem Street Church, 1874.

MOORE, MARTIN. *Boston Revival, 1842*. Boston: John Putnam, 1842.

NEWMAN, A. H. *A History of the Baptist Churches in the United States*. Philadelphia: American Baptist Pubn. Soc., 1898.

POLLOCK, J. C. *Moody*. New York: Macmillan Co., 1963.

The Preservation of Park Street Church. Boston: George H. Ellis, 1903.

REED, ANDREW, and MATHESON, JAMES. *A Narrative of The Visit to The American Churches*. New York: Harper & Bros., 1835, Vol. II.

ROSS, MARJORIE DRAKE. *The Book of Boston, The Federal Period, 1775-1837*. New York: Hastings House Pubs., 1961.

SAFFORD, ANN ELIZA. *A Memoir of Daniel Safford*. Boston: American Tract Soc., 1861.

SANTVOORD, C. VAN. *Memoirs of Eliphalet Nott, D.D., LL.D*. New York: Sheldon & Co., 1876.

The Semi-centennial Celebration of The Park Street Church and Society. Boston: Henry Hoyt, 1861.

SHAW, CHARLES. *A Topographical and Historical Description of Boston*. Boston: Oliver Spear, 1817.

SPRAGUE, WILLIAM B. *Memoir of The Rev. Edward D. Griffin, D.D.* New York: Taylor & Dodd, 1839.

———. *The Life of Jedidiah Morse, D.D.* New York: Anson D. F. Randolph & Co., 1874.

STOWE, LYMAN BEECHER. *Saints, Sinners, and Beechers*. Indianapolis: Bobbs-Merrill Co., 1934.

STRONG, WILLIAM E. *The Story of The American Board*. Boston: Pilgrim Press, 1910.

A Volume of Records Relating to The Early History of Boston, with Selectmen's Minutes, 1799-1810. Boston: Municipal Printing Office, 1904, Vol. XXXIII.

WARNER, JR., SAM B. *Streetcar Suburbs*. Cambridge: Harvard University Press & MIT Press, 1962.

WHEILDON, WILLIAM W. *Sentry, or Beacon Hill*. Concord, Mass.: William W. Wheildon, 1877.

WHITTIER, JOHN GREENLEAF. *Poems.* Boston: Sanborn, Carter & Bazin, 1857.

WOOD, NATHAN E. *The History of The First Baptist Church of Boston.* Philadelphia: American Baptist Pubn. Soc., 1899.

WOODS, LEONARD. *History of The Andover Theological Seminary.* Boston: James R. Osgood & Co., 1885.

RECORDS

Articles of Faith and Covenant, Park Street Church, and Membership List, 1809-77.

Catalog of Sabbath School Library, Park Street Church, 1868.

A Compilation by Alfred H. Colby of Names of Persons Pledging Toward Payment of Mortgage, 1922.

Index to Historical Committee Records, Park Street Church.

Minutes of Annual Business Meetings, Park Street Church, 1952-56.

Proceedings of Business Meetings, Park Street Church, 1809-34; 1834-54; 1854-71; 1871-99; 1899-1922; 1922-38; 1939-46; 1946-52.

Prudential Committee Records, Park Street Church, 1824-30; 1884-98; 1898-1911.

Receipt of Boston YMCA to Park Street Church, November 25, 1864.

Records of Examining Committee, Park Street Church, 1828-34; 1854-58.

Records of Maternal Association of Park Street Church, 1816-71.

Records of Park Street Congregational Society, 1835-86; 1887-1916.

Records of Park Street Society, 1810-23.

Records of Pulpit Supply Committee, Park Street Church, 1866-68.

Records of Park Street Benevolent Sewing Circle, 1882-1911.

Records of Park Street Ladies Auxiliary to The Women's Board of Foreign Missions, 1879-93.

Records of The Park Street Singing Society, 1810-27.

Records of Religious Improvement Society, March 13, 1804, to November 14, 1808.

"A Statement of The Results of The June 20, 1904, Meeting Relative to The Future of The Edifice, Park Street Church."

Subscriptions for Park Street Meetinghouse, n. d.

Subscriptions to New Church Lot, December 5, 1808.

ARTICLES AND PERIODICALS

'Adirondack Murray in Boston," *Shooting and Fishing,* (February 22, 1906), pp. 408-9.

BACON, LEONARD W. "A Forgotten Glory of Park Street Church," *The Congregationalist and Christian World,* (July 9, 1904), p. 52.

The Boston Courier, (April 5, 1858), p. 1.

    Ibid., (April 12, 1858), p. 1.

Boston Gazette, (February 27, 1809), p. 1.

Boston Recorder, (April 17, 1819), p. 63.

    Ibid., (October 30, 1819), p. 179.

    Ibid., (November 6, 1819), p. 183.

"Churches or Music Halls," *The Congregationalist,* (January 1, 1874), p. 1.

The Congregationalist, (May 6, 1875), p. 140.

    Ibid., (October 7, 1875), p. 316.

    Ibid., (April 9, 1885), p. 124.

    Ibid., (October 14, 1886), p. 339.

    Ibid., (February 21, 1889), p. 61.

The Congregationalist and Boston Recorder, (November 19, 1868), p. 372.

CONRAD, ARCTURUS Z. "The Hinge of Destiny," *Christian Faith and Life,* (January, 1935), pp. 8-9.

"Contrast Between Calvinism and Hopkinsianism," *The General Repository and Review,* (April, 1813), pp. 324-78.

"Crush The Hohenzollern Hyena, Says Dr. Conrad," *The Boston Post,* (July 1, 1918), p. 6.

DORCHESTER, DANIEL. "Religious Progress in Boston," *The Congregationalist,* (January 26, 1881), p. 25.

"Dr. Withrow's Farewell," *The Congregationalist,* (January 6, 1887), p. 5.

DWIGHT, JOHN S. "The History of Music in Boston," *The Memorial History of Boston, 1630-1880,* ed. Justin Winsor. Boston: James R. Osgood & Co., 1881, IV, 415-64.

FARNHAM, LUTHER. "Park Street Church—Rev. Andrew L. Stone, Pastor," *Gleason's Pictorial Drawing-Room Companion,* Boston Pulpit Series, No. 10, n. d., p. 156.

GARRISON, JR., WILLIAM LLOYD. *Boston Anti-Slavery Days,* (The Bostonian Society Publications, 1905). Boston: Old State House, 1905, II, 81-104.

GREGG, DAVID. "Is The Church of Christ in Danger?" *The Congregationalist,* (October 20, 1887), p. 363.

———. "Park Street Church," *The Congregationalist,* (December 11, 1890), p. 440.

KINGSBURY, JOHN D. "Silas Aiken," *The Congregational Quarterly,* (April, 1870), pp. 179-98.

The Liberator, (January 1, 1831), p. 1.

MALEFYT, LOUISE L. "Sunday School," *The Park Street Spire*, (October, 1955), pp. 24-25.

MARINER, ELWYN E. "Park Street Church and Missions," *Twentieth Annual Missionary Conference*, (Park Street Church, 1959), pp. 8-14.

MARSHALL, J. MURRAY. "History of The Mayflower Pulpit," *The Park Street Spire*, (June, 1955), pp. 13-15.

MATTHEWS, ALBERT. *Early Sunday Schools in Boston*, (Reprint from the publications of The Colonial Society of Massachusetts). Cambridge: John Wilson & Son, 1919, XXI, 259-85.

MURRAY, WILLIAM HENRY HARRISON. "A Metropolitan Church," *The Congregationalist*, (December 11, 1873), p. 393.

"A New Pastor at Park Street Church," *The Congregationalist*, (March 16, 1893), p. 428.

OCKENGA, HAROLD JOHN. "The New Evangelicalism," *The Park Street Spire*, (February, 1958), pp. 2-7.

———. "The Pastor's Study," *The Park Street Spire*, (January, 1958), pp. 6-7.

———. "What 25 Years of Missionary Conferences Have Taught Me," *World Vision Magazine*, (March, 1964), pp. 22-25.

"Park Street Church Means Business," *The Congregationist and Christian World*, (February 3, 1906), p. 152.

The Park Street Spire, (April, 1959), front cover.

The Park Street Spire, (December, 1961), pp. 4-5.

PHELPS, AUSTIN. "The New England Clergy and Anti-Slavery Reform," *The Congregationalist*, (April 24, 1884), p. 135.

———. "The New England Clergy and The Abolitionists," *The Congregationalist*, (May 1, 1884), p. 143.

RANKIN, ISAAC O. "The Story of Park Street Church," *The Congregationalist and Christian World*, (February 7, 1903), p. 197.

Review of *Music-Hall Sermons* (2d series), *The Congregational Quarterly*, (April, 1873), pp. 326-28.

Review of A Review of "A Sermon Preached January 10, 1810, at The Dedication of The Church in Park-Street, Boston, by Dr. Edward D. Griffin, D.D.," *The Panoplist and Missionary Magazine United*, (June, 1811), III, 20-35.

"Rev. Mr. Gregg's First Sunday at Park Street Church," *The Congregationalist*, (February 24, 1887), p. 63.

"A Sermon Preached January 10, 1810, at The Dedication of The Church in Park-Street, Boston, by Dr. Edward D. Griffin, D.D.," *The Monthly Anthology and Boston Review*, (February, 1810), VIII, 128-36.

"The Service of Song," *The Congregationalist and Boston Recorder,* (January 7, 1869), p. 1.

"Survey of Churches," *The Panoplist,* (October, 1806), pp. 210-16.

TARBOX, INCREASE N. "The Congregational (Trinitarian) Churches," *The Memorial History of Boston, 1630-1880,* ed. Justin Winsor. Boston: James R. Osgood & Co., 1881, IV, 401-20.

"What Dr. Conrad Thinks of Modernism," *The Boston Post,* (July 18, 1926), p. B-7.

WITHROW, JOHN LINDSAY. "The Anchored Ones," *The Congregationalist,* (April 17, 1884), p. 125.

———. "The Sale of Park Street Church, Boston," *The Congregationalist and Christian World,* (December 20, 1902), p. 953.

SERMONS AND ADDRESSES

BEECHER, LYMAN. *The Bible A Code of Laws.* Andover, Mass.: Flagg & Gould, 1818, p. 51.

CONRAD, ARCTURUS Z. *Invisible Collisions: Two Goblets of Wine.* Boston: Hamilton Bros., 1928, p. 19.

GARRISON, WILLIAM LLOYD. *Dangers to The Nation.* ("Old South Leaflets," Vol. VIII); Boston: Directors of the Old South Work, Old South Meetinghouse, n. d., pp. 1-12.

GREGG, DAVID. "The Quakers; or Ideal Civilization," *Makers of The American Republic.* New York: E. B. Treat, 1896, pp. 213-48.

GRIFFIN, EDWARD DORR. *A Series of Lectures Delivered in Park Street Church.* Boston: Nathaniel Willis, 1813, p. 327.

———. *An Address Delivered Before The American Education Society, May 23, 1825.* Boston: Ezra Lincoln, 1825, p. 15.

———. "Christian Boldness," *The American Pulpit.* Edinburgh: T. & T. Clark, 1852, p. 334.

———. *Sermon at Dedication of Meetinghouse at Sandwich, Massachusetts, Preached October 20, 1813.* Boston: Nathaniel Willis, 1813, p. 35.

———. *A Sermon Preached January 10, 1810, at the Dedication of the Church in Park Street, Boston.* Boston: Lincoln & Edmands, n. d., p. 34.

———. *The Kingdom of Christ, A Missionary Sermon.* Philadelphia: Jane Aitken, 1805, p. 30.

LANSING, ISAAC J. "Church and State, Their True Relations," *National Danger in Romanism.* Boston: Arnold Pub. Assn., n. d., pp. 261-84.

———. "Despotism in Church and State The Principle of Romanism," *National Danger in Romanism.* Boston: Arnold Pub. Assn., n. d., pp. 75-98.

———. *Rome's Avowed Purpose to Control The State, and Her Success in Great Cities.* (Envelope Series, enlarged, No. 3B.) Boston: Arnold Pub. Assn., 1892, II, 285-318.

———. "Rome's Despotic Intolerance of Free Opinion," *National Danger in Romanism.* Boston: Arnold Pub. Assn., n. d., pp. 99-126.

LINSLEY, JOEL HARVEY. *Lectures on The Relations and Duties of The Middle Aged.* Hartford: D. F. Robinson & Co., 1828, p. 180.

MASON, LOWELL. "Address on Church Music," *The Christian Examiner and Theological Review,* (November-December, 1826), III, 489-98.

MURRAY, WILLIAM HENRY HARRISON. *Deacons.* Boston: Henry L. Shepard & Co., 1875, p. 82.

———. *Music Hall Sermons.* Boston: Fields, Osgood & Co., 1870, pp. vi 276.

———. *Music Hall Sermons* (2d series). Boston: James R. Osgood & Co., 1873, p. 207.

———. *Park Street Pulpit: Sermons.* Boston: James R. Osgood & Co., 1873, p. 372.

———. *Park Street Pulpit: Sermons* (2d series). Boston: James R. Osgood & Co., 1872, p. 372.

———. *Words Fitly Spoken.* Boston: Lee & Shepard, 1873, p. 417.

OCKENGA, HAROLD JOHN. "Boston at The Crossroads." Boston, 1950.

———. *Park Street Church Again Votes No.* Boston: Park Street Church, n. d., p. 16.

———. *Park Street Church Votes No.* Boston: Park Street Church, n. d., p. 16.

———. *The Church God Blesses.* Pasadena: Fuller Missions Fellowship, 1958, p. 48.

———. *The Unique and Unparalleled Position of Park Street Church in Boston's Religious History.* Boston: Park Street Church, 1939, p. 22.

———. "The Unvoiced Multitudes," *Evangelical Action,* comp. and ed. by Executive Committee of National Association of Evangelicals for United Action. Boston: United Action Press, 1942, pp. 19-39.

STONE, ANDREW LEETE. *A Discourse Occasioned by The Death of Abraham Lincoln.* Boston: J. K. Wiggins, 1865, p. 21.

———. *An Oration Before The Municipal Authorities of The City of Boston.* Boston: J. H. Eastburn, 1854, p. 42.

———. *Emancipation.* Boston: Henry Hoyt, 1862, p. 28.

———. *Memorial Discourses.* Boston: Henry Hoyt, 1866, p. 305.

———. *Praise for Victory.* Boston: T. R. Marvin & Son, 1862, p. 15.

———. *The War and The Patriot's Duty.* Boston: Henry Hoyt, 1861, p. 24.

SUMNER, CHARLES. *The War System of The Commonwealth of Nations.* Boston: Ticknor, Reed & Fields, 1849, p. 71.

WISNER, BENJAMIN BLYDENBURG. *The History of The Old South Church in Boston in Four Sermons.* Boston: Crocker & Brewster, 1830, p. 122.

WORCESTER, SAMUEL. *The Foundation of God Sure and Sealed.* Boston: Samuel T. Armstrong, 1811, p. 48.

LETTERS AND UNPUBLISHED MATERIAL

Annual Reports and Supplementary Records, Park Street Church, January, 1957, to November, 1961.

Beecher Family Collection, Yale University Library.

BUMSTEAD, JOSIAH. "The Origin of Park Street Church, Boston," March 7, 1845, Congregational Library.

Evarts Letterbook, January, 1820, to August, 1826, in Evarts Family Papers, Yale University Library.

Historical Report on Various Topics Made Before the Annual Meeting, 1845, Park Street Church.

JENKINS, JOSEPH W. Personal Remarks and Observations Concerning Origin of Park Street Church, March 7, 1845, Congregational Library.

Letter of Andrew Leete Stone and Louis Dwight to Rev. William T. Dwight, December 6, 1850.

Letter of Andrew Leete Stone to Park Street Church, January 3, 1849.

Letter of Arcturus Z. Conrad to The Committee for The Preservation of The Park Street Meetinghouse, March 5, 1906.

Letters of Chaplain Andrew Leete Stone to Park Street Church, December, 1862, to June, 1863.

Letter of David Gregg to Park Street Church and Society, November 15, 1890.

Letter of Deacons, Park Street Church, to Arcturus Z. Conrad, November (?) 15, 1932.

Letter of Dismission from Old South Church, February 19, 1809.

Letter of Ebenezer Parker to Edward Beecher, March 22, 1830.

Letter of Elias Boudinot to Edward Dorr Griffin, October 26, 1809.

Letter of Ezra Farnsworth to Charles C. Litchfield, May 23, 1869.

Letter of Harold John Ockenga to Park Street Congregational Church, n. d.

Letter of John Lindsay Withrow to Edwin Lamson, June 13, 1876.

Letter of Josiah Bumstead, Jeremiah Evarts and John C. Proctor to Park Street Church, November 20, 1824.

Letter of Lowell Mason to William T. Eustis, October 5, 1840.

Letter of Peter Hobart to John Lindsay Withrow and Park Street Conference Committee, n. d.

Letter of Sereno Edwards Dwight to Park Street Church, April 24, 1826.

Letter of William Lloyd Garrison to Jacob Horton, June 27, 1829.

Letter to Members of Park Street Church Protesting The Proposed Demolition of The Church Edifice, June, 1904.

MURRAY, WILLIAM HENRY HARRISON. *To The Members of The Committee Appointed by Park Street Church and The Committee Appointed by The Parish to Confer with The Pastor Touching an Associate Pastor.* Boston: Rand, Avery & Co., 1874, p. 20.

Petition of Committee of Proprietors, Park Street Church, to City of Boston, 1823.

Report of Committee on Church Meetings, February 7, 1827.

Report of Committee on The Expediency of Settling A Colleague, April 20, 1846.

Report of Music Committee on The Subject of Lowell Mason's Request, n. d.

SMITH, SYLVIA. "History of The Mason Street Mission," n. d.

Specifications of Park Street Church Tombs, n. d.

Treasurer's Authorization to Secure Loans, April 23, 1810.

Treasurer's Memorandum, April 24, 1810.

Treasurer's Reports, 1892-96.

Undated letter of A. B. to Charles Bulfinch.

PAMPHLETS AND BROCHURES

An Appeal for Two Hundred Thousand Dollars, 1921, p. 11.

An Historical Sketch of Eighty Years, 1816-1896. Paper read by J. A. Hamilton at annual meeting of the Congregational Home Missionary Society, New Haven, Conn., June 3, 1896, p. 7.

MORRIS, GEORGE K. *Present Condition and Needs of the Church.* Boston: Evangelistic Association of New England, 1900, p. 14.

Report of The Society for The Moral and Religious Instruction of The Poor, October 8, 1817.

Review of A Pamphlet on The Trust Deed of The Hanover Church. Boston: T. R. Marvin, 1828, p. 37.

Sesquicentennial Program, February 22 to March 1, 1959.

75th Anniversary of Park Street Congregational Church. Boston: Brown & Clark, 1884, p. 74.

Twenty-fifth Anniversary, Pastorate of Rev. A. Z. Conrad, Ph.D., D.D. Boston: Park Street Church, 1930, p. 49.

PUBLIC DOCUMENTS

Boston, Massachusetts. Registry of Deeds, Suffolk County, Libro 228, Folio 181.

 Ibid., Folio 182.

 Ibid., Libro 237, Folio 74.

 Ibid., Libro 395, Folio 177.

Commonwealth of Massachusetts. *Special Acts and Resolves Passed by The General Court of Massachusetts in The Year 1916.* Boston: Wright & Potter Printing Co., 1916, p. 603.

OTHER SOURCES

Bulletin of Point Breeze Presbyterian Church, Pittsburgh, Pa., September 27, 1936.

Exercises of Celebration of American Independence, July 4, 1831.

MERIDETH, ROBERT. "Edward Beecher, The Deacon of The Civil War Generation." Unpublished Ph.D. dissertation, University of Minnesota, 1963.

Twenty-fifth Annual Missionary Conference Program.

APPENDIX I

ARTICLES OF FAITH AND GOVERNMENT ADOPTED
FEBRUARY 23, 1809

We, the Subscribers, having agreed to unite in the establishment of a new Congregational Church in Boston, by the name of *Park Street Church,* think it proper to make a declaration of that Faith which is the bond of our ecclesiastical union, and which we shall expect to find in all those who shall hereafter participate in our religious privileges and communion.

First. We believe that the Scriptures of the Old and New Testament are the Word of GOD, and the only perfect rule of Christian faith and practice.

Second. We profess our decided attachment to that system of the Christian religion which is distinguishingly denominated *Evangelical;* more particularly to those doctrines, which in a proper sense, are styled the Doctrines of Grace, viz.: "That there is one and but one living and true GOD, subsisting in three persons, the FATHER, the SON, and the HOLY GHOST; and that these Three are the one GOD, the same in substance, equal in power and glory; that GOD from all eternity, according to the counsel of His own will, and for His own glory, foreordained whatsoever comes to pass; that GOD in His most holy, wise and powerful providence preserves and governs all His creatures and all their actions; that by the Fall, all mankind lost communion with GOD, are under His wrath and curse, and liable to all the miseries of this life, to death itself, and to the pains of hell forever; that GOD out of His mere good pleasure, from all eternity elected some to everlasting life, entered into a covenant of grace, to deliver them from a state of sin and misery, and introduce them into a state of salvation by a Redeemer; that this Redeemer is the Lord JESUS CHRIST, the eternal Son of GOD, who became man, and continues to be GOD and man in two distinct natures and one person

271

forever; that the effectual calling of sinners is the work of GOD'S Spirit; that their justification is only for the sake of CHRIST'S righteousness by faith." And though we deem no man or body of men infallible, yet we believe that those divines that were eminently distinguished in the time of the Reformation, possessed the spirit, and maintained in great purity, the peculiar doctrines of our holy religion; and that these doctrines are in general clearly and happily expressed in the Westminster Assembly's Shorter Catechism, and in the Confession of Faith owned and consented unto by the Elders and Messengers of the Churches, assembled at Boston, (N. E.) May 12th, A.D. 1680.

Third. In regard to our ecclesiastical government and discipline, with our sister churches in this Commonwealth we adopt the Congregational form, as contained in the Platform of Church Discipline, gathered out of the Word of God, and agreed upon by the Elders and Messengers of the Churches, assembled in the Synod at Cambridge, (N. E.) A.D. 1648.

Fourth. In order to gain admission to membership in this Church, it is understood that every Candidate shall be previously examined, and give credible evidence of a ground of the comfortable hope of a personal condition of grace, through the renovation of the soul, by the special influences of the HOLY SPIRIT, implying repentance for sin and faith in JESUS CHRIST the Redeemer.

Finally. We hereby covenant and engage, as fellow Christians of one faith, and partakers of the same hope and joy, to give up ourselves unto the Lord, for the observing of the ordinances of CHRIST together in the same Society, and to unite together into one body for the public worship of God, and the mutual edification one of another in the fellowship of the Lord Jesus: exhorting, reproving, comforting, and watching over each other, for mutual edification;—looking for that blessed hope and the glorious appearing of the great GOD, even our Saviour JESUS CHRIST, who gave Himself for us that He might redeem us from all iniquity, and purify unto Himself a peculiar people zealous of good works.

FORM OF ADMISSION

ADDRESS. You have presented yourselves in this public manner before God, to dedicate yourselves to His service, and to incorporate yourselves with His visible people. You are about to profess supreme love to Him, sincere contrition for all your sins, and faith in the Lord JESUS CHRIST; to enter into a solemn covenant to receive the FATHER, SON, and HOLY GHOST, as they are offered in the Gospel, and to walk in all the commandments and ordinances of the

Lord. We trust you have well considered the nature of these professions and engagements. The transaction is solemn, and will be attended with eternal consequences. GOD and holy angels are witnesses. Yet be not discouraged. In the name of CHRIST you may come boldly to the God of grace, and provided only you have sincere desires to be His, may venture thus unalterably to commit yourselves, and trust in Him for strength to perform your vows.

Attend, now, to the COVENANT.

In the presence of GOD, His holy angels, and this assembly, you do now solemnly dedicate yourselves to GOD the FATHER as your chief good; to the SON of GOD, as your Mediator and Head, and to the HOLY SPIRIT as your Sanctifier, Comforter, and Guide. To this one GOD, FATHER, SON, and HOLY GHOST, you do heartily give up yourselves in an everlasting covenant to love and obey Him.

Having subscribed the *Confession Faith and Rules of Government* adopted by this Church, you promise to walk with us in conformity to them, in submission to the requirements of the Gospel, and in attendance on its ordinances, and that, by the aid of the Divine Spirit, you will seek to make this profession a reality in your life.

This, you severally profess and engage?

In consequence of these professions and promises, we affectionately receive you as members of this Church, and in the name of CHRIST declare you entitled to all its visible privileges. We welcome you to this fellowship with us in the blessings of the Gospel, and on our part engage to watch over you, and seek your edification, as long as you shall continue among us. Should you have occasion to remove, it will be your duty to seek and ours to grant a recommendation to another Church; for hereafter you can never withdraw from the watch and communion of the saints, without a breach of covenant.

And now, beloved in the Lord, let it be impressed on your minds, that you can never again be as you have been. You have unalterably committed yourselves. Hereafter the eyes of the world will be upon you; and as you conduct yourselves, so religion will be honored or dishonored. If you walk worthy of your profession, you will be a credit and a comfort to us; but if it be otherwise, you will be to us a grief of heart. "But, beloved, we are persuaded better things of you, and things that accompany salvation, though we thus speak." May the Lord guide and preserve you till death, and at last receive you and us to that blessed world where our love and joy shall be forever perfect. AMEN.

APPENDIX II

ACT OF INCORPORATION, PARK STREET
CONGREGATIONAL SOCIETY, 1835

Section 1. Be it enacted by the Senate and House of Representatives in General Court assembled and by the authority of the same, That the proprietors of pews in Park Street meeting-house, in the City of Boston, and their successors, are hereby made a corporation, by the name of the Park Street Congregational Society, with all the powers and privileges, and subject to all the duties and liabilities by law incident to religious societies legally established in the Commonwealth.

Section 2. Be it further enacted, That said society shall have power to take, purchase and hold the said meeting-house and other estate, real or personal, for the use of said society, and the ministry thereof, and the same to sell, mortgage, or otherwise dispose of, as they may see fit: provided the income thereof, exclusive of their meeting-house, and land under and adjoining the same, shall not at anytime exceed the sum of three thousand dollars annually.

Section 3. Be it further enacted, That said society shall have power to assess upon the pews in said house, (which now are or hereafter may be held on a condition, or subject to a liability, to pay assessments thereon, for the support of public worship in said house) according to the valuation thereof heretofore made, or which may be hereafter agreed upon by said society, such sums as shall be by them voted to be raised for the support of public worship in said house, and for other parochial charges of said society; and all such assessments may be collected in the manner provided by the statute of one thousand eight hundred and seventeen, chapter one hundred and eighty-nine.

APPENDIX III

Form of Pew Deed, 1835

KNOW all Men by these Presents, That the PARK-STREET CON-
GREGATIONAL SOCIETY, in Boston, in consideration of . . . .
. . . . Dollars, to them paid by . . . . the receipt
whereof they hereby acknowledge, do hereby grant, sell and convey
unto the said . . . . the Pew No. . . . . in
the Meeting-House of the said Society in Park Street, in said Boston,
with all the rights and privileges that appertain thereunto under and
by virtue of the Act of Incorporation and the By-Laws of the Society,
and the Indenture by which the said Meeting-House was conveyed to
the Society by Trustees, in their Deed, dated August 18th, A.D. 1835,
and recorded with Suffolk Deeds, to all which reference is to be had
herewith.

To Have and to Hold, the granted premises unto the said . . . .
. . . . executors, administrators and assigns forever. Provided,
nevertheless, and this grant is made and accepted upon the following
express conditions: That the said . . . . executors, administrators or assigns shall pay unto the said Society the sum of
. . . . Dollars, quarter yearly, and every quarter, as the
same shall become due, until said . . . . shall surrender
said Pew to the Society by a written notice to the Treasurer, for sale
for the benefit of said . . . . or for occupancy by another, and also shall pay or cause to be paid as aforesaid such further
sum or sums as shall be assessed on said Pew by vote of said Society
at any meeting called for that purpose, and in case of default of
payment of said taxes and assessments or either of them, for more
than six months from the time they became due, the said Pew shall
revert to said Society, and the Society may cause the same to be
offered at public auction and may, at their option, sell the same to
the highest bidder or retain the same as the absolute property of the
Society at the highest price then bid therefor, and after deducting from
the proceeds of such sale, or from the price at which the Society may
so retain said Pew, all expenses and arrearages of every kind, shall
pay any remaining surplus unto the said . . . . executors,
administrators or assigns whenever thereto requested.

No alteration or addition shall be made in or unto said Pew with-

out the consent of the Prudential Committee of the Society, nor shall
said Pew if surrendered to the Society for occupancy by others be re-
occupied by the said . . . . executors, administrators or
assigns within twelve months from the time of such surrender, except
with the consent of the Prudential Committee and the payment of all
taxes that may have become due thereon during the time it has been
surrendered, nor shall the said . . . . be entitled to any
vote on said Pew while the same is surrendered to the Society. No
sale or other transfer of said Pew to any person or persons shall be
valid unless the same shall have been first offered to the Society,
through their Prudential Committee or Treasurer, in writing, upon
the same terms, and the purchase thereof shall have been refused or
neglected for five days, from the date of such offer, nor unless such
transfer be duly recorded in the Books of the Society.

In testimony whereof, the said PARK-STREET CONGREGATION-
AL SOCIETY hereunto affix their Corporate Seal, and the Clerk and
Treasurer thereof subscribe their names on this . . . .
day of . . . . in the year of our Lord one thousand eight
hundred and . . . .

Clerk of Park-Street Congregational Society.
Treasurer of Park-Street Congregational
Society.

APPENDIX IV

CONFESSION OF FAITH ADOPTED FEBRUARY 27, 1877

I believe in GOD, the FATHER ALMIGHTY, Maker of heaven and earth; and in JESUS CHRIST, His only Son, our Lord, and in the HOLY GHOST, and that these three are one GOD.

I reverently receive the Scriptures of the Old and New Testaments, and believe them to be the inspired Word of God, the only infallible rule of faith and practice.

I believe in the Lord JESUS CHRIST, who, in the beginning "was with GOD," and "was GOD," and "who His own self bare our sins in His own body on the tree."

I believe the HOLY SPIRIT has led me to repent of all my sins, and to turn from them, and to obey CHRIST where He says, "If any man will come after me, let him take up his cross and follow me."

I believe in the resurrection of the dead, and in the final judgment of all men. "He that believeth on the SON hath everlasting life; and he that believeth not the SON shall not see life; but the wrath of God abideth on him."

I do not believe that we are saved for the sake of our good works, but " by grace through faith" in the Lord JESUS CHRIST, and that good works are the certain fruit of such faith. I therefore offer myself for Christian service as a means of expressing my gratitude to Him, and to extend His cause.

I cheerfully submit myself to the INSTRUCTION and government of this Park Street Church, as constituted under Congregational form, February 27, 1809, and I promise to promote its purity, peace, and prosperity by all means within my power, so long as I shall continue to be a member of its communion.

APPENDIX V

ARTICLES OF FAITH ADOPTED JUNE 26, 1916

We profess our decided attachment to that system of Christian religion which is designated EVANGELICAL.

WE BELIEVE that the Scriptures of the Old and New Testaments are the Word of God and the all-sufficient rule of faith and practice.

WE BELIEVE that there is one and but one living and true God, subsisting in three persons, the Father, the Son and the Holy Spirit, equal in power and glory; that this triune God created all, upholds all and governs all.

WE BELIEVE that Jesus Christ is the Son of God, the Saviour of the World, and that through his life, death and resurrection an atonement was made for sin and redemption was provided for all mankind.

WE BELIEVE that repentance for sin and the acceptance of Jesus Christ as a personal Saviour is the one and only way whereby sinful man can inherit Eternal Life.

WE BELIEVE the Holy Spirit regenerates the soul of the believer and brings man into saved relations with God, and that He is the Comforter and Guide of all who receive Jesus Christ as a personal Saviour.

WE BELIEVE in what is termed "The Apostles' Creed" as embodying fundamental facts of Christian Faith.

APPENDIX VI

COMPARISON OF CONTRIBUTIONS FOR CHURCH EXPENSES
AND MISSIONS, 1935-64

Year	For Church Expenses	For Missions
1935	$ 18,885	$ 2,235
1936	19,833	4,460
1937	24,039	6,099
1938	25,730	6,381
1939	28,442	9,043
°1940	31,286	17,871
1941	33,233	25,427
1942	36,062	29,852
1943	41,103	39,196
1944	46,389	45,134
1945	51,561	49,571
1946	53,435	75,573
1947	58,309	82,086
1948	59,317	104,421
1949	62,901	117,565
1950	65,641	141,453
1951	67,356	152,401
1952	70,083	175,239
1953	73,067	192,676
1954	78,800	216,768
1955	81,248	224,013
1956	83,885	240,527
1957	84,745	246,066
1958	90,970	248,871
1959	96,815	277,587
1960	94,048	284,754
1961	99,794	306,486
1962	98,204	307,413
1963	103,026	308,534
1964	105,704	321,031
1965	116,054	291,017
1966	121,220	308,233

°First Missionary Conference

APPENDIX VII

EDWARD DORR GRIFFIN, b. East Haddam, Conn., January 6, 1770; Yale, 1790; married Frances Huntington May 17, 1796; daughter, Ellen; pastor, Congregational Church, New Hartford, Conn., June 4, 1795; First Presbyterian Church, Newark, N. J., October 20, 1801; PSC, July 31, 1811; Second Presbyterian Church, Newark, N. J., June 20, 1815; D. D., Union College, 1808; president, Williams College, November 14, 1821-37; d. November 8, 1837, Newark. Major works: *Park Street Lectures; The Doctrine of Divine Efficiency; The Kingdom of Christ; A Missionary Sermon.*

SERENO EDWARDS DWIGHT, b. Greenfield (Fairfield), Conn., May 18, 1786, of Timothy and Mary Dwight; Yale, 1803; married Susan Edwards Daggett; admitted to the bar, New Haven county, 1810; lic., October 8, 1816, by West Association, New Haven county; chaplain, United States Senate, 1816-17; pastor, PSC, September 3, 1817; D. D. Yale, 1833; pres., Hamilton College, N. Y., 1833-35; d. November 30, 1850, Philadelphia; buried in New Haven. Major works: *Memoirs of Rev. David Brainerd; The Life and Works of President Jonathan Edwards; The Hebrew Wife.*

EDWARD BEECHER, b. East Hampton, Long Island, N. Y., August 27, 1803, of Lyman and Roxana Foote Beecher; Yale, 1822; tutor, Hartford public schools, Yale, 1822-26; married Isabella Porter Jones, October 27, 1829; eleven children; pastor, PSC, 1826-30; pres., Illinois College, 1831-44; D. D., Marietta College, 1841; pastor, Salem Street Church, Boston, 1844-55, Galesburg (Ill.) Congregational Church, 1855-71; pioneer educator and antislavery leader in Illinois; a founder of *The Congregationalist,* May, 1849; senior editor until 1853; d. July 28, 1895, Brooklyn. Major works: *The Conflict of Ages; The Concord of Ages; Baptism with Reference to Its Import and Modes; The Papal Conspiracy Exposed; The Nature, Importance, and Means of Eminent Holiness Throughout The Church; Narrative of The Riots at Alton.*

JOEL HARVEY LINSLEY, b. July 15, 1790, Cornwall, Vt., of Joel and Lovinia Gilbert Linsley; Middlebury College, 1811; admitted to bar, state of Vermont, 1815; Andover Seminary, 1821; lic., 1822, as missionary in South Carolina; pastor, South Congregational Church, Hartford, Conn., 1824-32; PSC, 1832-35; Second Congregational Church, Greenwich, Conn., 1847-68; D. D., 1837; married (1) Phoebe Henderson Smith, July 17, 1817, (2) Hannah Miner Thompson, April 23, 1860; children: Charles, Joel, Jeannette, Mary; d. March 23, 1868, Greenwich, Conn.

SILAS AIKEN, b. Bedford, N.H., May 14, 1799, of Phinehas and Elizabeth Patterson Aiken; Dartmouth College, 1825; studied under President Bennett Tyler, 1825-28; ord. March 4, 1829; pastor, First Congregational Church, Amherst, N.H.; PSC, 1837-48; Congregational Church, Rutland, Vt., 1849-63; D. D., Vermont University, 1852; married (1) Mary Osgood, March 4, 1829, (2) Sophia W. Parsons, May 24, 1837; children: Edward, Mary, Susan, Henry, Harriett; d. April 7, 1869.

ANDREW LEETE STONE, b. Oxford, Conn., November 25, 1815, of Dr. Noah and Rosalind Stone; Yale, 1837; married Matilda B. Fisher, July 4, 1842; six children; pastor South Congregational Church, Middletown, Conn., 1844-49; ord. September 3, 1844; PSC, 1849-66, First Congregational Church, San Francisco, 1866-80; D. D., Amherst College, 1861; Union Army Chaplain, September, 1862-June, 1863; editor, *The Congregationalist*, 1853; d. January 17, 1892.

WILLIAM HENRY HARRISON MURRAY, b. Guilford, Conn., April 26, 1840, of Dickinson and Sally Murray; Yale, 1862; Hartford Theological Institute; pastor, Second Congregational Church, Greenwich, Conn., 1864-66, Congregational Church, Meriden, Conn., 1866-67; PSC, 1868-74; pioneer naturalist and sportsman, Adirondack wilderness, New York; author, lecturer, horse breeder, businessman, editor; pastor, New England Church, 1875-78; married (1) Isadora Hull, 1862 (divorced, 1886, desertion), (2) Frances M. Rivers, 1886; children: Ruby, Maude, Grace, Ethel; d. March 3, 1904, Guilford, Conn. Major works: *Adventures in The Wilderness; Adirondack Tales; Daylight Land; Deacons; The Busted Ex-Texan; How John Norton The Trapper Kept His Christmas*.

JOHN LINDSAY WITHROW, b. Coatesville, Pa., March 19, 1837; College of New Jersey, 1860; Princeton Seminary, 1863; ord. by second presbytery of Philadelphia, May 22, 1863; married Annie Judson

Hinkel, 1863; pastor, Abington (Pa.) Presbyterian Church, 1866-72; Second Presbyterian Church, Indianapolis, Ind., 1873-76; PSC, 1876-87; Third Presbyterian Church, Chicago, 1887-98; PSC, 1898-1907; moderator, General Assembly, 1896; D. D., Lafayette College, 1872; Ll. D., Knox College, 1896; d. September 24, 1909, Brookline, Mass.

DAVID GREGG, b. Alleghany, Pa., March 25, 1846, of David and Mary Margaret Rafferty Gregg; Washington and Jefferson College, 1865; grad., Reformed Presbyterian Theological Seminary; married Kate Etheridge, 1870; children: Robert, David, Margaret, Catherine; pastor, Third Reformed Presbyterian Church, New York City, 1870-86; PSC, 1887-90; Lafayette Avenue Presbyterian Church, Brooklyn, 1890-1903; D. D., New York University, 1888; Ll. D., Washington and Jefferson College; president Western Theological Seminary, 1903-9; d. October 11, 1919, New York City. Major works: *Makers of The American Republic; Ideal Young Men and Women; Facts That Call for Faith; Between the Testaments; Testimony of The Land to The Book.*

ISAAC J. LANSING, b. Waterville, N.Y., October 3, 1846; grad. Wesleyan University, Middletown, Conn.; married Ella T. Lansing; children: Gilbert, Elysabeth, Helene, Miriam; pastor and lic., New York East Conference, Methodist Episcopal Church, 1873-87; pastor, Embury Church, Brooklyn, 1873-75; president, Clark University, Atlanta, Ga., 1875-76; pastor, Lloyd Street Church, Savannah, Ga., 1876-77; agent, Freedman's Aid Society, 1877; pastor, First Methodist Episcopal Church, Meriden, Conn., 1878-81; First Church, Stamford, Conn., 1881-83; Summerfield Avenue Methodist Episcopal Church, Brooklyn, 1884-86; Salem Street Congregational Church, Worcester, Mass., 1886-92; PSC, 1893-97; West Side Presbyterian Church, Ridgewood, N. J., 1912-20 (supply); agent for National Security League, 1918; lecturer, Liberty Bond campaign; d. August 4, 1920. Major works: *Romanism and The Republic.*

ARCTURUS Z. CONRAD, b. Shiloh, Ind., November 26, 1855, of Rev. Jacob and Margaret Slagle Conrad; Carleton College, 1882; Union Theological Seminary, 1885; married Harriet Narcissa Adams, August 26, 1885; ord. by Brooklyn presbytery, June 20, 1885; pastor, Ainslie Street Presbyterian Church, Brooklyn, 1885-90; Old South Congregational Church, Worcester, Mass., 1890-1902; PSC, 1905-37; Ph.D., New York University, 1891; D.D., Carleton College, 1892; married Jean Livingston, November 9, 1932; staunch champion of numerous religious, moral and civic causes; associated with the Lord's

Day League, the Anti-Saloon League, Gordon College, Evangelical Alliance of Boston, etc; assoc. ed. *Christian Faith and Life;* d. January 22, 1937. Major works: *Boston's Awakening; Comrades of The Carpenter; The Gospel For An Age of Thought; Radiant Religion; Jesus Christ at The Crossroads; The Seven Finalities of Faith; Secret of The Life Sublime; Flashes From My Forge; You Must Go Right On.*

HAROLD JOHN OCKENGA, b. Chicago, Ill., July 6, 1905, of Herman and Angie Ockenga; grad., Taylor University, Upland, Ind.; Westminster Theological Seminary, 1930; student pastorates, Methodist Church, Avalon, N.J.; Chelsea Methodist Episcopal Church, Atlantic City, 1929-30; married Audrey Laura Williamson, 1935; children: Audrey Starr, Aldryth Sabra, Harold John, Jr.; pastor, Point Breeze Presbyterian Church, Pittsburgh, Pa., 1931-36; PSC, 1936—; a founder of National Association of Evangelicals and its first president, 1942-44; chairman, NAE International Commission; president, American Board of The World Evangelical Fellowship; cofounder and first president, Fuller Theological Seminary, Pasadena, Calif., 1947-54, 1960-63; chairman, Board of Trustees, Fuller Seminary, 1955-60, 1963—; president of board, *Christianity Today;* trustee, Gordon College, Wenham, Mass.; a director, Christian Freedom Foundation, New York City; editor, Evangelical Book Club; D.D., Taylor University, 1937; Ph.D., Pittsburgh University, 1939; Litt. D., Suffolk University, 1939; D. Hum., Bob Jones University, 1944; Ll.D., Houghton College, 1946; D.D., Wheaton, 1960; Litt. D., Norwich University, 1962; Litt. D., Seattle Pacific College, 1963; D.D., Fuller Seminary, 1963. Major works: *Our Protestant Heritage; The Comfort of God; Our Evangelical Faith; The Church in God; Protestant Preaching in Lent; Power Through Pentecost; Women Who Made Bible History; Epistle to The Thessalonians.*

Index

Date Due